"It practically **holds your hand** with its step-by-step itineraries."—Conde Nast's Traveler

"...a **new appro**
venerable city."-

"...the **perfect solution** for travelers making brief stays in that wonderful town."—Minneapolis Star-Tribune

"...for travelers **who don't have time to plan** and don't want to go on a group tour, who want hints on seeing the city's famous sites as well as some equally **fascinating places** that aren't as well known."—Associated Press

"...a chatty, **good-natured** tone make her book a cheerful, **helpful companion.**"—Davis Enterprise

"...a **coordinated way** to do London in a short time, with tours based on **traveler interests**, hobbies or professions." —World News Features

"...**puts it all together** for you and plans your brief time so that you **won't miss** a single feature"—Active Senior Lifestyles

Also by Ruth Humleker

New York
for the
Independent Traveler*

*Winner of the Benjamin Franklin Award for "**best published travel book**" in 1989 from Publishers Marketing Association. *New York for the Independent Traveler* is also a MARLOR PRESS book.

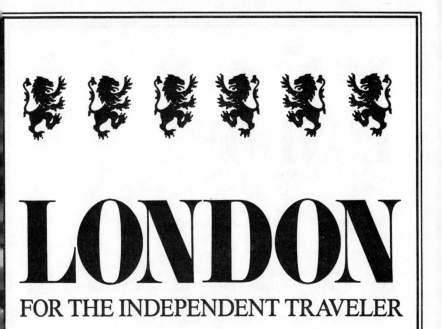

LONDON

FOR THE INDEPENDENT TRAVELER

Ruth Humleker

ML

MarLor Press

LONDON

FOR THE INDEPENDENT TRAVELER

A Marlin Bree Book

Library of Congress Cataloging-in-Publication Data:

Humleker, Ruth
London for the independent traveler.
"A Marlin Bree book."
1. London (England)---Description---1981---Guidebooks. I. Title
DA679.H86 1987 914.21'04858 86-33175

Distributed to the book trade by Contemporary Books/ 180 North Michigan Av./ Chicago, ILL 60601/ Telephone (312) 782-9181
ISBN 0-943400-43-0

Revised edition

ML
MarLor Press
4304 Brigadoon Drive
Saint Paul, Minnesota 55126

Maps by **Dick Humleker**

For Dick

Who is on a
new journey

Illustrations

Contents

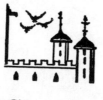

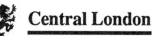

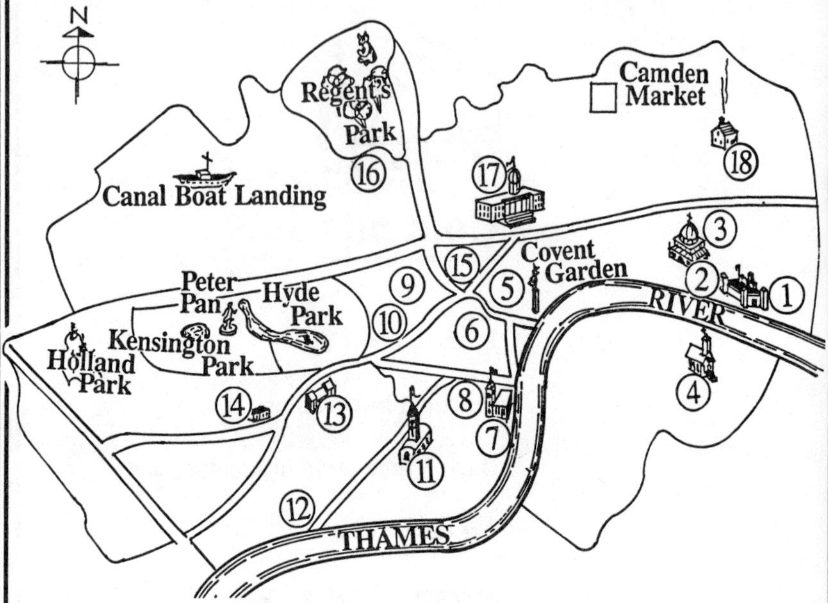

Central London

1/ Tower of London
2/ The Monument
3/ St. Paul's Cathedral
4/ Southwark Cathedral
5/ Trafalgar Square
6/ St. James's Park
7/ Parliament
8/ Westminster Abbey
9/ Green Park
10/ Buckingham Palace
11/ Victoria Station
12/ Chelsea
13/ Harrod's
14/ Victoria and Albert Museum
15/ Picadilly Circus
16/ Madame Tussaud's
17/ British Museum
18/ Dicken's House

Introduction

Most guidebooks give you information on restaurants, hotels, museums, parks and historical monuments, but they let you sort out your own tours. The result is often that you are at one end of town, with the next place you want to see at the other — so you waste time and effort. Other books feature walking guides, which in reality take too long and are too complex. These books can be useful for people who will be in London for weeks at a time, but are too detailed for the average visitor with only days to spend in this great city.

In this book, I try to assemble all the pieces of this traveler's jigsaw puzzle into chronological, geographical and special interest tours for the independent traveler. Each day is arranged into a tour following a special map, so you can see at a glance where you are going and what you have left to do. I have a timetable and make specific recommendations so that, while you may not see everything, at least you will be seeing the major features.

My goal is to make each day as pleasant and inclusive as possible without exhausting either the traveler's body or pocketbook. You do that by traveling smarter, not harder. The result is that many travelers tell me they can do as much in three great days as most do in a week.

The chapters are arranged in three-day tours, since that is often the amount of time a visitor spends in London — before renting a car and touring Britain or crossing the channel to Europe.

As you read, you'll probably find a theme that will interest you, whether it's "Basic" London, London for "Romantics," "Literary" or "Mariners" London or even "Children's" London. For example, my first plan is the "Basic Three Days in London." This is for travelers who want to see "all of London" during their brief visit, and of course I want to help them see the major points of interest. They'll visit London's great attractions, including the Tower of London, St. Paul's Cathedral, Westminster Abbey, the Houses of Parliament and Big Ben, Buckingham Palace, the British Museum, Regent's Park and finally, they'll even take a boat trip down the Thames River to see the illuminated city. It's really maximum London — in just three days.

Another tour I have designed is for "romantics," which includes a visit to Mayfair and Shepherd's Market, an outdoor theatre production at Regent Park, a river trip down the Thames to Henry VIII's Hampton Court with its beautiful State Apartments and magnificent gardens, the charming shops along Piccadilly, Jermyn and St. James's streets; a picnic in St. James's lovely park, with groceries purchased at Fortnum and Mason's elegant store, a stop at the Queen's Gallery and a walk around Buckingham Place. The tour culminates with dinner at St. Katherine's Dock and the 700-year-old Ceremony of the Keys at the Tower of London.

Perhaps your interest is "Literary London," which includes Southwark, where Chaucer and Shakespeare worked, Carlyle's and Dicken's fascinating houses, and the not-to be-forgotten Poet's Corner at Westminster Abbey. "Mariner's London" takes a voyage up the Thames to Greenwich to visit the famous clipper Cutty Sark, go aboard the H.M.S. Belfast, and take a ride on one of London's famous canal boats.

If your interest is gardening, "Gardener's London" is three days among the plants and flowers, featuring the world-famous Chelsea Flower Show with a side trip to the Chelsea Physic Garden. A day trip to the Royal Botanic Gardens (better known as the Kew Gardens), and the Syon House Garden, will be a gardener's delight.

There's even a "Children's London" so that travelers with children can have a special three days visiting the Tower of

London, have a swim in the Serpentine in Kensington Gardens, ice skate at the Queen's Ice Skating Club, and take a canal boat ride on their way to the world famous London Zoo.

That's just a sample. There are many places to go and see if you have a special interest. You can combine tours and days — or turn them upside down. There is no reason an art lover could not combine a day from Art Lover's London, one from Gardener's London and one from Romantic London. In most instances that will work. Just be careful to notice opening and closing times of public buildings. The plans are arranged to accommodate those hours.

As you follow the tour plans, try to stay on the time schedule if you want to see all the places recommended. I have walked all these tours at a moderate pace and they do work. This assumes, of course, that you will not loiter, drag your feet or become absolutely fascinated with some particular place. And of course you will. Don't worry about it. Just use these tours to help you steer your own course through London..

My rule of thumb regarding restaurants, pubs, shops or public buildings is that if it was not there for at least 100 years, I would not mention it. Not quite true, but close. There are no trendy fern bars in this book. Many of these places are located in central London and are convenient stops on more than one tour. They are also my favorites: restaurants and pubs which have never failed me; shops which provide attentive service and museums which are endlessly fascinating. I hope you find them so, too.

A visitor can have it all in London: sightseeing, shopping, art, gardens, parks, castles, good food and the best theatre in the world. It's all there for the taking.

This is my advice, with all my biases and loves and hates showing, but I think it can be your London, too. I hope so because I want you to love this city as much as I do.

Two hundred years ago Dr. Samuel Johnson said, "When a man is tired of London he is tired of life; for there is in London all that life can afford." It is still true.

Practical Information

London: The Changing City

London is a living, breathing, changing city. This is important to remember because many of us tend to think of it as a static museum city. I know I did for a long time.

I was annoyed when the Royal Mews were not open on a Wednesday afternoon because the horses were at Windsor. I was furious when I realized I could no longer get a clear look at St. Paul's Cathedral as I walked up Ludgate Hill because a new office building blocked the view. I huffed and puffed my way around Bankside's new construction and was irritated when Boulestins restaurant changed its entrance from Southampton to Henrietta Street. I wanted it all to remain the way it was when I first saw it. But it didn't and it won't.

Be prepared for such changes. Some may occur between the time this book is written and when you take it with you on your walks around London. The information is as accurate as possible, but there will be changes.

Travel Safety

The very idea of travel makes many people uncomfortable. The first time I went to Europe it was like going to the moon. The excitement of travel is usually accompanied by a certain amount of anxiety. Added to one's normal nervousness from tales about pickpockets, motorcycle gangs, muggers and now terrorists, it is no wonder that travelers have second thoughts about going to new places.

While the average tourist can do little to change the climate of our times, there are specific things you can do to look after yourself. To put it in perspective, you have more chance of hurting yourself in a car accident or even by falling in a bathtub, than you have in traveling about London, which has always been among the safest cities in the world.

Many tourists tend to travel in large tour groups, which are visible and tempting targets for all kinds of pickpockets and con artists. As an independent traveler, you will fit in more with the London scene by avoiding becoming highly visible. Avoid crowds, which pickpockets seem to work with great success. Visit major sights early in the morning or late in the afternoon instead of mid-day, when tour groups are visiting. When possible, travel in the spring or fall instead of the busy, crowded summer months.

Dress down. Leave your gold chains, Rollex watches and diamonds at home. Do not carry more money or traveler's checks than you need for the day. Do not put your wallet in your back pocket, with or without the ubiquitous rubber band. These pickpockets are good!

Be sensible. You wouldn't walk down a dark alley at home; don't do it abroad. Use your head and don't let a few strange sights or imposing buildings make you lose your common sense.

Airlines have instituted more stringent security check-in procedures and inspections. Get to the airport at least two hours ahead of your flight time; go through the security checks quickly, so you are not in the unsecured part of the airline terminal any longer than necessary. When possible, take non-stop flights to avoid sitting around in airports. Report suspicious behavior to airline personnel.

Do not carry anybody else's luggage aboard if that person is not traveling with you. Listen to the flight instructions. It is the sophisticated traveler who knows how to use the life jacket, if necessary, not the one who was too blase to pay attention to emergency directions.

When to Visit

The weather may influence the time you choose to visit London. The temperature in winter is in the 40's, in spring the upper 50's, summer the mid 60's to low 70's, and fall in the low 60's. Those are all Fahrenheit temperatures. Though it may rain mostly in the spring and winter, my fall trips have included many rainy days. If you just face the fact that it probably will rain no matter when you go, you'll be prepared.

August is London's busiest tourist month. Personally, I like to go in early spring and late fall in order to miss the bulk of the tourist travel. But whatever your travel constraints, go whenever you can arrange it.

Tips on Flying

On a long flight, seat selection can make a big difference in your comfort. Some airlines book seats at the time of reservation; ask if your airline provides that service. Others are not equipped with computers to make advance seating reservations, but will take advance seating preference, such as smoking or non-smoking as well as passenger location on the plane. Incidentally, many airlines automatically book you on the same seat for the return flight. If I have a choice, I ask for a bulkhead seat. These are located on aisles and near the exit doors and have much more leg room because there is not a seat in front of them. The disadvantages are that you often have people crossing in front of you and some of the seats near the doors are drafty. Personally, I put up with the disadvantages to get the leg room.

At the time you make your flight reservation, you can also order the special meal you want for dietary or religious reasons, such as vegetarian, kosher, diabetic, no or low salt, or fruit plates.

When you board, put your carry-on baggage either under your seat or in the overhead storage bins. This is a good time to take one of the small pillows, to tuck in the small of your back or for sleeping, and one of the blankets. They are much easier to get now than when they are buried under luggage and coats. Change your shoes for slippers and switch your jacket for a more comfortable sweater.

If the flight is not crowded, move into adjacent empty seats where you can stretch out when the plane begins to depart. You will notice the regular flyers making this move as soon as the plane begins to taxi from the gate.

Listen to the flight instructions and keep your seat belt fastened. I loosen my belt but keep it buckled all the time I am in my seat. You never know when an unexpected air pocket or other emergency will occur. The flight crew does everything to warn you in advance, but most seasoned fliers just leave their belts secure during the trip.

And finally, remember to reconfirm your flight when you are ready to return home.

Passport

A passport and money in some form are the two essentials for your trip. They won't let you out of the country without the passport and without money you aren't going very far, either. Contact the appropriate government agency to get passport applications and information.

Get your passport early, long before your trip, so you won't have to worry about it. In most countries, the best time to apply is between September and January. The heaviest demand is usually in March. Once you have your passport, guard it with your life. Either photocopy the first two pages or write the number of your passport, date and place of issue on a piece of paper; keep it in a separate place. In case of loss this precaution will be useful in helping you secure a replacement. If your passport is lost, notify the police in London and your embassy. The embassy can issue a replacement or a temporary passport for the duration of your trip.

But do not lose it. Carry your passport with you or leave it in the locked safe in your hotel. Do not leave it in your room, even locked in your bag. Incidentally, depending on the kind of hotel you stay in, check to be sure it has a safe — and is not just tucking things underneath the counter.

Customs

I won't even attempt to spell out the Byzantine custom regulations which change periodically. Write your Customs Service for their most recent publications concerning customs requirements.

I will add just one note, which you might otherwise overlook: Customs can impound (that means take and keep) "counterfeit merchandise," including fake Gucci bags or shoes, imitation Vuitton luggage, and other bootlegged merchandise. This is done to protect the trademarks of a foreign country, but it can come as a shock to travelers who thought they had made some great buys.

Also check the regulations on gifts which can be mailed to friends or relatives which are not deducted from your duty-free allowance.

Currency

Everyone you talk to will give you different information on how to take your money abroad. So take my advice with a grain of salt and decide how you will be most comfortable. I will just tell you what I have learned — and how I do it.

It took me a while to understand that money is a commodity that is bought and sold like anything else. Since banks handle so much money, they can usually give the best deals.

First, I locate a bank at home which has an international department and buy a small amount of British currency before departing. This is for immediate expenses, such as taxis, tipping or bus tickets. If you are not near such an international center, don't fret. London airports have exchange desks in their air terminals. I advise using the local bank because it saves time on your arrival.

When the money market is volatile and the rates are changing rapidly, the following tips may prove useful:

- If the dollar is rising, don't change dollars into pounds ahead of time and don't buy traveler's checks in the currency of the country. Don't change all your money into pounds when you arrive. Use your credit card for payment.
- If the dollar is falling, exchange your dollars as soon as possible or buy your traveler's checks in the currency of the country.

Plan to take some of your own currency in small denominations. It can come in handy both in London and when you return home. I use traveler's checks. Many banks provide their customers with these, commission free. It is possible to get your traveler's checks in British currency, which eliminates changing money twice. While convenient, it may not be the best buy.

Credit cards may not be as widely accepted as traveler's checks, but can be used in most establishments. Just remember, your purchases are charged at the prevailing rate when the merchant bills your credit card company, not at the moment of purchase. This can make a big difference in a fluctuating currency market.

When changing money in London, always go to a bank for the best rate. Even then you may want to check more than one bank to find the best rate. Ask what the bank is adding as a service charge. It can vary several pounds. One final warning: do not exchange money at the 24-hour credit exchanges. Their rates may be competitive but they can charge up to 10 per cent as a service charge.

Best advice: Exchange only as much as you expect to spend; use traveler's checks, which are insured if lost or stolen; and have enough British currency when you arrive to cover immediate expenses. Remember to record the serial numbers of your traveler's checks and mark off the ones you use. Keep this record in a separate place, for it is important to have these numbers if you lose the checks.

British currency is in the form of pound sterling: each pound contains 100 pence. Spend some time before you leave home or in your hotel room studying and getting acquainted with the currency. You do not want to be flashing around your money in public. A little hand converter is very handy, but you really do not need it unless you are traveling to a number of countries with a variety of currency.

And one final piece of advice: "Everyone" will tell you that no one will accept a personal check. I carry some with me and they have come in remarkably handy; indeed, many merchants and hotels have been delighted to take them.

Don't Leave Home Without

What else should you take, now that you have your passport and money? The most important things to me are an adventurous spirit, good manners and a positive attitude. Good manners and enthusiasm cover a multitude of evils. Remember that you probably will find pretty much what you expect, so expect the best, try the new, laugh at the snags, and enjoy.

Other than the all-important mental conditioning, here are some suggestions to make you a better and more comfortable traveler.

First of all, the more experienced the traveler, the *less* he or she carries. Ask any bellboy or porter. Everything in life is a trade-off, so why should travel be any different? Make up your mind whether you want to see or be seen. Best advice: take half of what you think you will need.

Be sure to take any necessary medications on the plane with you; do not pack them. It is also sensible to take a copy of your prescriptions, just in case you need a refill. Take your prescriptions in their original, labeled bottles for identification going through customs. If you have any physical conditions which might demand medication, take it with you. If you wear glasses or contact lenses, an extra pair may come in very handy.

I am not going to give you a list of clothes. This choice is very personal, and how do I know whether you wear pants or skirts or shirts or turtlenecks? Just some broad observations: Color coordinate. Lay your clothes on your bed and match the colors of your shirts and skirts or pants with your shoes and scarves or ties. Remember clothes can be washed, thrown away or purchased in London.

Two absolute essentials for London: a light raincoat and a folding umbrella. I never leave my hotel or apartment in London without a folding umbrella in my bag. You can almost bet it will rain sometime during the day. I suggest a light raincoat because I dress in layers: a cotton shirt, cardigan and coat. As the day goes on, I can peel or add clothes.

My feet are my number one priority. Take comfortable, well-broken-in shoes. Here is where style goes overboard and comfort wins. I use lambswool to pad tender spots on my feet, wear heavy socks in my clunky tie shoes with non-slip crepe soles. Needless to say I wear pants to disguise my less-than-chic foot fashion. The new light weight running shoes are wonderful.

I do not take very dressy clothes. A silk shirt or a black cashmere sweater will take a woman almost anyplace. Grey slacks and a blazer will work for a man.

Of course I have a few idiosyncrasies. The first thing I put in the bottom of my bag is some flat brown wrapping paper, tape and string because I mail things home, particularly books which are my passion and can weigh a ton. Book rate by ship is very cheap. If you want to send by ship the package must be tied with string so that it can be opened easily by the postal authorities. Otherwise, either string or tape can be used. When the package arrives months later, (ship travel is cheap but very slow), it is like Christmas.

I add a flat-folded nylon suitcase for the things I buy and do not mail. In addition to the regular toiletries, I add soap and a washcloth, since some of the less-than-three-star hotels I stay in do not provide them; a universal bath plug for the same reason; bandaids; and some kind of medication in tablet form for stomach distress. I know you can buy it there, but when I am in trouble, it is usually three o'clock in the morning. I also take small packets of tissues which can be used as toilet paper.

My stomach always takes priority. I take an immersion heater to make coffee, soup or tea from the instant packages I carry. To do this you need an electrical adaptor, since Britain's electrical current is different from many other countries. If you want to have bottled drinks in your room, take a cork screw and bottle opener. Plastic forks, spoons and knives are light and handy. A Swiss army knife with its assortment of tools and blades can be very helpful.

Despite all my advice about traveling light, I used to take a terry cloth robe, but I have weaned myself from that. I still want it, but I do not want to carry it. I dream of the fancy hotels which provide them.

IMPORTANT: Though you have carefully packed your bags, there are still some items you want to keep on or near you at all times. In your purse, carry on bag, on your person or a combination of these, take your passport, currency, tickets, credit cards, glasses, medications, folding slippers, and trail mix, chocolate or whatever you like for snacks, in case the plane is delayed and you cannot get food. Never check anything essential in your check-in luggage.

Luggage

Basically there are just three types of suitcases: hard, made-of-metal or plastic for rock stars and photographers; soft-sided with a rigid frame; and soft with no frame. What you gain in protection, you pay for in weight.

My advice: The best suitcase is the least suitcase. If you use vinyl or nylon, check on its durability and seams. Make sure it cannot be punctured and that it is as rainproof as possible. Almost nothing is completely waterproof since moisture can come in through zippers and other minute openings. Luggage is a personal thing, so in determining your needs, look carefully and check prices. Just remember, you have to carry it. Look for bags with locks which will deter amateur thieves and prevent opening in transit.

Personalize your bag with colored tape or any other device for identification purposes. In the luggage line, all bags begin to look alike. Put tags with your name, home address and destination inside and outside your bag. The sticky tags available from airlines work fine inside the bags. Your business card will fit in some luggage tags. Some tags are covered to avoid easy identification by anyone but the owner. Remove any old tags. Give up the appearance of being a world traveler to avoid confusing the already baffled handlers. If you want wheels, buy separate lightweight carts for your bags. I love them. Wheels attached to bags invariably are knocked off during handling. Most airlines will not check these carts at the luggage check-in, but will accept them as you board the plane. They will be the first articles unloaded at the baggage pickup.

Check baggage allowance, both weight and size. Usually two bags per person are free. Remember: Traveling light is the next best thing to having someone carry your bag.

Help Assure Arrival of Baggage

One good way to insure the arrival of your luggage, in addition to your identification tags, locks, and removal of old tags, is to check in one to two hours before departure. Double check the tag which the airline puts on your bag and don't be afraid to ask questions. When you arrive, go directly to the baggage claim area to pick up your bags.

In the unlikely event your bags do not arrive, report the loss immediately to the airline baggage office. Check the airline's limit of liability printed on the back of your ticket. Remember the liability is per passenger, not per bag. You hear about the lost bags; you do not hear about the hundreds of thousands of bags which arrive safely, on time and in the right place.

Jet Lag

There have been whole books written on how to avoid jet lag. My advice is fairly simple: Eat and drink lightly for a few days before you leave, and especially during your flight. Go easy on alcoholic drinks or avoid them altogether at this time. Try to get some sleep during your flight. Take it easy on your arrival day. Don't plan to attend the theatre on your first night - you will probably doze off during the first act. And synchronize your body clock with the local time as soon as possible.

Arrival and travel into London

The two main airports in London are Heathrow and Gatwick. All charter flights fly to Gatwick, which prides itself on fast baggage reclaim. It has a little lounge near the escalators which lead to the baggage hall. This lounge is equipped with TV sets which announce the arrival of baggage. Free baggage carts and the porters in brown uniforms are there to help you. If you need to change money, look for the currency exchange window.

You can take a bus or a very expensive cab ride, but the train is the most sensible way to get to and from Gatwick. The train stops inside the terminal on a lower floor. As soon as you pick up your bags and go through passport control, take an escalator downstairs to the train platform. Trains leave every 15 minutes from 5:30 a.m. to 10 p.m., then every hour through the night. The new Gatwick Express has cut the trip to about 30 minutes. The fare is between $8 and $9. The train will take you to Victoria Station, where you can take a cab to your hotel. Gatwick is smaller than Heathrow and its compact, modern design makes it quicker and easier to go through.

Get your bags, go through customs, take the short train ride and a cab to your hotel. Unpack, take a rest and you are ready to tackle London.

Heathrow, the world's busiest international airport, has opened a new three-story terminal, complete with its own subway station on London Transport's Piccadilly Line. It handles incoming and outgoing passengers on different floor levels, which speeds up the handling of passengers and baggage.

From Heathrow, the best way into London will be via the subway station at the terminal. If you want a more scenic, but slower route, try the red double-decker Airbus, which goes to Victoria Station with several stops along the way. Or you can take a cab. It is expensive for a single traveler, but if there are several people in your group, it can be a pleasant and sensible alternative.

Traveling in London

The best way to get around in London is on foot. When crossing the street, remember that London traffic moves the reverse of traffic in most other countries. The British have tried to make it easier and safer for you by markings, "Look Right" and "Look Left," on the street, near the curbs. They must have been losing too many of us. Be careful. It is hard to get used to looking the "wrong way" for cars and buses.

Pedestrians also are provided right of way in areas designated by white stripes. Be careful because while cars almost always stop, bicycles and motorcycles often do not. The British also help walkers with their stop-and-go lights. The green walk light shows a little walking green man; the red stop light shows a little red man standing still. And finally, look for the pedestrian underground walkways which are provided at many of the busiest intersections, such as the entry to the subways. They are well marked, indicating exactly which way to go to arrive at the side of the road you are trying to reach, and can be real life savers.

The next best way around is the Underground or subway, known affectionately as the Tube. Get a "Tube" map. It is color-coded and very easy to read and use. The maps are posted in every underground station as well as in the trains themselves. You can buy a "Go As You Please" ticket for use on any underground or bus for three, four, seven or fourteen days. This ticket is cheaper and easier to use, since you do not have to stand in line to buy one for each trip or worry about the right change. If you will be in London for a week, buy a Zone 1 ticket for under $6, which will enable you to go anywhere in Central London on a tube or bus.

The tube runs from 5:30 a.m. to midnight and from 7:30 a.m. on Sunday to midnight. The subways are built deep underground and have enormously long escalators which take you from the bowels of the earth to ground level. Stand to the right on them to let people in a hurry pass you. A few stops, such as the one at Russell Square, use an elevator to take you topside.

Buses are more complicated, but seeing London from the top of a double decker bus is worth figuring it out. Or just get on one and ride around a bit. Do avoid rush hours; they are horrendous. Bus stops are marked by red signs with "Request" in white letters. Buses do not automatically stop; hail them by extending your arm. When you want to get off, ring the bell — well in advance.

Or, you can always hail one of London's 13,500 cabs. London's boxy black cabs are as much a part of this city as the Tower of London or Westminster Abbey. All you have to do is wave your arm. If the "Taxi" or "For Hire" sign is illuminated, the cab is available. Most cabs cruise, although they often line up around hotels. If you need to pre-book a cab, call ComputerCab (286-0286) run by the Licensed Taxi Drivers' Association. You pay for the distance the driver travels to you, up to a maximum of 1 pound, 20 pence.

Visitor Centers

The London Tourist Board maintains information offices at Victoria Station, open daily; Selfridge's on Oxford Street, Harrod's on Knightsbridge and at Heathrow Central Station. The City of London Information Centre is on the south side of St. Paul's Cathedral.

The newest and most complete information center is on Regent Street, just off Piccadilly Circus. Run by the British Tourist

Authority, American Express and British Rail, it offers full information and reservation service for all of Britain, seven days a week. The center includes nine television monitors showing a variety of tapes about Britain, its sights and traditions, as well as a fine bookshop. Perhaps most important, it is staffed by informed, pleasant people to assist you with information, theatre tickets, hotel reservations, package tours and car rentals. It also operates a currency exchange.

The center is open from 9 a.m. to 6:30 p.m. Monday through Saturday; 10 a.m. to 4 p.m. on Sunday. Telephone 730-3400.

Theatre Information

You can order theatre tickets before you leave home through your travel agent or booking agents, or you can get them after you arrive, through your hotel, bookers or from the individual box offices. Just like home, you will pay more buying through the hotel or booking agent. Box offices often do not answer their phones, so you best go directly to the theatre.

Some theatres now have a telephone number listed in the newspapers or magazines through which you can order tickets and use your credit card to reserve. You are charged for the tickets even if you do not pick them up.

You can get half-price tickets on the day of performance at a booth on Leicester Square, which is right in the middle of the theatre district. It is open from noon to 2 p.m. for matinee tickets and from 2:30 to 6:30 p.m. for the evening performances. There is a small service charge.

When ordering, note that the expensive seats are in the "Stalls" and "Dress Circle," the less expensive ones in the "Upper Circle" and the cheapest seats in the "Gallery." In hot weather avoid the "Upper Circle" seats, which are in the top balcony, except at the National and Barbican theatres, which have air conditioning.

Latecomers are not admitted until the end of the first act; be on time or you will find yourself watching Act One on closed circuit television in the foyer. Theatre programs are not free; they usually charge 60 to 80 pence. Theatres do provide cast lists free of charge, however. Check newspapers and the publication, *London Theatre Guide*, which you can get at the air terminals, theatre booking offices and most hotels, to find out what is playing where. My only advice is to consider a performance by the Royal Shakespeare Company, now at the new Barbican Center, as well as a show at the National Theatre. Incidentally, the National Theatre has guided backstage tours at 10:15 a.m., 12:30 and 5:30 p.m. The 5:30 p.m. tour is convenient since it is just before performance time.

Most evening performances begin at 7:30 or 8 p.m; matinees usually on Wednesday, Thursday or Saturday at 1 or 1:30 p.m. Some theatres have early Saturday evening performances at 5 or 6 p.m.

One special theatre to consider is the Players on Villiers Street, just off Trafalgar Square, underneath the train arches. They present old-time music hall or variety shows, during which you can have drinks and snacks. Remember the old song, *Underneath the Arches*? This is where it was written and sung at the turn of the century. You need to be a "member" to attend, but visitors can become temporary members by paying a nominal fee and waiting a certain number of hours. Often the waiting period can be waived.

One last tip. Almost all theatres have bars in the foyers. If you want a drink during the interval (intermission) you can order in advance, as you arrive at the theatre. You will find your drink placed on a table or ledge with your name on a slip of paper, waiting for you at intermission. It is a nice way to avoid the crush of people trying to get a drink. One warning: drinks at these bars tend to be expensive and luke-warm.

Opening Times

The following are the open hours of some of the most widely visited places in London.

Banks: Monday - Friday 9:30 a.m. to 3:30 p.m.

Pubs: Hours since 1988: 11 a.m. to 11 p.m., Monday to Saturday; noon to 3 p.m. and 7 to 10:30 p.m. on Sunday. Opening hours are often at the discretion of the owners.
Restaurants: Generally serve from 12:30 to 2:20 p.m. and 7 to 10:30 p.m
Shops: Monday - Saturday 9 a.m.to 5:30 p.m.

Telephones

Local calls are never free. Ask your hotel what they charge. DO NOT MAKE LONG DISTANCE PHONE CALLS FROM YOUR HOTEL ROOM . The surcharges can be astronomical. The Post Office has recently opened the Westminster Inter- national Telephone Bureau at 1 Broadway, near St. James tube stop. It is open from 9 a.m. to 5:30 p.m. every day. They can help you call overseas.

Helpful Telephone Numbers
If you need **Directory Assistance**, Dial **142.**
If you need the **Operator**, Dial **100**
Teletourist (Information about events) 246-8041
American Express Touristline (40 to 60 cents a minute, depending on time of day; messages last about 5 minutes. Three lines offer shopping, leisure and general information. Shopping 0898-121860; leisure 0898-121961; general information 0898-121862.
Doctorcall, a service directing callers in London to a physician: 935-9535. Open 24 hours every day of the year. The doctor's standard consultation fee is $56.
Weather Forecast:: 246-8091
Time: 123
Heathrow Airport: 759-7702-4; 759-7115-7; After 10 p.m. 759-7432
Gatwick Airport: For inquiries: 668-9311; For reservations: 668-4222

Tipping

Tipping should be considered on the same basis in London as it is in your own country. You might want to remember what the word Tips meant originally: "To Insure Prompt Service." So tip the 10 to 15 percent you would anywhere. Just one piece of advice: A service charge of 10 to 15 percent is often added to your bill. No extra tipping is necessary in that event, so check your bill carefully.

VAT (Value Added Tax)

England has a complicated Value Added Tax of 15 percent on purchases. However there exists something called the Personal Export Scheme, which exempts visitors from paying if the object is to be carried out of the country.

You need to show your passport and sometimes your return ticket to the shopkeeper, who will give you a VAT relief form to fill out. This completed form and the purchased goods must be presented to a Customs Officer in the VAT booth at the airport as you leave the country. You can then send the approved form back to the shopkeeper who will return your 15 percent.

This is a complicated and unwieldy operation. Hand carrying the goods through customs is only half the problem; cashing the checks often results in a loss, depending on the exchange rate and service charges I recommend this scheme only in the event you make a substantial purchase and then only if you are willing to carry the object through customs.

For Up To Date Information

Read any of London's newspapers or weekly publications such as *What's On*, *Where to Go*, *Time Out* or *City Limits*.

Drugs

Do not attempt to carry any form of illegal drugs in or out of the country. The United Kingdom, along with most countries, takes a very dim view of this kind of undertaking. Jail terms of five years for possession of cannabis and seven years for heroin or LSD possession would extend your trip, but in very unpleasant surroundings.

LONDON

FOR THE INDEPENDENT TRAVELER

Three Day Tours

Basic Three Days
Art Lover's London
Romantic London
Royal London
Literary London
Mariner's London
Shopper's London
Gardener's London
Children's London
Legal London
Author's Special London

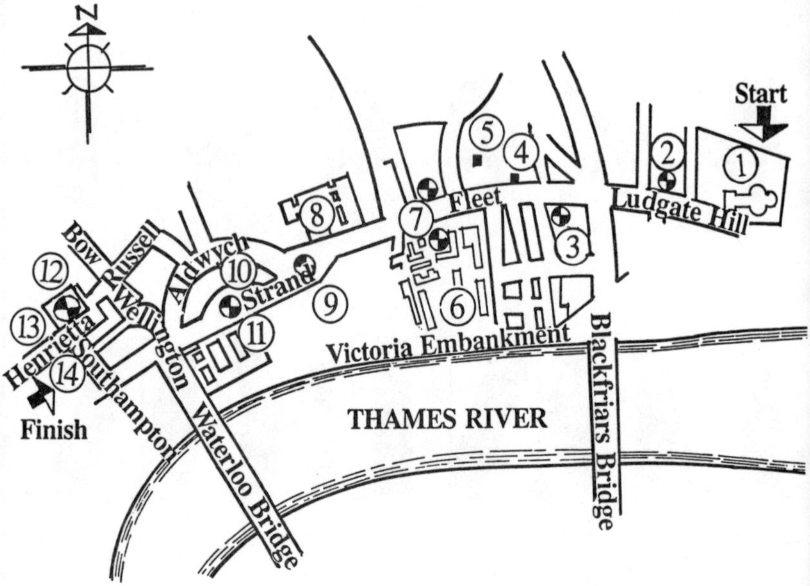

Day 1

1/ St. Paul's Cathedral
2/ St. Martin's Ludgate
3/ St. Bride's Church
4/ Cheshire Cheese Pub
5/ Dr. Johnson's House
6/ Middle and Inner Temples
7/ Temple Bar
8/ Royal Courts of Justice
9/ St. Clement's Dane
10/ St. Mary Le Strand
11/ Somerset House
12/ Covent Garden
13/ Rules Restaurant
14/ Boulestin's Restaurant

Basic Three Days in London

The **Basic Three Days in London** tour is for visitors to the city who are absolutely, positively sure they will never come back. Probably not true, but that is what they think. Tours in other chapters are planned for people with special interests, but this one is for the generalist who wants a sense of this great city in a few short days.

Day 1

Highlights: Tower of London and the Ceremony of the Keys, St. Paul's Cathedral, Cheshire Cheese Pub and Covent Garden.

Reservations: Ceremony of the Keys at the Tower of London. Write Resident Governor, Tower of London, London, England, EC3N, for free tickets, well in advance of your visit to London. Indicate number of tickets and date desired. Rules Restaurant for dinner, 35 Maiden Lane. Telephone 836-5314

Morning

Depending on the location of your hotel, either take a cab or the tube to the **Tower of London**. The closest tube stop is **Tower Hill**. As you leave the underground station, walk toward the street separating you from the Tower. As you reach the sidewalk, you will find a stairway immediately on your left leading to the *pedestrian underpass*, which will take you safely under a very busy street to the Tower side. It is a short walk to the Tower. Try to arrive when it opens at 9:30 a.m., before the tour buses arrive.

The 800-year-old **Tower of London** is the *most important* castle in England and the *oldest* continuously occupied, fortified building in Europe. It overlooks the Thames River and was intended to deter attackers from the river and to intimidate rebellious Londoners. Its 20 towers and 18 acres have held a mint, an observatory, a menagerie in the appropriately named Lion's Tower, an arsenal and a state prison. **Sir Walter Raleigh** was held in the "Bloody Tower" for 13 years and it was here that the alleged murders of the "little princes" by Richard III took place in 1483. The exteriors of many of the buildings are modern restorations but blend in wonderfully with the old fronts.

Walk from the entrance directly to the **Jewel House**, which contains the **Crown Jewels** and other royal regalia. If you arrive early, there should not be long waiting lines or queues, as they call them in London. The guards inside the Jewel House will move you along very smartly but you will have plenty of time to see the wonderful jewels, many of them so large it is hard to believe they are real. Be sure to especially notice Queen Victoria's Imperial State Crown, with the Star of Africa cut from the Cullinan Diamond, and the Crown of Queen Elizabeth (consort of George VI) set with the 108-carat

The Tower of London

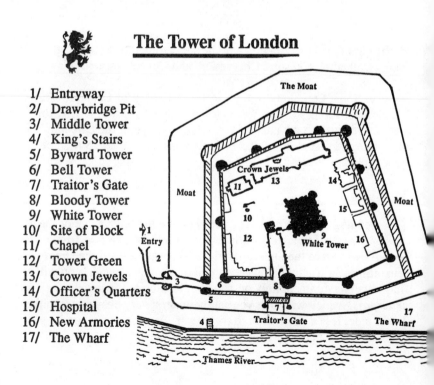

1/ Entryway
2/ Drawbridge Pit
3/ Middle Tower
4/ King's Stairs
5/ Byward Tower
6/ Bell Tower
7/ Traitor's Gate
8/ Bloody Tower
9/ White Tower
10/ Site of Block
11/ Chapel
12/ Tower Green
13/ Crown Jewels
14/ Officer's Quarters
15/ Hospital
16/ New Armories
17/ The Wharf

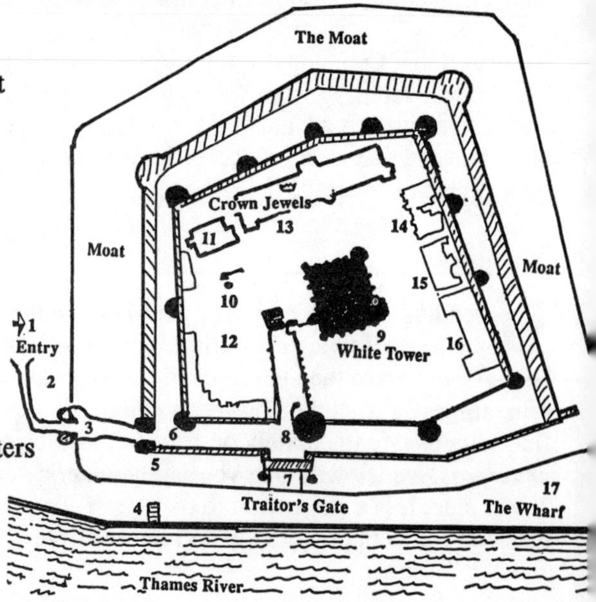

Koh-i-Noor diamond. My favorite is Queen Victoria's "little" crown which she wore for less important occasions and which was not so heavy for her small head. It is a humane touch among the glittering array of royal trappings.

After you leave the Jewel House, walk across the green and back to the **Entrance** where you can join one of the **"Beefeater' Tours."** These men are really Yeoman Warders, an order founded in 1485; 39 guard the tower and guide visitors. I will not recommend many guided tours, but this is a special mini-one. It will enable you to see and learn more in a brief period of time than you could do on your own. Be prepared to tip your guide as he leaves you, usually at the Chapel Royal of St. Peter ad Vincula where two of Henry VIII's wives, Anne Boleyn and Catherine Howard, are buried.

As you walk around you probably will see the **ravens;** the Crown protects and supplies them with food. It is said that the fall of the British Empire will occur if they ever leave the Tower. In order to provide double insurance, their wings are clipped. You may also see the **Changing of the Guard** on Tower Green which occurs at 11:30 a.m. daily in summer.

Now on to **St. Paul's Cathedral.** Either take a cab from the entrance of the Tower or tube to St. Paul's Station. I recommend a cab for this short trip since the tube ride involves a change of stations and is a bit awkward. Ask the driver of your nice black London cab to drive you through The City, the financial center of London, past the Bank of England and the Stock Exchange.

St. Paul's Cathedral is architect Sir Christopher Wren's masterpiece. Modeled after St. Peter's, its dome is second in size only to the church in Rome. As you walk through its imposing doors, turn left. **All Souls Chapel,** the first you will see on your left (North Aisle), contains a monument to World War I leader Field Marshal Earl Kitchener. Further along the North Aisle is the Duke of Wellington's elaborate monument. Statues of Sir Joshua Reynolds and Dr. Samuel Johnson were hit by a bomb in 1941 and were refurbished in 1962.

Take time to examine the **Great Dome,** which rises 218 feet above the floor. It bears paintings of scenes from the life of St. Paul by Sir James Thornhill. The 62,000-ton dome appears to be suspended in mid-air, despite the fact it is supported by eight piers with Corinthian capitals which are buttressed by four huge supports.

Directly below the center of the dome is a plaque to **Sir Winston Churchill**; another plaque here contains Wren's epitaph, "If you seek his monument, look around" ("Si Monumentum requiris, circumspice" for you Latin scholars).

Move up and around the choir stalls to see the carvings by Grinling Gibbons (you will hear his name when you see fantastic carvings throughout England) and the gorgeous wrought iron sanctuary gates by Jean Tijou. You now will be behind the main altar in the **American Chapel** (formerly the Jesus Chapel) which contains an American Memorial to the 28,000 Americans based in England who were killed during World War II. Each day a page is turned in a huge book containing the names of the fallen. In one small corner of the memorial you can still see a hole left by one of the bombs. It is a very moving experience to stand quietly in this place.

In the **South Choir Aisle**, you will see the bizarre statue of the poet and Dean of St. Paul's, **John Donne**, wrapped in his funeral shroud. It serves to reinforce the story that Donne occasionally slept in his coffin. This is the only monument from the old church which survived the Great Fire.

As you leave the South Choir Aisle, you will see the entrance to the **Crypt**. Here you will find the tomb of **Sir Christopher Wren**, with the original tombstone containing the famous epitaph you saw earlier on the main floor of the Abbey; Wellington's tomb; the painters corner with graves of J.M.W. Turner, Sir Joshua Reynolds, Sir John Millais and the American Benjamin West; and the tomb of Admiral Lord Nelson.

Go up the stairs to the south aisle, where you will find the entrance to the galleries, all 627 steps of them. You might want to climb the first 259 steps to the **Whispering Gallery** where you can hear whispers from one side of the dome to the other. You must walk up 542 steps for the magnificent view from the Golden Gallery at the very top of the dome, but I do not recommend the whole climb unless you are in great aerobic shape.

You are now back at the main entrance and ready to leave the Abbey.

Noon

By now you must be starved. As you walk down **Ludgate Hill**, turn and look back at St. Paul's to admire the recent restoration of its magnificent exterior.

Ludgate Hill becomes **Fleet Street** as you pass under the Holborn Viaduct (a 1/4 mile connection between Holborn Circus and Newgate Street). You will pass **St. Martin Within Ludgate**, a church rebuilt by Wren. Look ahead of you, across Fleet Street and to your left, to see the soaring steeple of **St. Bride's Church**. A local baker took his inspiration for what is now our traditional wedding cake from that spire. St. Bride's was burned out during the air raid (Blitz) in 1940 but was rebuilt by 1957.

After crossing Shoe Lane, look for a narrow opening on your right. The overhead sign, which says Wine Office Court, leads the way to **Ye Olde Cheshire Cheese**, a charming and popular tavern, rebuilt in 1667. It is said that Dr. Johnson and Boswell as well as Oliver Goldsmith were regular visitors. Dr. Johnson's house is located just a few steps beyond in Gough Square.

As you enter the low-ceilinged, smoky inn with its sawdust-covered floor, chances are you will be seated in the dining room to your left, at long tables with other people. There is often a fire burning in an open fireplace in the dining area. The two favorite items on the menu are roast beef and Yorkshire pudding, or steak and kidney pie.

To your right is a small, noisy and crowded bar with tiny tables. If the weather is nice, you are apt to see people standing outside the tavern, drinking large mugs of ale or bitters. Ask to see the wine vaults in the basement. If they are not too busy, they will walk you down the narrow steps into the cellar with its wine storage and private rooms for entertaining.

Afternoon

Walk west on Fleet Street: on your left, across the street, you will see little entrances to **The Temple**, the name for both the Inner and Middle Temple, two of the Inns of Court. The other two

Inns of Court are Lincoln's Inn and Gray's Inn. These comprise the English University of Law. At one time students slept, ate and studied in these courts. As you walk along, you will see the street which leads to Lincoln's Inn on your right where **Charles Dickens** worked as an office boy at the age of 14. Now you will pass the **Royal Courts of Justice**, a magnificent building which houses the courts of appeal, probate, divorce, and others. If you detour into either of the courts of law on your right or left, you will be swept up in the world of the scholar and surrounded by winding walks, gardens, cul de sacs, sculpture and ancient, ivied buildings.

But don't delay: proceed down Fleet Street in the direction of **Covent Garden**, which is your goal this afternoon. As you walk along, you come to **Temple Bar**, a strange dragon-like memorial in the middle of the road which marks the dividing line between The City of London and the City of Westminster. It is not very attractive, but at least it no longer displays the heads of executed prisoners which used to be stuck on top as late as 1745.

Now past **St. Clement Danes**, the official church of the Royal Air-force Academy. Remember the old nursery rhyme, "Oranges and lemons, say the bells of St. Clement's?" Well, this is it. For any needleworkers on this tour, take a quick look at the beautiful petit point hassocks hanging on hooks in each pew. In the middle of the road, further on, you will come to **St. Mary-le-Strand**, a Roman-looking church with beautiful blue windows.

Go past the sweeping arc of Aldwych on your right and Somerset House across the street on your left, occupied by public offices. Turn right on Wellington Street, which becomes Bow Street at Russell Street. When you arrive at Russell Street, if you look a block ahead you will see the **Royal Opera House**; a block to your right is the **Royal Theatre** (Drury Theatre). Turn left on Russell Street. It will bring you to the area known as **Covent Garden**.

In the Middle Ages, this was the convent garden of Westminster Abbey. By 1670, the Earl of Bedford had received a royal charter "to hold forever a Market" for fruits, flowers and vegetables. It remained London's main produce market until 1974, when it was moved to Nine Elms on the other side of the Thames across the Vauxhall Bridge. Nine Elms is covered by the largest stressed steel skin roof in Europe. It processes 4,000 tons of fruit and vegetables and 14,000 packages of flowers and plants daily.

Today's Covent Garden has been restored as a pedestrian shopping area and includes a wide variety of shops, bars and restaurants as well as the Jubilee Market, a crafts market adjacent to the garden. Be sure to visit nearby **St. Paul's** church. The Earl of Bedford also commissioned the great architect, Inigo Jones, to design a church for his property, but did not want to spend very much money: "Not much better than a barn" was his instruction. But Jones gave him "the handsomest barn in England." Notice particularly the church portico; you will recognize the site where **Henry Higgins** finds **Eliza Dolittle** selling her violets in the musical, *My Fair Lady.* Today you probably will find jugglers and fire eaters entertaining the crowd.

The rather odd little church garden can be entered from Henrietta Street or through the main gates on Bedford Street. Inside the church, look for the silver casket on the south wall bearing actress **Ellen Terry's** ashes. It is up a step or two, just to the right of the altar. This church is also the resting place for the famous carver, Grinling Gibbons

Dinner

As you walk around the market place, begin to think about dinner and the special treat tonight at the Ceremony of the Keys at the **Tower of London**. There are a number of places right in the central market, several within a block or two, but if you followed my advice at the beginning of this chapter, you have your reservations at **Rules Restaurant** at 35 Maiden Lane. This fine eatery opened in 1798 and is one of London's oldest and most cherished restaurants. It is very British, slow and careful of service and a wonderful reward to yourself after a long day of sightseeing. They will take very good care of you.

After dinner, (if you wrote for your tickets to the **Ceremony of the Keys** at the Tower of London), you will cab to the main entrance of the Tower and arrive before 9:30 p.m. Allow about 20 minutes for this trip. For 700 years, the Chief Warder of the Tower has locked the gates at this hour and presented the keys to the Resident Governor. This is an **ancient and moving ceremony** — just one of the many beloved traditions still taking place in this remarkable city.

Get a good night's sleep. Tomorrow is another busy day and an early one.

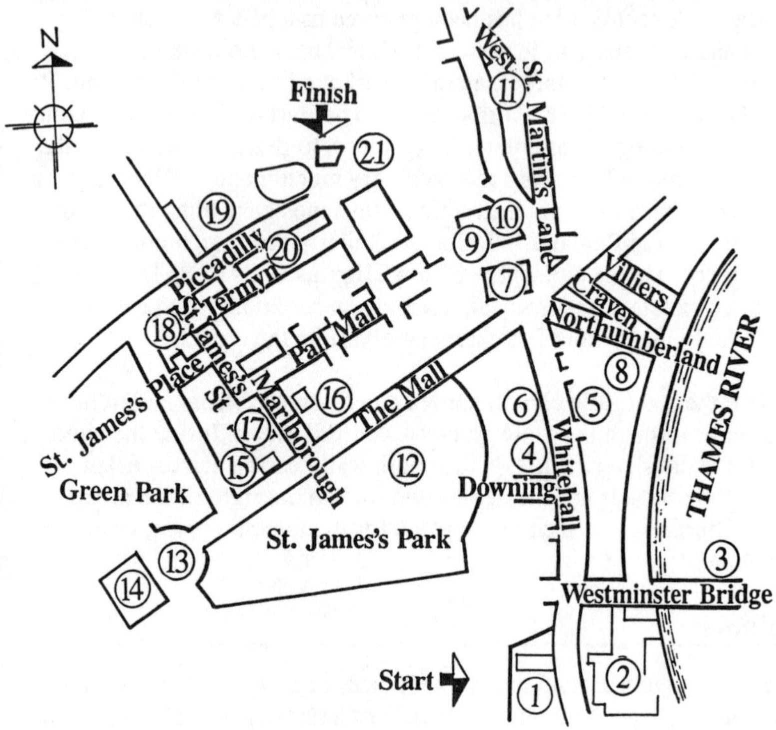

Day 2

1/ Westminster Abbey
2/ Parliament & Big Ben
3/ Westminster Bridge
4/ 10 Downing Street
5/ Banqueting House
6/ Horse Guards
7/ Trafalgar Square
8/ Sherlock Holmes Pub
9/ National Gallery
10/ National Portrait Gallery
11/ The Ivy Restaurant
12/ St. James's Park
13/ Victoria Memorial
14/ Buckingham Palace
15/ Clarence House
16/ Marlborough House
17/ St. James's Palace
18/ Ritz Hotel
19/ Burlington Arcade
20/ Fortnum & Mason
21/ Piccadilly Circus

Day 2

Highlights: Westminster Abbey, the Houses of Parliament and Big Ben, Trafalgar Square, the National Portrait Gallery and Buckingham Palace.

Reservations: Plan to go to the theatre this evening. Check the theatre schedules in the daily newspapers or weekly magazines to select the performance you want to attend. See Practical Information chapter for advice on getting tickets.

Morning

Start the day early at **Westminster Abbey**. It opens at 8 a.m., but the royal chapels do not open until 9 a.m., so plan to be there shortly after 9 a.m. You should still be early enough to avoid the bulk of the tour groups. The tube stop is Westminster.

If you took the tube to the abbey, you will arrive just opposite the **Houses of Parliament** and **Big Ben**. Take the pedestrian underpass toward Parliament and walk out onto **Westminster Bridge**. Look back at the famous view of Parliament. You can see up and down the Thames River. If you have decided to cab to the abbey, take a few minutes after your tour to walk onto the bridge.

As you leave the bridge and walk down Bridge Street, notice the statue of Winston Churchill directly ahead. On the other side of the grassy square is a statue of Abraham Lincoln.

Walk around the outside of **Parliament** to admire this beautiful building, which is very often closed to visitors. Even if it is open, I do not recommend a tour on this quick tour of London. Do, however, notice the statues of Oliver Cromwell and Richard the Lion Heart on horseback, alongside the buildings. Cross over to visit the abbey; alongside, look up to see the gargoyles. If it is raining you will see their tongues acting as little water spouts.

Westminster Abbey was begun by Edward the Confessor in 1050; here William the Conqueror was crowned William II on Christmas Day in 1066, the first British coronation. Since then, every British monarch has been crowned here, and it has been the scene of many marriages and burials of British monarchs. Here Prince Andrew and his Sarah were married in 1986.

As you enter the abbey through the **West door**, you will see a memorial to Winston Churchill and the **Tomb of the Unknown Warrior**. Your eyes immediately will be drawn toward the vaulted ceiling of this English Gothic cathedral. Just walk around for a few minutes and let feelings of wonder wash over you. Then walk down the main aisle toward the altar and at the sanctuary turn left: note the remarkable sculpture of Isaac Newton just inside the altar rail.

At this point you must pay an small admission to the **chapels** behind and surrounding the main altar. It is worth every pence. Walk up the **North Ambulatory**, noting the **Queen Elizabeth** marble tomb in the same chapel with the small memorial containing the remains of bones found in the Tower, thought to be those of the little murdered princes. Read the label referring to "Richard's perfidy."

The **East Chapel** is dedicated to Royal Air Force fighters who fell in the Battle of Britain. Note the stained glass window which includes Shakespeare's lines, "We few, we happy few, we band of brothers (Henry V)." Oliver Cromwell's stone is directly in front of this chapel, indicating he was buried here from 1658-1661, only three years. He was then disinterred, and buried at Tyburn at Marble Arch. Later he, or at least his head, was buried in the Sydney Sussex Chapel in Cambridge.

When you enter the jewel of the church, **Henry VII's Chapel**, your eyes automatically will go to the ceiling, the banners, the carvings and the statues. When you lower your eyes, you will find equally remarkable sights: the carvings on the choir stalls, great double gates, bronze panels and the tombs of Henry VII and Elizabeth of York.

Move on to the *most sacred* part of the abbey, the **Chapel of St. Edward the Confessor**. Cross a small bridge to enter; the chapel, in addition to Edward's marble shrine, contains the **Coronation throne** on which every English monarch has been crowned. For coronations, the chair is moved to the high altar and covered with a cloth of gold. Below the seat is the **Stone of Scone**, of legendary and mythic importance.

Westminster Abbey

1/ Entrance
2/ Unknown Warrior
3/ North Choir Aisle
4/ North Ambulatory
5/ Battle of Britain Memorial
6/ Henry VII's Chapel
7/ Chapel of St. Edward the Confessor
8/ Coronation Throne
9/ Poet's Corner
10/ Faith's Chapel
11/ Chapter House
12/ Cloisters

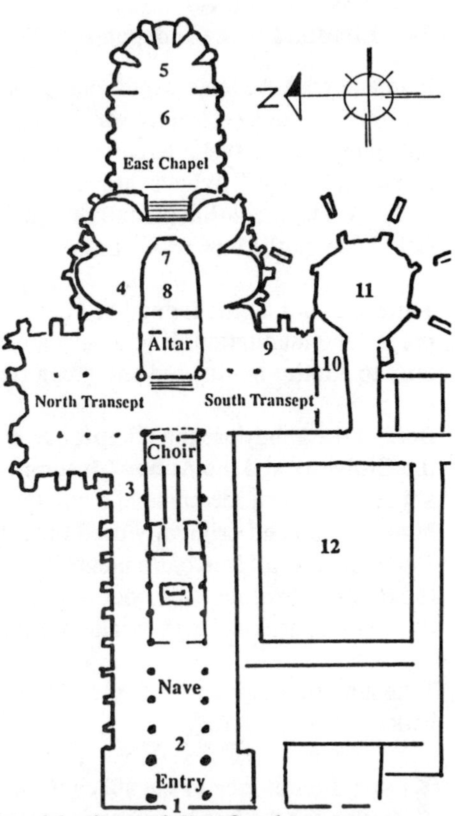

As you leave St. Edward's Chapel *look carefully* for the entrance to the next **chapel.** Many people miss the doorway. This chapel includes the tombs of **Mary, Queen of Scots,** and Lady Margaret Beaufort, the mother of Henry VII. Some think hers is the *finest tomb* in Westminster. Notice the details such as the wrinkles in her statue's hands.

Walk further on and you arrive at the **Poet's Corner**. Here are **buried** or **memorialized** the **most famous British writers**, as well as an American, Henry Wadsworth Longfellow. Look for the fine Chaucer tomb, made of very dark marble almost hidden in the dark wall. The writings are so old they are almost illegible. Visit the not-so-fine memorial to Shakespeare; the strange bust of William Blake, and the memorials to such men of letters as Shelley, Milton, Browning, Byron, Dickens and Kipling.

I was in the abbey in 1973 for the dedication of the W. H. Auden stone. It was an extraordinary experience to see the laurel wreath laid on the stone, hear the boys' choir with their high soprano voices, listen to Stephen Spender and John Bjetleman, England's poet laureate, read Auden's words and extol him. I happened to arrive at the abbey as this ceremony was beginning, one of those happy coincidences every traveler experiences somewhere along the way. Actor **Lord Laurence Olivier's** ashes were laid in the abbey in the spring of 1990. The memorial plaque can be found beside Irving and Garrick, beneath the bust of Shakespeare.

Faith Chapel, at the far end of Poet's Corner, is intended for private prayer and meditation. If you have a moment, enter and sit quietly, if only to admire its fine red and green frescoes.

Behind the abbey are the **Chapter House**, the **Norman Undercroft**, the **Cloisters** and the **Abbey Museum**. On this brief tour of the abbey, I will just recommend a quick visit to the Chapter House, built in 1250 and originally used for early meetings of Parliament, "the cradle of all free parliaments." As you enter, you will be asked to put on little cloth overshoes to protect the floor's red and gold tiles. Note particularly the wall paintings.

Take a minute to visit the Little Cloister with its fountain and flower beds.

If you did not tube to the abbey, walk over to the **Westminster Bridge** for the lovely view of the Houses of Parliament and Big Ben.

Walk back to Parliament Street, which becomes Whitehall, then past the Commonwealth offices and Treasury on your left, to Downing Street, also on your left but which is often blocked off for security reasons. **Number 10**, the home of the Prime Minister, is unassuming except for the guard and the groups of tourists.

Back to Whitehall, with the Ministry of Defence on your right and walk down to the **Horse Guards**. Stop to admire the guards in their full-length capes which almost cover their knee-high polished black boots. If you timed this right, you will arrive at 11 a.m. for the **changing of the guard**. I like this much better than the one at Buckingham Palace, primarily because the crowds are smaller and you can see this one. People insist on petting the horses, which either stand politely or snort at their visitors.

Across the street is the **Banqueting Hall**, built for just what its name implies. The great building, designed by architect Inigo Jones, is worth a quick stop to see the magnificent ceiling paintings by **Rubens.** Although this great room was intended primarily for royal revelries, it was from here that Charles I stepped through a window onto a scaffolding for his beheading in 1649.

Proceed straight ahead on Whitehall with the Old Admiralty on your left and Great Scotland Yard on your right and you will debouch (a wonderful British word I just love) into **Trafalgar Square.** It was built to memorialize Nelson's victory over the French and Spanish fleets at Trafalgar in 1805. Nelson's 185-foot column, topped with his 18-foot likeness, overlooks the entire square. The four bronze lions at the base were created by Sir Edwin Landseer. The square is always filled with pigeons, tourists, and often with political demonstrations.

Backing up the square is the **National Gallery of Art**, and to your right, the church of **St. Martin in the Fields.**

Noon

By now you are ready for lunch. Nearby Northumberland and Craven streets have numerous pubs and quick lunch places. The famous **Sherlock Holmes Pub** is located where Craven and Northumberland intersect. The **National Gallery** has a cafeteria with acceptable, inexpensive food.

Afternoon

Go to the **National Portrait Gallery**, located directly behind the National Gallery of Art. You can "do" this museum fairly rapidly for a *quick look* at British history. Every king, queen, artist, musician, writer, actor, prime minister and military person who was anybody in Britain is here; it is a collection of about 10,000 portraits, including photographs. Not all are on view at any given time.

Take the stairs or the elevator to the **second floor.** The collection is arranged chronologically, from the top floor to the bottom. Then walk down.

On the **mezzanine** are portraits from the Middle Ages. Room one is home to the Tudors: the wonderful Henry VIII cartoon, which was sketched for a fresco, and the portraits of Elizabeth I and Lady Jane

Grey. Look for the famous Chandos portrait of Shakespeare, the first picture the gallery acquired.

Walk through the rooms at a steady pace just looking at what particularly interests you. **Room 13** has the only authentic portrait of Shelley, one of his wife Mary (the author of *Frankenstein)*, and a painting of his friend, Lord Byron, dressed in a Greek costume. **Room 15** contains Jane Austen's image, painted by her sister, Cassandra, and considered one of the gallery's treasures.

To reach the first floor and **Room 16** walk down the back stairs. In Room 16 is the elegant painting of Queen Victoria in her coronation regalia. **Room 17** has my favorite, the Bronte sisters painted by their brother, Branwell. It was found folded up; the creases still show. **Room 21** has Margaret Cameron's photographs of Carlyle and Tennyson, and Watts *Choosing*, for which he used his wife-actress, Ellen Terry, as model.

All the royal portraits are on the **Main Floor** including those of **Princess Diana** and **Prince Charles.** The bookshop has black and white cards of every item in the collection as well as a large selection of other attractive gifts.

London is filled with lovely parks; no visit would be complete without a stroll through at least one of them. Walk back to Trafalgar, cross the square, walk under the Admiralty Arch and you will be on **The Mall.** An entrance to **St. James's Park** is just opposite the broad steps to Carlton House Terrace on your right and Horse Guards Road on your left. Walk to the lake with its ducks, geese and pelicans. The surprising pelicans are the offspring of a pair given to Charles II by the Russian Ambassador to England.

Walk along the lake to the first main path to your right, which will take you back to The Mall. Walk left down the Mall to the **Victoria Memorial**, in front of **Buckingham Palace.** If the standard is flying atop the palace, the royal family is in residence. I suggest you walk back up the Mall to Marlborough Gate and St. James's Street on your left. You will pass **Clarence House**, the residence of Queen Elizabeth (the Queen Mum).

As you turn left into Marlborough Street, **Marlborough House,** residence for important visitors, is on your right and **St. James's Palace** on your left. None of these buildings are open to the public on a regular basis, but you can walk into some of the courtyards. Jog a few steps to your left and then right on St. James's Street.

You will pass **Lobb's**, the bootery; **Lock & Co.**, for hats; and **Berry Bros. & Rudd** for wines; all in business since the 18th century. Do stop in one or more of them for a giant step into the past. Tiny little **Pickering Place**, next to Berry Bros., opens into a little square which is said to be the site of the last duel fought in London.

Continue on St. James's Street to **Jermyn Street**. If you go one block further on you would come to Piccadilly with the Ritz Hotel just around the corner to your left. I suggest Jermyn Street. Visit the royal perfumer **Floris**; the cheese-and-ham shop **Paxton and Whitehead**; and **Dunhill's** for pipes and tobacco.

At **Duke Street** you are at the back end of **Fortnum and Mason**, unlike any grocery you ever saw. The clerks are dressed in tails; ladies of the realm wander around buying caviar and quail's eggs. It is a good place to look and to ship home gifts of marmalade and shortbread. You can also have tea here, or just a sweet, as the British say. Try the first floor bar or the mezzanine restaurant. Or, sit at the counter and have the best bitter chocolate soda in town.

Out the front door of Fortnum's and you are on **Piccadilly**. The **Burlington Arcade** is directly across the street, a glass enclosed shopping mall. Walk up one side and back the other. Look for the beadle's (guards) in their fancy dress who have been here for a century. Out on Piccadilly, and turn left, where you can walk to **Piccadilly Circus** and the statue of **Eros**, with hundreds of young people sitting at the base of the fountain, waiting for something or someone.

Evening

You are now in the center of the **theatre district**. If you took my advice you will have your tickets for the theatre this evening. Time for a quick supper, if your tea at Fortnum's was not sufficient, or on to the theatre. Remember most curtains in London are at **7:30** p.m. A final reminder: if you want to eat after the theatre, restaurants usually do not take orders after 10:15 p.m.; the tubes stop running at midnight.

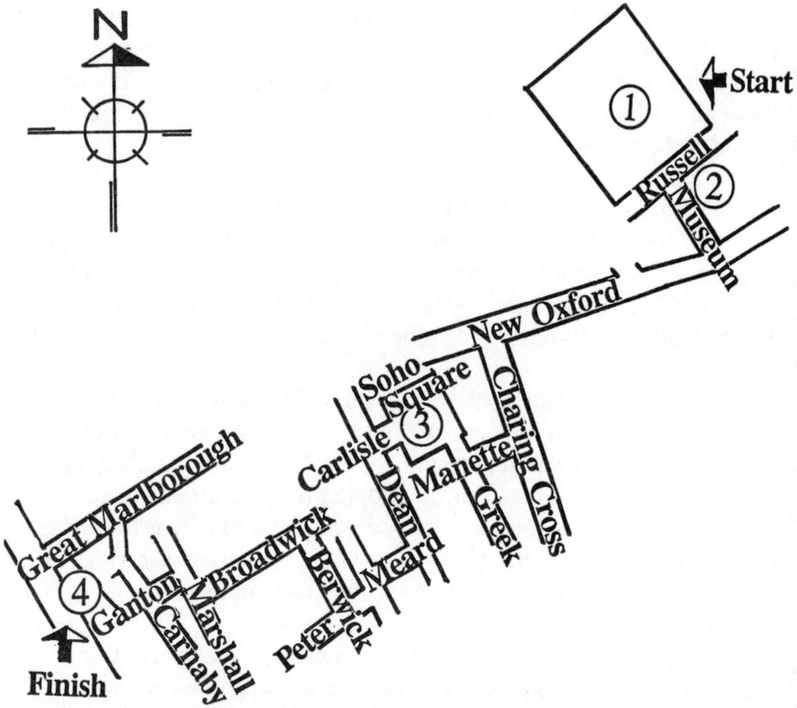

Day 3

1/ British Museum

2/ Museum Tavern

3/ Soho Square

4/ Liberty's

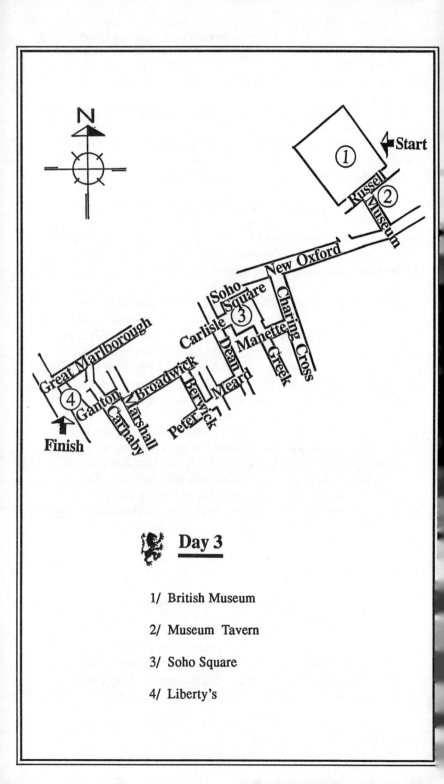

Day 3

Highlights: British Museum, SoHo, Carnaby Street, Liberty's Department Store, Regent Park and the Queen's Garden, and Madame Tussaud's Waxworks.

Reservations: Evening cruises on the Thames. Check schedules and get reservations by calling the Riverboat Information telephone, 730-4813.

Morning

You can start *a little later* this morning since the **British Museum** does not open until 10 a.m. On Sunday it is open at 2:30 p.m. Take the tube to Tottenham Court Road or cab to the museum.

Walk up the long, impressive steps into the **Great Hall.** The **Reading Room** of the **British Library** is directly opposite the front door. Tours begin at 11 a.m. You may be allowed to just look in to see the huge 106-foot-high dome and to hear the strange quiet of the room.

I suggest you spend from an *hour-and-a-half* to *two hours* in the museum, enough for you to see a small number of the most important objects in the collection. I think most people overload their minds when they go to a museum and end up remembering very little of what they have seen. It will be hard to walk through some galleries without stopping, but in the long run I suspect you will carry away *happier memories, if you are selective.*

Turn to the left as you come in the front door, and walk past **Gallery 26 to 25.** The **Great Egyptian Gallery** contains the famous **Rosetta Stone**, which was discovered in 1797 and provided the key to Egyptian hieroglyphs, a script previously unreadable. Note the huge statues of **Ramses II** and the giant **Scarab Beetle**, as if you could miss them. On your left in **Room 16** are the Assyrian winged bulls.

Walk to **Gallery 8**, the **Duveen Gallery**, which contains the **Elgin Marbles**, remarkable fragments of the Parthenon. The Greek frieze at eye level is a procession to Mt. Olympus. Either spend time in this gallery, reading labels and walking slowly around the room, or don't bother at all. Without spending some time here, it all looks like a bunch of rubbish. I suggest spending the time; it's well worth the effort.

Go to **Gallery 14**, just to your left as you leave the Duveen Gallery, to see the **Portland Vase**, a cameo glass from the 1st century B.C., with the top white layer carved away to reveal the lovely blue underneath. **Room 17** displays the royal lion hunts from Nineveh. Zigzag left and right past the **Balawat Gates**, a reconstruction, and the postcard shop. You will be back in the Great Hall again.

Take the stairs to the second floor. Incidentally, you will find toilets on either side of the stairway.

Cut through **Galleries 68-73** without stopping, back to the **Egyptian Rooms Numbers 60-65** with their mummies, mummy cases and other objects. Room 62 displays the splendid Egyptian burial masks. Do take time to visit little **Gallery 66**, with its Coptic portraits, one of my favorite places in the museum.

Retrace your steps to the stairway; return to the main hall and manuscript **Rooms 29-33. Room 30** contains two of the four existing original copies of the **Magna Carta** and **Room 31** features an original **Gutenberg Bible**.

Here you can look over all kinds of manuscripts, writings and letters, including a first folio of **Shakespeare** and letters from **Lewis Carroll.** The cases are well labeled to help you find your favorite objects. **Scott's** diaries of his last trip to the Antarctic are in a corner with other historical documents.

Noon

Time for lunch. Just across the street from the British Museum on Museum street is, you guessed it, the **Museum Tavern**, open at 11:30 a.m. This is one of my *favorite* pubs.

The last time I was there I had the best shepherd's pie I ever ate, with fresh vegetables and some wonderful kind of pickle relish on the side. Be prepared for the hard-working, no-nonsense women behind the counter who sort of yell at everybody and call you dearie. Get your food at the counter, your drink at the bar, and carry them to one of the tiny tables lining the walls.

Afternoon

After lunch, walk up Museum Street to New Oxford Street. Turn right and go to Giles Circle where you will turn left into **Charing Cross Road.** This is the *"street of books."* Walk down to Manette Street (Remember Dr. Manette from Dickens' *The Tale of Two Cities* ?). The great book store, **Foyles,** is here and you could spend the whole afternoon browsing.

Resist, if you can, and walk down Manette Street, under the arch of the Pillars of Hercules pub, turn right on to Greet Street and in a block or so you will be at **Soho Square.** This area was originally the hunting fields outside the walls of what was then The City of London. "Soho" was the hunting call heard as foxes and rabbits were pursued across these grounds. During the 19th century, this was the worst slum area in London. Today, trendy Soho is the center for good food, drink, the movie industry, strip shows and other variations of the sex industry. It continues to be a hangout for artists, actors and craftspeople as well as the "global village" for people from around the world.

Soho Square was laid out in the 17th century. A poorly maintained statue of Charles II and a funny mock Tudor cottage in which gardeners can rest are in the center of the square. To your right, on Greek Street, is the **House of Barnabas,** built in 1750 and still a haven for homeless women.

Walk part way around the square to Carlisle Street, take a short block to **Dean Street**, then turn left. Number 88 Dean Street is an 18th century shop; number 26 is where **Karl Marx** lived in a room above the present Italian restaurant; and number 49 is the old French Pub. Turn right on Meard Street to see some of Soho's earliest buildings. Jog left a few steps to Peter Street, which looks like an alley, but will take you to Berwick Street, where you will turn right to see the vegetable, fruit and flower markets, complete with sex shops.

Turn left on Broadwick Street with its noisy collection of shops. Jog right a few steps on Marshall Street and left on Ganton; you will arrive at **Carnaby Street,** once the home of the flower children's culture of the 60's. Look to your left on Carnaby to see what remains of those wild days. Go right on Carnaby to Great Marlborough Street, where a left turn will bring you to Regent Street and the great department store, **Liberty's**, a Tudor-style building with a maze of shopping rooms. One whole floor contains fabrics including Liberty's silks. The Liberty scarves are a standard tourist purchase. Don't neglect the excellent bargain basement if you feel like shopping. **Hamleys** toy store is just beyond Liberty's, a child's and parent's paradise.

A note: Do not think you saw all of Soho. You just had a taste, and not even a look at the Chinese area on Gerrard street, the Italian and Greek shops and restaurants on Old Compton Street or Frith Street, where unemployed waiters gather, "waiting" to be hired.

After all the noise and hurly-burly of Soho, and shopping on Regent Street, take a cab or the tube to the tranquil area called **Regent Park.** Its original design was to link a park via Regent Street to the now-vanished Carlton House. It is a nice change for this busy afternoon.

Walk up Regent Street to Oxford Circus and take the tube to Bond Street on the Central Line; then change to the Jubilee Line to Baker Street. Notice the new images of Sherlock Holmes on the walls of the Baker Street station.

If you are not inclined to take the tube, hail a cab and take it to the entrance of Regent's Park at York Bridge Road. A reminder: cabs are a good bargain in London. Fees change, but at last count they were charging about $1.10 for the first two-third of a mile or four minutes, with a charge of 30 cents for each additional third of a mile or two minutes.

If you haven't taken the tube, walk down **Marylebone Road**, past London's **Planetarium** and **Madame Tussaud's** remarkable waxworks. You will see St. Marylebone Church where **Elizabeth Barrett** and **Robert Browning** were married. Famous Wimpole Street is just beyond. Turn left at York Gate and walk to the entrance to John Nash's park. The park is surrounded by magnificent buildings called terraces. It would be a day's trip to walk around the exterior of the park; today, just walk into the park but look to your right, left and ahead to glimpse those glistening terraces. On your left, look for the octagonal domes of Sussex Place and the exotic Mosque.

Walk past Regent's College on your left, across the Inner Circle, to **Queen Mary's Gardens**. If the roses are in bloom when you visit you will be in for a special treat.

A restaurant is on your left, near the boating lake; an open air theatre is just ahead with a tearoom beyond it. If you walk to your right you will come to the **Broad Walk** which will take you to the **London Zoo** with all its giant pandas from China and much, much more.

Whether you choose to walk in Queen Mary's Gardens, to explore the streams, flower beds and lake, or opt for a much longer trek to the zoo or around the perimeter of the park, you will sense the grandeur of the planning and construction of this magnificent part of London.

Evening

In this, your final evening, plan a **boat trip** to see illuminated London. During the summer months, boats from Westminster Pier go up and down the Thames River, often with a basket supper available..

If you followed my advice at the beginning of today's tour, you will have made a reservation for a supper cruise. Or you can have supper on one of the restaurant boats moored on the Thames along Victoria Embarkment. The floating restaurant,the Hispaniola, and the paddle steamer, the Tattershall Castle, both serve meals near the floodlit sights.

These three days have given you a taste of this great city. I hope it will encourage you to come back again to sample more.

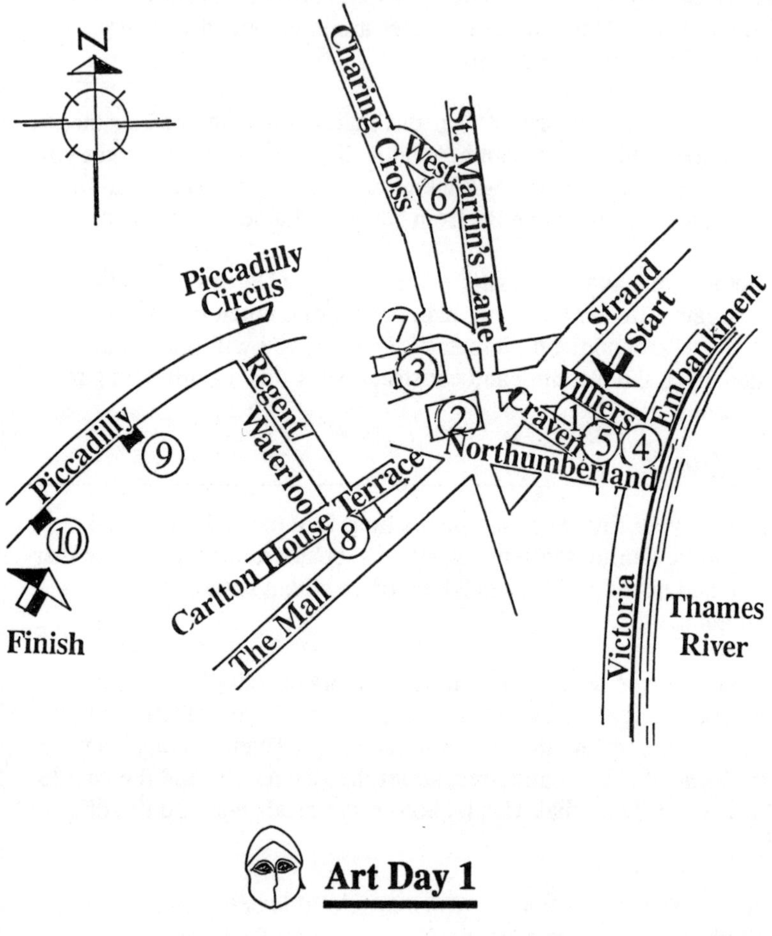

Art Day 1

1/ Charing Cross Tube
2/ Trafalgar Square
3/ National Gallery
4/ The Players
5/ Sherlock Holmes Pub
6/ Ivy Restaurant
7/ National Portrait Gallery
8/ Institute of Contemporary Art
9/ Fortnum and Mason's
10/ Ritz Hotel

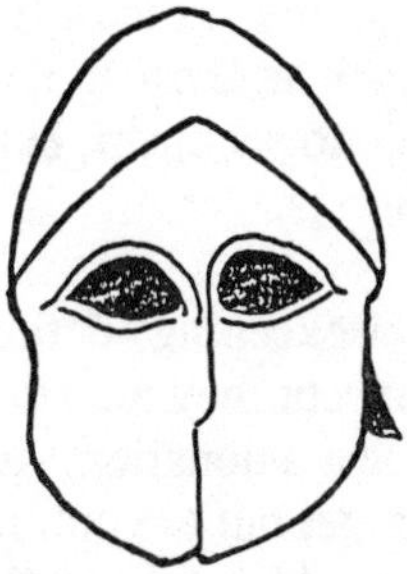

Art Lover's London

London is the home of more than 150 museums and galleries, ranging from great houses chock full of gorgeous paintings and furniture, to huge buildings filled with the treasures of the centuries.

Remember Britain was once the greatest empire in the world and, as great conquerors are wont to do, they collected treasures from all over the world to bring home to their capitol, London. The Elgin Marbles, those wonderful friezes removed from the Parthenon in Greece and now in the British Museum, were not the only objects "liberated" by the British during years of empire building. Many great British collections were developed by individuals with enormous wealth and impeccable taste. It is these fine individual collections which form the basis for most of the great museums in London.

It would be impossible to get more than a glimpse of some of these collections in three days, but let's have a go at it. I have chosen **three major museums** and several smaller, but no less important ones, to visit. More importantly, I am going to suggest **specific objects or rooms** to view. I have learned that if I go to a museum and look at 400 objects, I cannot remember any of them; but if I go and have a good look at 12 objects, I may remember eight of them.

Once in the Pitti Palace in Florence, I left in tears when I realized I could not remember what I had just seen in the gallery I had just visited. I had over-dosed on art. Try it my way. I know it will be hard, often impossible, to walk through rooms of gorgeous things and not really look, but try it on this short visit and see if it works.

My selections are just that: my choices. If you have different and more specific interests such as German Expressionism, which is not one of my passions, do go to see them, but try my technique and look at only a few of the paintings.

Now for a couple of "housekeeping" details. Museums in London are just like those at home except they are still *free*. A few, such as the Victoria and Albert, request a donation. Recently, the government attempted to attach a charge, but the public uproar was such that they rescinded the order. What a blessing for all of us.

Just one other tip: Do visit the museum shops. Most of them are superior and have gorgeous, inexpensive catalogues of their collections and special exhibitions.

You can check your coat and parcels in most museums, usually free of charge. Some places require checking of umbrellas and other objects.

A caution: These are changing collections. Works of art are loaned, reinstalled, and taken down for conservation. My suggestions for touring museums will help, but no tour can be totally accurate given the nature of a living organism such as a museum.

I suggest attending the theatre **each** of the three evenings in this tour. I also recommend having supper *following* the performances. Since I cannot possibly know exactly where you will be attending a production, it is equally impossible to suggest a nearby restaurant. But here are a number of excellent suggestions for supper following the theatre. They all serve dinner till at least 11 p.m.; some until midnight. Do make *reservations*. There are a limited number of restaurants in London, which serve late in the evening, and they are always crowded. *Reserve*.

On or near St. Martin's Lane: **Giovanni's**, 10 Goodwin Court. Telephone 240-2877. Serves until 11 p.m. Monday through Saturday. Serves excellent pasta and great desserts. **Cafe Pelican**, 45 St. Martin's Lane. Telephone 379-0309. Art deco setting and attractive clientele. **Salisbury Pub**, 90 St. Martin's Lane. Very chic and kicky place with lots of stained glass, brass fittings and fashionable folks.

Near **Covent Garden: Rules,** 35 Maiden Lane. Telephone 836-5314. Serves until midnight, Monday through Saturday. Oldest restaurant in London. British food. Excellent. **Le Cafe des Amis du Vin,** 11 Hanover Place. Telephone 379-3444. Across from the Royal Opera House. Wall covered with theatre posters and restaurant filled with theater crowd. Serves until 11:30 p.m., Monday through Saturday. **Joe Allen,** 13 Exeter, south of Covent Garden. Telephone 836-0651. Hangout for actors and artists. Good American food. Difficult to find; look for a tiny light over the door and a brass plaque. Basement restaurant.

Near **Shaftesbury,** the theatre street: **Soho Brasserie,** 25 Old Compton Street (runs parallel and north of Shaftesbury). Telephone 439-3750. Open until 11:30 p.m. Monday through Saturday. Lively place.

Soho: Leoni's Quo Vadis, 26-29 Dean. Telephone 437-4809/ Photos of actors on wall and tables filled with the art crowd. Karl Marx lived upstairs of this 60 year old restaurant. The owners will take you on a tour of his apartment, a tour by flashlight.

Now, on to your exploration of Art Lover's London.

Day 1

Highlights: The National Gallery, The National Portrait Gallery, and the Institute of Contemporary Art.

Reservations: The Ritz Hotel for tea. Telephone 493-8181. Supper after the theatre at the restaurant of your choice.

Morning

Start the day at **Trafalgar Square**; Charing Cross is the closest tube stop. At the north end of the square, facing Lord Nelson's monuments, the fountains and the pigeons, is a huge building, the **National Gallery.** It began in 1824, when Parliament purchased 38 paintings from the collection of John Julius Angerstein, a City banker, and has been expanded five times since then.

As you walk past the elegant columns and up the stairway, note the mosaic floor with images of famous people representing ideas: Churchill as *Defiance* and Margot Fonteyn as *Delectation*, for example. All paintings are on view; some which are considered minor or damaged work are located on the lower floor. Incidentally, Rosa Bonheur's famous *The Horse Fair* and Delaroche's *Execution of Lady Jane Grey* are located on this lower floor.

As I said earlier, the galleries are often rearranged and paintings are moved or loaned. My suggestions on what to see and where to see it may not be totally accurate, but the galleries do tend to stay within various schools of paintings, so my advice will lead you to the areas where these paintings most likely will be on view. Even room numbers change, so do get a printed guide at the information desk or shop to update any changes.

I am going to move you around the museum from **Room 1**, in a sort of bulbous circle through Room 46, where you will return to the main foyer. Some rooms I will not even pause in. One final reminder: my choices are arbitrary, capricious and personal.

Room 1 displays *The Wilton Diptych*, for many years at Wilton House. It is in a little alcove on the far side of the room opposite the entrance. It shows Richard II being presented to the Virgin and Child. The origin and purpose of these paintings are unknown, but the panels are exquisite.

Rooms **2 through 13** are filled with Italian 13th to 15th century art, including Ucello's large *Battle of San Romano* in Room 2. Note the five panels by Fra Angelico, *Christ Glorified* in the *Court of Heaven*; Bellini's *Doge Leonardo Loredan*, a sculptured bust which is very lifelike; the Botticellis in room 5; and the Leonardo da Vinci cartoon of the *Child with S. Anne and S. John* in Room 7.

Rooms **15 to 19 and 26 to 28** are filled with the Dutch Paintings. Notice that although these numbers jump, they are together in the museum. The Flemish and Netherlander paintings are in adjacent galleries from 20 to 25.

The Dutch galleries have some of my favorite paintings: the round *Winter Scene* by Avercamp; Hobbema's *The Avenue*; *Middelharnis* with its illusion of depth; De Hoogh's *The Courtyard of a House in Delft*; and van Hoogstraten's *A Peepshow with views of the interior of a Dutch House* with its odd perspectives.

My favorite room is **number 28**, actually two long rooms separated by a circular room. And of course, the fabulous collection of Rembrandt paintings, from self portraits to the one of his wife Saskia, *Belshazzar's Feast* and and the moving portrait of *Old Man in an Armchair.*

Every one of his paintings is worth time. These are exquisite and, as with so many of the National's treasures, in excellent condition; the museum does take good care of its paintings. And finally, two of the great Vermeer paintings, *Young Woman Standing at a Virginal* and one of the same young woman seated.

In **Room 24** you will find the Jan Van Eyck painting, *Marriage of the Arnolfini.* Everything in this portrait of two people at their betrothal is meaningful. Note the mirror at the back of the painting, which reflects the entire scene in the foreground. Incidentally, the lady is not pregnant; it was the style to emphasize the belly. It is an extraordinary painting.

In **Room 29**, Italian, 17th Century, you will find the Caravaggio painting, *Supper at Emmaus.* Worth more than a glance. Recent construction has resulted in moving many of the British school of paintings. Room 43 now holds Constable's *The Haywain.*

Look for Hogarth's six satiric paintings, *The Marriage Contract*; Gainsborough's *Mrs. Siddons*, portrait of the great actress and my favorite, *Mr. and Mrs. Andrews*, the oh, so self-conscious young couple.

Although most of the great Turner paintings are at the Tate, which you will see later on this tour, the National still has some, including the famous *The Fighting Temerarie* in **Room 43**. It shows the warship, Temerarie, named for a French ship which fought at Trafalgar, being towed to its last berth by a modern steam tug. This paintings is about age and youth as well as about the coming Industrial Age. It is a remarkable and moving painting.

And finally you come to **Rooms 41 and 42** with their Spanish paintings. There are some great Goya's, El Greco's painting of *Christ Driving the Traders from the Temple* and Velasquez's *Philip IV*. The French schools of Impressionists and Post-Impressionists in Rooms 40 to 46 are everybody's favorites. Especially lovely are Monet's *Beach at Trouville, Water-Lilies* and his glorious *The Thames below*

Westminster; Renoir's delightful *The Umbrellas* and of course Van Gogh's *Sunflowers* and his sad and poignant *Cornfield with Cypresses.*

You are now back in the **main entry** near the shop. I recommend the shop with its excellent and inexpensive postcards, catalogues and art books. Obviously, you could spend a lifetime in this great museum, but it should be about noon, time to eat.

Noon

The museum has an excellent and inexpensive **cafeteria** with both cold and hot dishes. If you would like to try a pub lunch, walk across Trafalgar Square and down Northumberland Avenue to the **Sherlock Holmes Pub**. This is an extremely popular spot; in nice weather you will find lots of customers standing in the street. A re-creation of Holmes' Baker Street study is on the first floor next to the pub and there are memorabilia of the fictional detective throughout the building.

The fine Greek restaurant **Beoty's** is on St. Martin's Lane, beside the National Gallery, if you want a slightly more expensive lunch. Lots of choices in this neighborhood.

Afternoon

This afternoon I suggest you visit the **National Portrait Gallery**, directly behind the National Gallery, and then the **Institute of Contemporary Arts** on the Mall, again not far from the National Gallery.

The **National Portrait Gallery** has paintings of everyone who was important in English history: statesmen, generals, kings and queens, artists, actors, scientists, writers, everyone.

Start on the **top floor** which you can reach by lift (elevator) or stairs. Just work your way *down*, pausing by the portraits of people you find most interesting. This is a smaller, very manageable museum and one of my very favorites in London. You can "do" it in an hour and a half unless you become totally fascinated by the images.

As you leave the gallery, walk across Trafalgar again, this time toward the Admiralty Arch, turn down The Mall; immediately on your right you will see the Carleton House Terrace. Walk down the Waterloo Steps to the **Institute of Contemporary Arts**. This will be a chance to see some of the contemporary work being done in London and environs, a big change from the museums you visited earlier.

Evening

Time for a rest and food again. If you plan to go to the theatre this evening, I recommend a good tea since you will not have time for a leisurely dinner before curtain time. Remember: most curtains are at 7:30 p.m.; you can always have supper after the theatre.

You could walk up to Piccadilly and have tea at **Fortnum and Mason's** or at the **Ritz Hotel**. The latter will require reservations. If you decide to have supper after the theatre, check to see how late your restaurant of choice serves and make a reservation. Since so many restaurants do not serve late in the evening, remember, the rush on those that do is tremendous. Check the recommendations at the beginning of this chapter.

Day 2

Highlights: British Museum, Wallace Collection, and the Thomas Coram Foundation for Children.

Reservations: Theatre tickets for this evening and supper reservations.

Morning

Your destination is the **British Museum** and **British Library** on Great Russell Street. Tottenham or Russell Street tube stops are closest. The BM, don't you love the abbreviation, was founded in 1753 and housed at Montague House, the site of the present museum.

In 1823, the library of George III formed the basis for the British Library, which is part of the museum. The building has been expanded over the years, is still growing, and now is so enormous that a morning visit is barely an introduction.

Walk up the great stairs at 10 a.m. (It opens at 2:30 p.m. on Sunday.) Enter the Great Hall, turn left, after a few steps turn into **Gallery 26** on your right and on to **Gallery 25**. The **Great Egyptian Gallery**

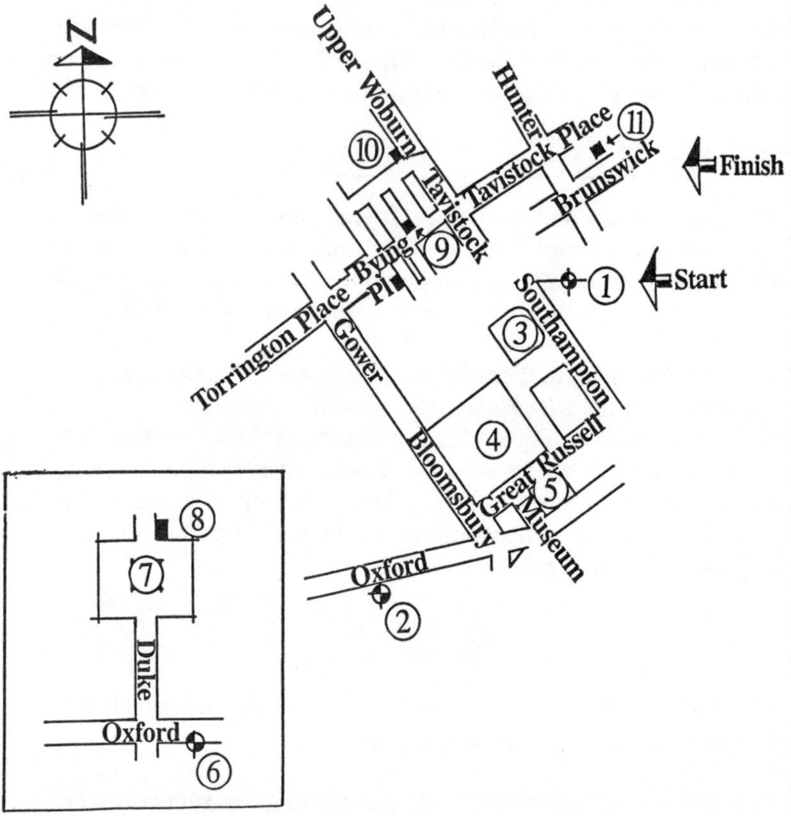

Art Day 2

1/ Russell Square Tube
2/ Tottenham Tube
3/ Russell Square
4/ British Museum
5/ Museum Tavern
6/ Bond Street Tube
7/ Manchester Square
8/ Wallace Collection
9/ Percival David Foundation of Chinese Art
10/ Jewish Museum
11/ Thomas Coram Foundation Art Gallery

contains the famous **Rosetta Stone** which was discovered in 1797 and provided the key to Egyptian hieroglyphs, a scrip previously unreadable. Note the huge statues of **Rameses II** and the giant scarab beetle.

Continue to **Gallery 8**, the **Duveen Gallery**, which contains the **Elgin Marbles.** In 1803, Lord Elgin rescued the fragments of the Parthenon which remained after an explosion in 1687. The frieze, which is at eye level, consists of human figures and horses in procession to Mt. Olympus. Either spend time in this gallery, reading labels and really looking or *don't bother at all.* I recommend spending the time here.

Just to your left as you leave the Duveen gallery is **Gallery 14** where you can see **the** Portland Vase, a 1st century B.C. cameo glass with the top white layer carved away to reveal the beautiful blue underneath.

Room 16 contains the Assyrian winged bulls; **Room 17**, the royal lion hunt sculptures from Nineveh. Zig zag left and right past the Balawat Gates (a reconstruction), through the postcard shop and you are back in the Great Hall again.

Take the stairs to the **second floor**. Incidentally, bathrooms are on either side of the stairway on the ground level. Cut through Galleries 68-73, back to the **Egyptian Rooms (60-65)** with their mummies, mummy cases, and sacred objects. **Room 62** displays portrait masks and Egyptian burial masks. Take time to visit little Gallery 66 with its Coptic portraits, one of my favorite places in the museum.

Cut up through Galleries 52 to **41** where you will find the **Sutton Hoo** treasure, the remains of a 7th century royal burial ship and its contents, excavated in 1939.

Room 44 is the unusual clock room and **Room 45** contains the Waddeson Bequest, an extraordinary collection of fabulous jewelry, silver plate, Limoges enamels, elaborately decorated guns and other superb articles collected by Baron Ferdinand de Rothschild.

Back downstairs to the manuscript **Rooms 29-33.**

Room 30 contains two of the four existing original copies of the **Magna Carta** and Room 31 displays the **Gutenberg Bible.** The manuscripts include **Lewis Carroll's** original *Alice in Wonderland*; **Scott's** diaries of the Antarctic; the death warrant of the Earl of Essex, Elizabeth I's favorite; autographs of the world's famous and hundreds of other fascinating documents and letters. The labeling is very clear and helpful; just look at the signage at the top of the display cases to find the various documents.

Tour the British Library's great reading room at 11 a.m. or other announced times. Its dome is the world's third largest; St. Paul's Cathedral and St. Peter's in Rome are larger. Take a quick look if you have time. Be sure to visit the shop with its great selection of postcards, slides, catalogues, books and other artifacts. You can even buy Egyptian scarabs.

Noon

It should be time to eat. The popular **Museum Tavern** is right across the street; a sign on the door says "Private" Bar, but just ignore that. Grab a table if you can get in, then send one of your party to the bar for your ale and to get your lunch at a counter in the back, ruled over by the bossiest, nicest women in the world. They will take good care of you as they pile on the Shepherd's pie and fresh vegetables. Ask for the pickle relish, which is one of my favorites. It is not as busy on weekdays as on Saturday and Sunday.

Afternoon

This afternoon, you have your choice of two alternative tours. You can either visit the remarkable **Wallace Collection** of extraordinary 18th century French paintings, furniture and porcelain, or, you can visit some lesser known but fascinating collections just north of the British Museum. It will depend on your individual interests.

The Wallace Collection on Manchester Square, is open Monday through Saturday from 10 a.m. to 5 p.m., Sunday from 2 to 5 p.m. Take a cab this time; it is a long walk. Or, ride the tube from Tottenham Court Road to Bond Street and walk north on James Street (which becomes Mandeville Place) to Manchester Square.

The bulk of the collection was formed by the 4th Marquess of Hertford, inherited by his son, Sir Richard Wallace, who brought it from Paris to England. Lady Wallace gave the collection to the nation on the condition that nothing be added to or removed from it. The public was first admitted in 1900.

Here you will visit a grand house with its paintings, furniture, draperies, rugs and art objects in place; only the family is missing. Remember, the British ground floor is the same as our first floor and their first floor is our second floor and so on. I still get confused by this. Just walk leisurely through the rooms on the ground floor, looking at all the magnificent objects.

Rooms 5, 6 and 7 are filled with an extraordinary collection of European armor. **Room 10** has some charming paintings by Richard Bonington and one by that strange French artist Delaroche who painted *The Execution of Lady Jane Grey*. The painting here is *Edward V and the Duke of York in the Tower*. He did love these extravagant and melodramatic scenes. Look for the Sevres porcelain and the cabinet work by the French masters Boulle, Cressent and Riesener.

In **Room 12** notice the magnificent chandelier and the roll top desk, a copy of one now in Versailles.

In **Room 1**, just to the right of the entry hall is Reynold's famous painting *St. John in the Wilderness* and a romantic painting of *Ñellie Power* with her little white bird by Landseer. He is the man who sculpted the four lions at the base of Nelson's monument in Trafalgar Square. There are two more typical Landseer paintings on the walls of the bookshop.

Circle back to the Entrance Hall and walk up the white marble staircase to the **first floor** with the most popular galleries. Notice the Boucher and Fragonard paintings on the stairway as well as the wrought iron and bronze balustrade you are gripping and the bright red carpet.

In **Room 13** Guardi and Canaletto paintings vie for attention; **Room 15** has the Rubens oil sketches for tapestries; and **Room 16** has paintings by Teniers II and a lovely one by Netscher, *Child plucking a Rose*.

Room 19 is the largest room and holds the **most famous paintings** in the collection: Rembrandt's painting of his son Titus; Hals *Laughing Cavalier*, perhaps the best known painting in this collection;

Velasquez's *Lady with a Fan*; and great paintings by Reynolds and Gainsborough. Gainsborough's painting of Mrs. Robinson (Perdita) hangs next to Lawrence's painting of George IV.

Room 21 is filled with some of the best French 18th century paintings in the collection as well as gorgeous furniture. Again Fragonard and Boucher as well as Watteau and Lancret fill the room with their romantic and beautiful paintings. I specially like Fragonard's *The Swing*. Be sure to notice the fabulous furniture, including some made for Marie Antoinette. Do lift the covers off cases in the center of the room to look at the miniatures.

You can spend hours in this extraordinary house with its incredible collections.

Or...

You can visit the little **Jewish Museum** and the **Percival David Foundation of Chinese Art** with a late afternoon stop at the **Coram Art Gallery.**

The **Percival David Foundation of Chinese Art,** open Monday to Friday, 10:30 a.m. to 5 p.m., is at 53 Gordon Square and is part of the University of London. I only recommend this museum if you are particularly interested in porcelain. Its collection of 1400 Chinese ceramics was given to the university by Sir Percival David as a research aid. Other pieces have been added to provide an in-depth collection. The Ming Dynasty pieces and the Celadon ware are particularly beautiful.The collection is located on two floors; one long gallery on the ground floor and two rooms on the first floor.

Walk over to Woburn Place and turn left to Woburn House on Tavistock Square, the location of the small **Jewish Museum**. Open Tuesday through Friday, Sunday, 10 a.m. to 4 p.m. November to March, Friday 10 a.m. to 12:45 p.m. Enter Adolph Tuck Hall and take the elevator to the first floor. Jewish household and ritual objects fill the one large room which is the Jewish Museum. Especially note the 16th century Venice Synagogue Ark. They accept donations from visitors. This is a very small and specialized collection.
If you have any time or energy left, walk south on Woburn Place, left at Tavistock Place, right on Hunter and left at Brunswick Square where you will find the **Thomas Coram Foundation for Children** (formerly the Foundling Hospital). It is open Monday through Friday

from 10 a.m. to 4 p.m. It was Thomas Coram, horrified by the plight of abandoned children in London, who opened a hospital for the "foundlings" in 1739. Both the artist Hogarth and the composer Handel were benefactors of the hospital. Notice the fine sculpture of Sir Thomas Coram outside the gallery.

The foundation's collection includes many paintings and other art works which are appropriate to the mission of the organization. Murillo's *Feeding of the Five Thousand* and Benjamin West's *Christ presenting a little Child* are examples. Be sure to see the painting of Captain Thomas Coram by Hogarth, which is hung on the stair landing.

The **Courtroom** is just off the Lobby on the first floor (not the ground floor). Visit this bright room with a Hogarth painting, an early Gainsborough and the pitiful objects left with the abandoned children by their mothers. These are in covered cases near the windows. Just fold back the cloth coverings. The ceiling is from the original building.

The nearby **Picture Gallery** has a number of good paintings including a cartoon for the tapestry *Massacre of the Innocents* from the School of Raphael and a copy of the score of Handel's *Messiah*. The organ keyboard, on which Handel often played, is here. Notice the mannequins dressed in the uniforms worn by boys and girls at the hospital from mid 1740 to 1950.

There are some fine art pieces but that is not why you are here. You came to honor the memory of the generous and kindly man who helped so many poor and friendless children. It is quite a special place; I recommend it.

Evening

If you need a place to sit down and have a glass of something, there is a **wine bar** on Tavistock, just off Woburn Place. Otherwise just go back to your hotel for a rest and a quick bite to eat before the theatre tonight. Check the beginning of this chapter for suggestions of where to eat following the performance.

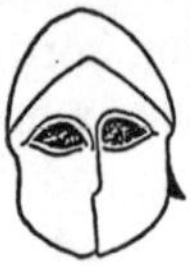

Art Day 3

Morning

1/ Pimlico Tube

2/ Tate Gallery

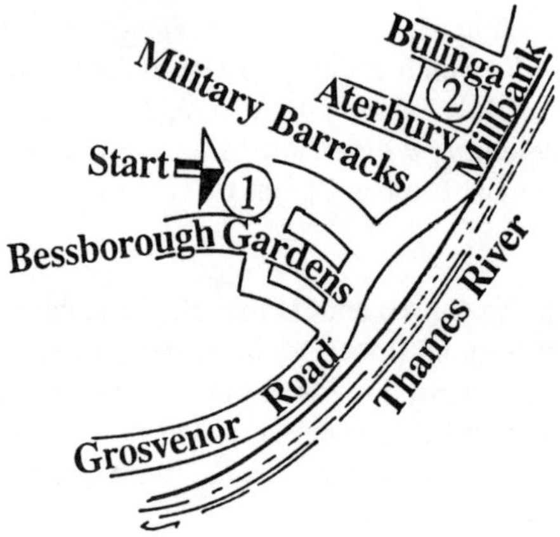

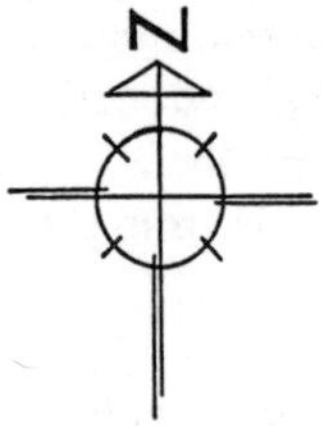

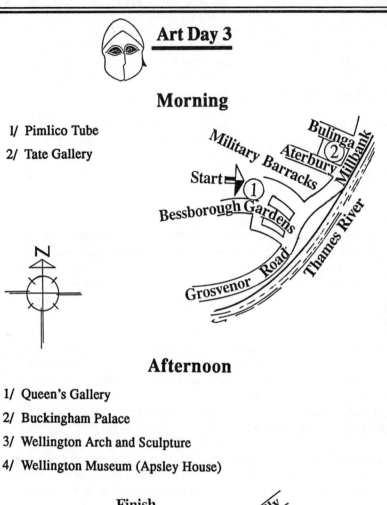

Afternoon

1/ Queen's Gallery

2/ Buckingham Palace

3/ Wellington Arch and Sculpture

4/ Wellington Museum (Apsley House)

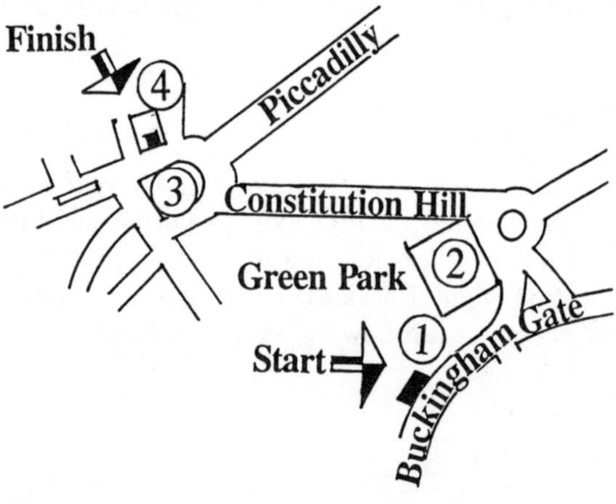

Day 3

Highlights: Tate Gallery, Queen's Gallery, Wellington Museum, and the Victoria and Albert Museum.

Reservations: Lunch reservations at the Tate Gallery restaurant. Telephone 834-6754. Theatre reservations.

Morning

Today it is the **Tate Gallery** on Millbank alongside the Thames. The closest tube stop is Pimlico. Open Monday through Saturday from 10 a.m. to 6 p.m.; Sunday from 2 to 6 p.m. Plan to have lunch in their first-rate restaurant. Reservations are essential.

This is the largest collection of modern works of art in Britain. The Tate also houses works by British artists from the 16th century. The British paintings by artists working in Britain and born before 1860 are left of the entrance on the ground floor. The modern collection of artists born after 1860 are right of the entrance.

The new **Clore Gallery**, designed by architect James Stirling, houses J.M.W. Turner's bequest of his works to the nation. The handsomely lit and designed galleries compliment the glowing sea paintings by Turner.

The French Impressionists and Post-Impressionists include everybody you ever heard of. Note especially Degas' sculpture of the *Little Dancer* with the satin ribbon in her hair just like the one in the Jeu de Paume in Paris; and Rodin's *The Kiss*. Everyone is represented: the Cubists, Abstractionists, Surrealists and Pop artists. There is a Pollock 'drip' painting, a Braque guitar and a Lichtenstein "WHAAM!"

Noon

Time for lunch at the **Tate** restaurant, if you made reservations. It is located on the lower level of the museum. The food is good, the wine list impeccable and the decorations by Rex Whistler beautiful.

Afternoon

This afternoon I will give you a choice again. In either event, take a cab from the front of the Tate. Either plan to go to the **Victoria and Albert Museum** or to the **Queen's Gallery** and the **Wellington Museum** in Apsley House. It depends on your taste.

The **Queen's Gallery** on Buckingham Palace Road, open during *Exhibitions only*, Tuesday through Saturday from 10:30 a.m. to 5 p.m., Sunday from 2 to 5 p.m, features special exhibitions, each drawn from the magnificent Royal Collection. Check listings in newspapers or magazines as to the details of the current exhibition. Whatever is there, it will be splendid. The Royal Collection is one of the world's greatest collections.

Walk up Constitution Hill, through Green Park to the Wellington Arch and across the way to **Apsley House** and the **Wellington Museum.** This is the busiest traffic circle in London, with hundreds of cars going round and round. The only safe way to cross is via the pedestrian subway.

The house is open Tuesday through Sunday from 11 a.m. to 5 p.m., Sunday from 2:30 to 6 p.m. It is closed Monday and Friday. Watch those closed days. This was the home of the **Duke of Wellington**, the 'Iron Duke', victor at Waterloo and Prime Minister from 1828 to 1830. Its collection is rich in Spanish paintings and memorabilia of Wellington's career.

The entrance hall has Lawrence's full-length portrait of Wellington. In the vestibule is Canova's almost nude marble statue of Napoleon Bonaparte; the Drawing Rooms are filled with fine Dutch paintings. But it is the rooms themselves you want to see, several designed by Adam and others by Wyatt. The great Waterloo Gallery, with its fine ceiling and windows, is magnificent. Notice particularly the Velasquez painting, *The Water-Seller of Seville*.

The Dining Room is now outfitted with its original oak chairs and table with a 26-foot-long silver Portuguese service as a centerpiece. I will never think of a centerpiece in quite the same way after seeing this one.

This magnificent house will give you some sense of the history of that time and the man who lived there.

OR

The Victoria and Albert Museum of fine and applied arts. Located on Brompton Road, it is open Monday to Saturday 10 a.m. to 5:30 p.m.; Sunday, 2:30 to 5:30 p.m. I have always found this one of the more difficult museums to explore because of its physical layout and because it has so many collections on view.

The museum is constantly renovating displays, which can involve closing galleries for months, and warns in its information brochure that "Galleries are sometimes closed without notice owing to shortage of staff." It is important to remember all of these admonitions so that you will not be too disappointed if you cannot see all the galleries I recommend.

Enter the museum at the **Cromwell Road** entrance. Walk through the entrance hall, Room 49; the shop will be to your left in room 48a. After you pay your donation and walk past the ticket seller you will be in a long hall which extends to your right and left. This is the **Index Corridor**. Directly ahead of you is the New Medieval Treasury room. On your right are the art of China gallery and the new Japanese Gallery.

Exit at the far end of the Japanese Gallery into Galleries **22, 23 and 24** with their collections of Gothic Art from Italy, England, France and Germany.

In **Gallery 25**, to your right, visit the large altar piece with scenes from the life of St. George. Continue along Galleries 26 and 27 to see art from the Northern European Renaissance. Cut through Gallery 29 to Gallery 38 to see the Medieval Tapestries.

Circle around the garden, which is to your left, to Galleries **16 and 15,** Italian Renaissance. Just beyond are *three extraordinary rooms:* the Poynter Room or Dutch kitchen, with its Minton blue and white tiles and stained glass window; the Gamble Room, with its decorated ceiling and columns; and the Morris Room or Green Dining Room, with its Burne-Jones panels. Follow the Italian Renaissance from Rooms 13 to 20. Turn right into Room 21 with objects from the High Renaissance 1500-1600.

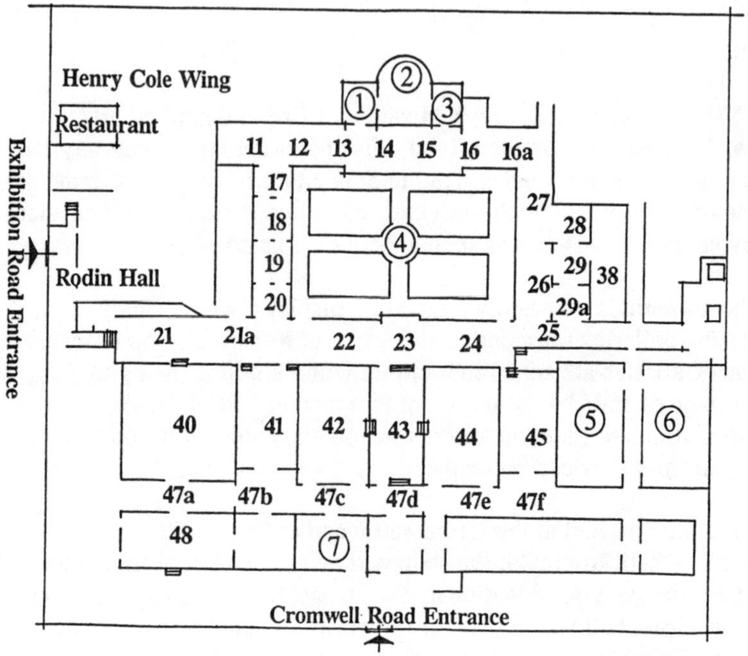

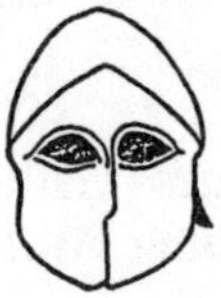

Victoria and Albert Gallery

Ground Floor

1/ Morris Room
2/ Gamble Room
3/ Poynter Room
4/ Garden
5/ Victorian Cast Court
6/ Italian Cast Court
7/ Shop

This would be a good time to stop for something to eat or drink. Walk through Room 21 to the entry way off Exhibition Road, turn right and walk through the Rodin sculpture to the steps which will take you downstairs to the **Henry Cole Wing** and the **restaurant.** The wing with its seven floors is filled with paintings, prints, photographs and watercolors.

And I am only taking you to the restaurant. If you insist, you might want to see the huge collection of Constable paintings, watercolors and drawings on the sixth level of this building. The restaurant is extremely handsome and the food is admirable and inexpensive.

Retrace your steps upstairs and back through **Gallery 21.** Turn to your right to see the famous **dress collection** in Gallery 40. The museum staff tells me that *25 percent* of visitors come to see this collection of costumes, which range from the 16th to 20th century.

Walk across the hallway to **Gallery 48** to see the enormous room containing the astounding Raphael Cartoons. The museum has *7 of the 10* **Raphael designs for tapestries woven in Brussels for the Sistine Chapel in Rome.**

Cross back to **Gallery 47b**, filled with Indian sculpture including Tipu's Tiger, a large wooden model of a tiger mauling a British officer. Inside is a small organ which reproduces the groans of the unfortunate victim, but that is not operational now, so it is not as gruesome as it sounds.

Gallery 41 is filled with Indian Art, including the fine Mughal rugs.

The Art of Islam in **Gallery 42** will bring you full circle and back to the **entrance** and shop

If you have either the time or interest, walk the length of **Corridor 47** to the Victorian and Italian **cast courts** , which opened in 1873. As you can tell from the name, these enormous skylit rooms are filled with *copies* of works of art. This kind of copying was very popular at the time but fell out of favor in the 20th century. Only recently has there been a revived interest in the collection because of its quality.

I have to admit I love these galleries and was totally astonished the first time I walked into one to see the exact copy of Trajan's enormous column sitting in the middle of the room.

As you walk around these two rooms, you will see *copies of many of the world's greatest sculptures*, from Michelangelo's David and Moses to the 12th century Portico de La Gloria from Santiago de Compostela.

However you may feel about copying works of art, I think you will be amazed at this collection and the architecture courts in which they are displayed.

I was amused to find a cast of a large fig leaf hanging behind the copy of the David statue. A sign read it was "hung on the cast on the occasion of visits by royal ladies". The fig leaf was originally used on the visit of Queen Victoria, and last used for the late Queen Mary when she was Queen Mother.

The **shop** is worth a stop. It has a fine assortment of material about the museum's collection and other art-related books and objects. At the side is a small alcove containing articles, especially fine glass work, made by British craftspeople.

Your visit has enabled you to see the art of the major civilizations, the art of the Renaissance including the tapestry collection, the great dress collection and several of the museum's fine period rooms.

And all of this on the main floor. On future visits you can go upstairs to see the jumble of British furniture and painting, the incredible iron-work, bronzes, jewelry, armor, embroidery, enamels, silver and musical instruments.

There seems to be no end to this museum, but you have made a start.

Evening

Walk up Brompton Road to **Harrods** for their spectacular **tea** at 4 p.m. or be content with resting in the museum restaurant.

Little **Beauchamp Place**, near Harrods, also has a number of places to rest and refresh. After walking through museums all day, the theatre would be a good place to spend the evening.

Check the beginning of this chapter for after-theatre restaurant suggestions.

No matter what choices you made during these three days, you will have seen wonderful things. I hope it will encourage you to stay longer and come back.

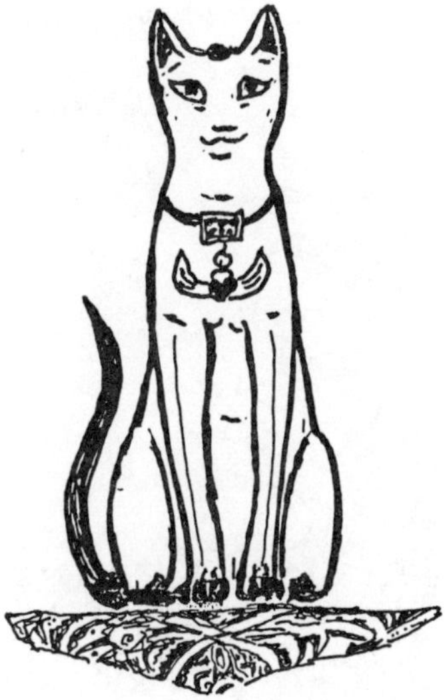

Romantic Day 1

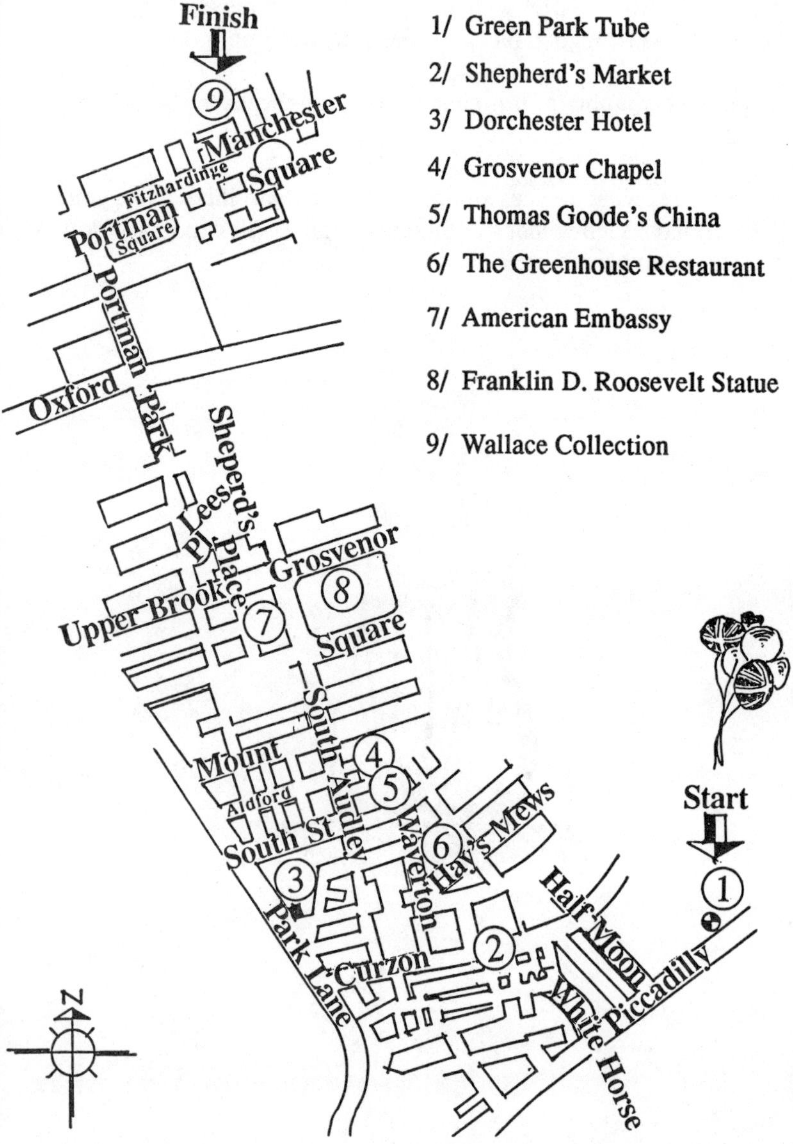

1/ Green Park Tube

2/ Shepherd's Market

3/ Dorchester Hotel

4/ Grosvenor Chapel

5/ Thomas Goode's China

6/ The Greenhouse Restaurant

7/ American Embassy

8/ Franklin D. Roosevelt Statue

9/ Wallace Collection

Romantic London.

When you think of romantic cities you may think first of Paris, Venice or Vienna, but probably not London. What makes a city *romantic?* Gardens, parks, pretty restaurants, lakes and rivers, strolling paths, flowers, music and art. London has them all.

Consider this: Your three days in London will include a leisurely walk through the most elegant part of this fabulous city, a boat trip following the path of kings and queens, a night cruise to see illuminated London, a picnic in an elegant park, rooftop dining and an outdoor theatre performance in the Queen's rose garden.

Your days will start later in the mornings, be more unhurried and not so filled with sightseeing as some of the other tours—all befitting your **"Romantic" London.**

Day 1

Highlights: Mayfair, Shepherd's Market, Grosvenor Chapel and Square, the Wallace Collection and the Dorchester Hotel.

Reservations: Lunch reservations at The Greenhouse, 27a Hays Mews. Telephone 499-3331.

Evening: Open air theatre in Regent's Park. Check newspapers or magazines to see whether there is a production and time of performance. Call to reserve tickets. Or, as an alternative, make dinner reservations at Boulestin's Restaurant, corner of Henrietta and Southampton streets. Telephone 836-7061.

What better place to start than in the most elegant part of London: **Mayfair** with its Rolls Royces; men in bowler hats and tightly furled umbrellas; ladies, hatted and gloved and sipping tea; and rows of town houses and antique shops.

The original May Fair, from which this part of London takes its name, was held in Shepherd's Market two weeks each year from late 1680 to the mid 1700's. This is the area which satirists Trollope and Thackeray wrote about in their novels of power and wealth and in which Evelyn Waugh's *Brideshead Revisited* was set. Shepherd's Market is now filled with small houses, shops, cafes, a little marketplace and the famous pub, Shepherd's.

Morning

Start the day in **Sheperd's Market** about 10 a.m. The **Green Park** tube stop is closest or cab to the market. If you take the tube, walk west on Piccadilly to either White Horse Street or Half Moon Street.

If you turn right on either one of them, you will arrive at the center of the market area. You will remember Half Moon Street is where P.G. Wodehouses's Jeeves took such good care of Bertie Wooster.

The **market area** stretches to your left and is filled with lovely shops, restaurants, pubs and interesting buildings. Explore the whole area, walking up and down the little mews, stopping for a cup of coffee or tea and a scone at one of the cafes.

After your exploration in the market, walk up to **Curzon Street.** Those of you who are bookophiles, look for 10 Curzon Street and the famous Heywood Hill Bookstore, filled with old and new books. Incidentally, the bookstore is located right next to Trumpers, the royal barbershop. Take a look in the window.

Walk west on Curzon Street to Park Lane, turn right and walk up past the fancy Dorchester Hotel until you come to **Aldford Street.** Turn right to see the Victorian houses and the lovely **Grosvenor Chapel** directly ahead. The chapel was built in 1730 and was adopted by the American forces in 1939-45.

When you come to South Audley, turn right for a block to see **Thomas Goode's**, purveyor of china to the Queen. Particularly notice the pair of seven foot ceramic elephants in the windows; the Minton pottery made them for the Paris Exhibitions in 1878 and 1889. Flowers are planted all around the shop. Go in and at least take a look.

Noon

Time for your lunch. Walk along the side of Goode's store on South Street one block, turn right on Waverton for about a block and a half, and turn left on Hays Mews. **The Greenhouse**, where you made your reservation, is just a few steps down the block.

The entrance to this restaurant is the prettiest in London. Flower beds on either side of the canopied walk take you into this romantic restaurant with its white linen cloths and Victorian chairs. Lunch for two will be moderate in cost.

Afternoon

After lunch, retrace your steps to South Audley. Right on Waverton, left on South Street and right on South Audley, remember? Two blocks further, you will come to **Mount Street.**

Walk either right or left and look at the pink terra cotta fronts from the late 19th century and the antique shops. Every time I come to this corner, I am startled by the beauty of the buildings. They are quite extraordinary.

Another two blocks north on South Audley will bring you to **Grosvenor Square**, where you will find the United States Embassy with its huge, menacing eagle hovering overhead. I have never liked this Embassy because of its brutal look. The square has been associated with the United States since John Adams was America's first minister to Britain and lived at #9 on the square.

The area is known as *Little America*. Particularly notice the fine statue in memory of American President Franklin D. Roosevelt. I have never been able to find out why the statue shows him standing, but I am sure there is a good reason.

Number 20 was headquarters for General Eisenhower in 1942 and 1944. Don't spend too much time around this rather sparse and uninviting square.

Walk back to Park Lane on Upper Brook Street to see great views of the city and the long terraces of homes. Turn right on Park Street to **Lees Place** to see a little cottage dated 1723 and Shepherd's Place with its antique street lamps.

Now head for the famous **Wallace Collection.** Continue north on Park Street which becomes Portman Street. Walk to the far (north) side of Portman square, turn right to Manchester Square where you will find the great Hertford House (Open weekdays 10 a.m. to 5 p.m.; Sunday 2-5 p.m.) which houses the Wallace Collection.

This is the **finest collection** of French paintings, furniture and objects of art outside France; it is the most romantic house and art collection in the city.

Here you will find a wonderful series of rooms filled with sculpture, porcelain, furniture, paintings and armor in which you can wander to your heart's content and not worry about whether you have seen all the right things. Everything is lush and beautiful.

The collection is particularly rich in ornate paintings by Boucher, Watteau and Fragonard. Room XVI contains the most important paintings in the collection; the best known being Frans Hals' *The Laughing Cavalier.* The house has recently been renovated and reinstalled and is a complete joy.

It should now be late afternoon and time for tea. I suggest a short cab ride from the Wallace Collection back to the **Dorchester Hotel** on Park Lane where you strolled earlier today. Their cream tea consists of little sandwiches and cakes and all manner of good things served in lovely surroundings. You might consider making this your light supper.

Evening

During the middle summer months there are performances at the open air theatre in **Regent's Park.** What could be more romantic than watching a production of *A Midsummer's Night Dream* in the rose gardens of the park?

If you have followed my earlier suggestions, you will have arranged for tickets for the park performance. An alternative is dinner at the fine French restaurant, **Boulestin's,** for which I suggested making reservations at the beginning of this chapter.

Relax and enjoy the evening and think about your long, meandering boat trip planned for tomorrow.

Day 2

Highlights: Westminster Pier, Thames River and Hampton Court.

Reservations: Information about sailing times of river boats. Telephone 730-4812. Double check sailing times since they are subject to change.

Alternative suggestion for the day: Sightseeing bus tours are not among my favorite ways to travel; however, Harrods Department Store has luxury sightseeing tours in double-decker Harrod green buses.

They are *extremely* comfortable, air-conditioned and have a"stewardess"aboard to bring you tea, coffee, soft drinks and bisuits. They even have a toilet on the lower deck. One of their specialties is a full-day tour to Stratford-Upon-Avon and Blenheim Palace for about $80 per person, which includes transportation, all entry fees, and a good three-course luncheon.

This is not quite as romantic as the trip down the river, but a double decker bus is not to be sneezed at, and you do see two great buildings in a relatively small amount of time and without undue effort. Book by calling 581-3603 or through your hotel porter. The coaches leave from Harrods Department store on Brompton Road. Check for departure times since these are subject to change.

Dinner reservations: Bombay Brasserie, Bailey Hotel, 1 Courtfield Close, Courtfield Road, South Kensington. Telephone 370-4040.

Romantic Day 2

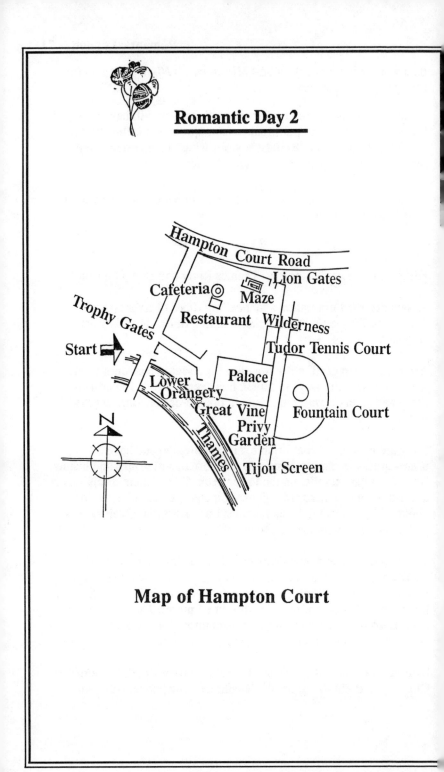

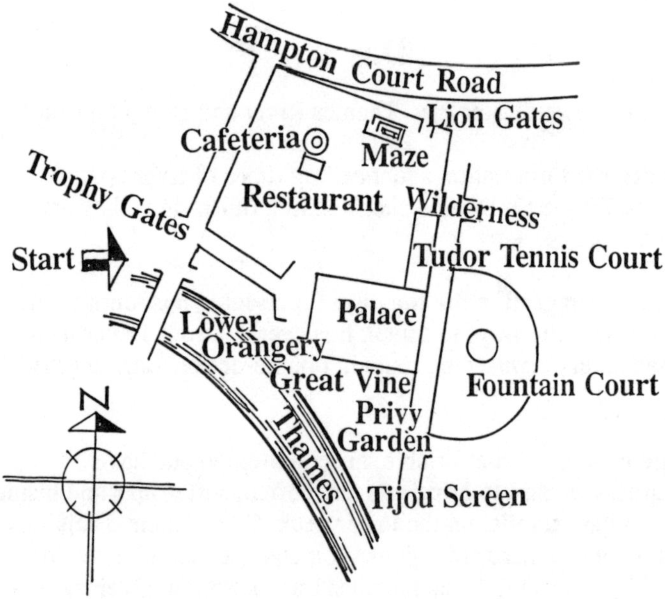

Map of Hampton Court

Morning

Today you are going to follow the **path of kings** down London's main highway and spend the afternoon in a royal palace and garden. The highway is the **Thames River** and your destination is **Hampton Court**, the palace built by Cardinal Wolsey, Henry VIII and William and Mary.

The monarchs and courtiers of England went to this idyllic spot by way of the river to spend weeks in pleasure and parties or to escape the various plagues which infested the city.

This morning you will take that same trip, leaving from **Westminster Pier**. The 21-mile trip takes about three hours and 45 minutes. I suggest you plan to take the boat to Hampton Court and return by train or bus from Hampton.

Sailing schedules are always subject to weather and are only operative in the summer months. The boats leave from the pier at 10 a.m., 10:30 a.m., 11 a.m., and 12 noon. They return from Hampton at 3, 4 and 5 p.m. I suggest you leave on the 10 a.m. boat.

I cannot imagine a more *romantic trip* than following this route, first past Parliament and the London bridges; alongside great country houses, the park at Richmond, Kew Gardens and finally Hampton, itself.

Plan to visit the **State Apartments** when you first arrive at Hampton Court. They are open March to late October daily from 9:30 a.m. to 5:30 p.m. Late October to late March, Monday to Saturday, 9:30 a.m. to 4 p.m.; Sunday, 2 to 4 p.m.

Take the *guided tour* of the **state apartments.** The red brick palace is complicated; you do not have the days you need to explore it on your own. Besides, you want time to roam the gardens, the maze, the tennis court, and all the other wonders on the grounds.

Let your imagination roam as you, too, walk up the **King's Staircase** with its incredible wall and ceiling paintings. The **Wolsey** rooms are at the top of the stairs; be sure to look out the windows in the various rooms to see magnificent views of the gardens. I will not attempt to describe the paintings, furniture and other objects you will see; the guides do an excellent job.

Remember to look in every direction: on the walls, on the floors and especially overhead. Your guides will take you into all the rooms open to the public. The **Great Hall** built by **Henry VIII** in 1531-36 has one of the finest hammer beam roofs in the world.

As you leave the magnificent living and sleeping quarters of the royal families, you will descend to Anne Boleyn's Gateway. There you will find the King's Beer Cellar which will give you some idea of what was involved in servicing a palace with more than 500 guests. Then come the Tudor kitchens and serving areas.

Noon

You will emerge into the gardens. It is time to visit the **tearoom** for lunch, a sweet and a"cuppa"tea. This is a pleasant and convenient place to eat and rest before exploring the gardens.

Afternoon

The **Broad Walk** runs across the front of the palace. Visit the nearby indoor tennis court. I was lucky enough one day to see men playing on the courts with the old, short handled rackets of Henry VIII's day. They have more modern courts on the grounds, but these old ones are very special.

The **Privy** gardens are on the south side of the palace near a fine screen by Jean Tijou and the knot garden of herbs. Incidentally, knot gardens are defined as 'neatly trimmed plants intricately laid out to form simple or complex patterns'. Further on is the Great Vine planted in 1768. Look for the Lower Orangery with the famous tempera paintings by Mantegna.

On the north side of the palace is the wilderness and the famous **Maze**. I think part of the fun is working through it by yourself, getting lost and finally deciding you are there for life. In a 1918 guide book I read that you take the first two right turns and then left at every next turn. I do not know if that still works, but you might want to try it.

On my first trip I vowed to walk the maze come hell or high water. No hell, but lots of water. It poured rain. But I walked it with my umbrella held, not only over my head, but up above the hedges. They are planted so close together I could not fit the umbrella between them. Someone in a helicopter would have seen a bright red umbrella making its way through this maze of plantings. I assure you, you will find your way out. They never leave anyone in it overnight. If you get claustrophobic, just signal the 'maze keeper' who sits on top of a tall ladder surveying the scene and he will send help.

A train will take you back from Hampton Court to the Waterloo station.

Evening

You will get back to London in time for dinner at the **Bombay Brasserie** in the Bailey Hotel. This skylighted pavilion with its wicker furniture, potted plants and romantic lighting will serve dinner for two for a moderate cost. Its splendid menu includes such delicacies as crisp Indian bread, stuffed quail, curries, a wonderfully colored mango sherbet and Kingfisher beer made in India.
Relax and enjoy this pretty place and prepare for tomorrow's picnic in the park and a final event at the **Tower of London** as it closes for the night.

Day 3

Highlights: Piccadilly Circus, Burlington Arcade, St. James's Park, Queen's Gallery, Royal Mews, and Tower of London for Ceremony of the Keys.

Reservations: Ritz Hotel for tea. Telephone 493-8181. **Dicken's Inn** by the **Tower,** St. Katharine's Way, for dinner. There are *two* restaurants, so take your choice: The **Pickwick Room** features English and Continental cooking. Telephone 488-2208. The **Dicken's Room** serves fish as its specialty. Telephone 488-9932.

Ceremony of the Keys at the Tower of London. At least *three weeks in advance,* write for **free** tickets, to: The Resident Governor, Queen's House H.M. Tower of London, London EC3. An international reply coupon (from your post office) must be enclosed. Give your name, alternative dates desired and the number of people in your party.

Romantic Day 3

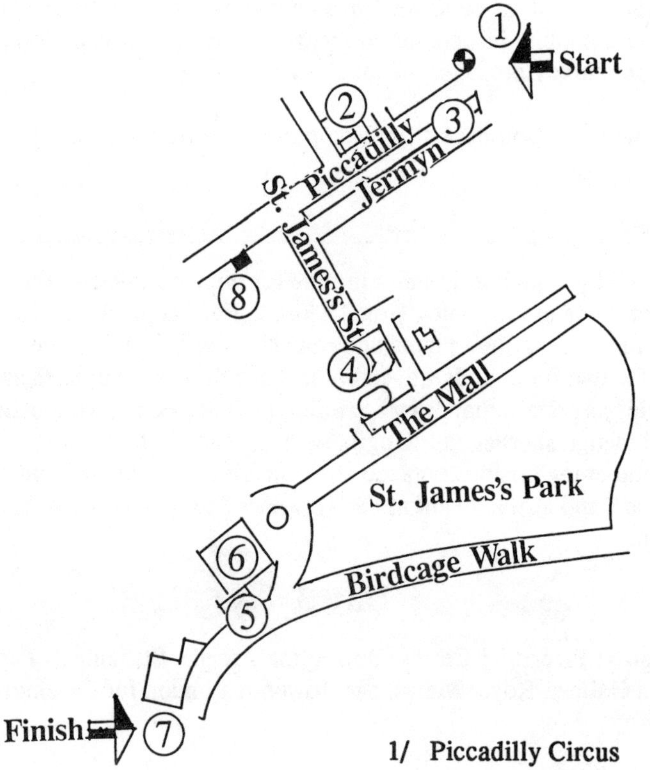

1/ Piccadilly Circus

2/ Burlington Arcade

3/ Fortnum & Mason

4/ St. James's Palace

5/ Queen's Gallery

6/ Buckingham Palace

7/ Royal Mews

8/ Ritz Hotel

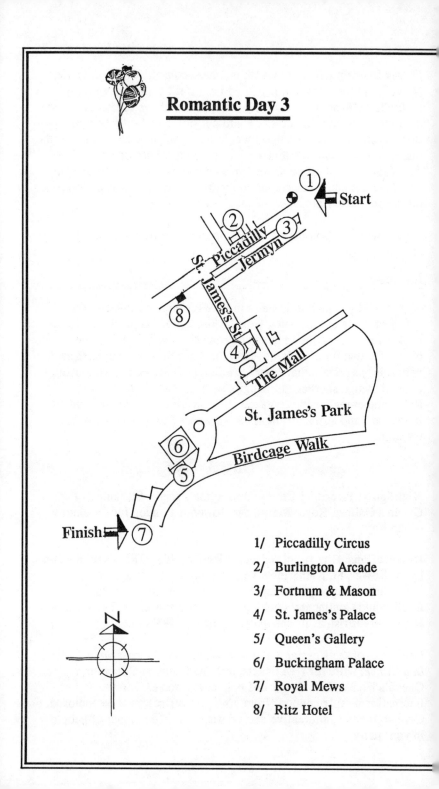

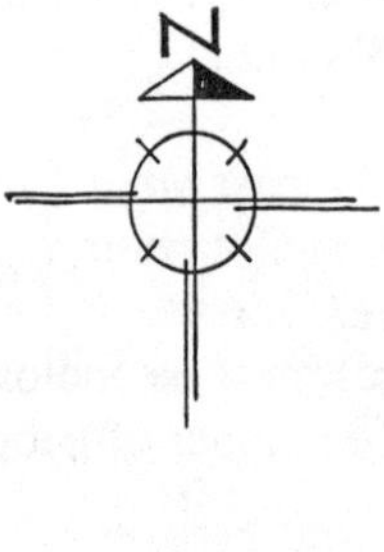

Morning

You will start today at **Piccadilly Circus** about 10 a.m. This is where Regent Street comes to an abrupt and awkward end; not at all where it was supposed to stop. But end it does, where about five or six streets pour into this busy intersection.

Right smack in the middle is a fountain at one time topped with **Eros**, the goddess of love. She has recently been moved to the side of the Circus in front of the Criterion Theatre. The statue is officially known as the Angel of Christian Charity and is a memorial to the philanthropist Lord Shaftesbury. But for our purposes Eros with his little winged cap remains a romantic symbol.

Make your way down Piccadilly, past the Royal Academy to the **Burlington Arcade**. It comes as somewhat of a surprise to find this glass-domed arcade built in 1819. It is still patrolled by beadles, ex-soldiers of the 10th Hussar, dressed in their uniforms and prepared to enforce the rules. Whistling, for some strange reason, is still against the law.

Your purchases might include a brocade vest to order at **S. Fisher's**; hand-rolled hankies at Irish Linen or one of **Peal's** cashmere sweaters.

Walk west on Piccadilly to St. James Street and one block to your left to **Jermyn Street** and turn left. Walk up one side of this street and back the other. All along the way are the old and still very active shops which have been there for many years.

Floris, purveyor of scents to the royal family, still sells its wild hyacinth and real bristle brushes; **Paxton and Whitehead** reaches out to you with both sight and smell with its cheeses and hams; and **Dunhill's** attracts with its tobacco and other appurtenances.

And finally you are at the backdoor of **Fortnum and Mason's.** Wander through and pick up some of the prepared foods, bread and a sweet to take to St. James's Park for a picnic with the ducks and swans.

Walk back to **St. James's Street**, turn right and walk on down to the park. You will pass some of London's oldest shops, **Locks** for hats and **Lobbs** for boots and some of the great palaces, St. James's and Marlborough House.

Noon

One of the great treasures of London is its green spaces and one of my favorites is little **St. James's Park** with its pretty lake and wildlife. Find a folding chair or a bench and sit in the sun, feed the ducks, eat your lunch and enjoy the beauty of the park and its people. An attendant will stop and collect a few pence rent for use of the chair.

Afternoon

After an hour in the park, it should be around 1:30 or 2 p.m. Walk up the Birdcage Walk to the **Queen's Gallery** (Open Tuesday to Saturday during Exhibitions only from 11 to 5 p.m.) Special exhibitions from the royal collections are often on display.

If you happen to be there on a Wednesday or Thursday (2-4 p.m.) the **Royal Mews** are open to the public.These stables (sometimes with and sometimes without the horses) include the harness rooms and coach houses. Of special interest is the Glass Coach which you will remember from"the wedding"and the Gold State Coach used at every coronation since 1820.

Even with these limited hours, the mews are often closed during these times, too. You have to remember this is a working stable and when the horses or coaches are required at Windsor or wherever, they go. It can be discouraging to arrive at the appointed hour and find the closed sign, but it happens often.

Walk around **Buckingham Palace.** This is not the time to see the changing of the guard, but you will see the guard at work. Amble back around the palace and up The Mall, to St. James's Palace and Clarence House.

Walk up St. James's Street to **Piccadilly** again and by now it should be 4 p.m. and time for tea in the **Palm Court** of the Ritz Hotel. The hotel is just to your left.

Evening

Back to your hotel for a rest before your dinner at **St. Katharine's Dock** and the ceremony at the Tower of London.

Take a cab to your dinner at **Dicken's Inn** at about **7 p.m.**

You need to be at the entrance to the **Tower of London** for the Ceremony of the Keys by **9:30 p.m**. This ancient ceremony has taken place each evening for nearly 700 years.

The Chief Warder of the Tower locks the gates and presents the keys to the Resident Governor. The words remain the same, except for the change in the name of the monarch:

"Halt! Who comes there?"

"The *Keys.*"

"Whose Keys?"

"Queen Elizabeth's Keys."

The lighted tower, the old and famous ceremony, and the costumed participants who are part of this enduring tradition are symbolic of the long and often romantic legacy of this city.

As you leave the tower and hail a cab to return to your hotel, you will know you have been a part of this romantic tradition.

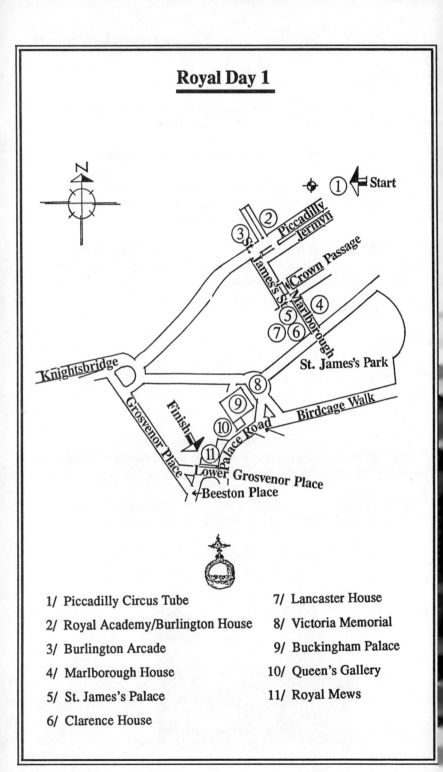

Royal Day 1

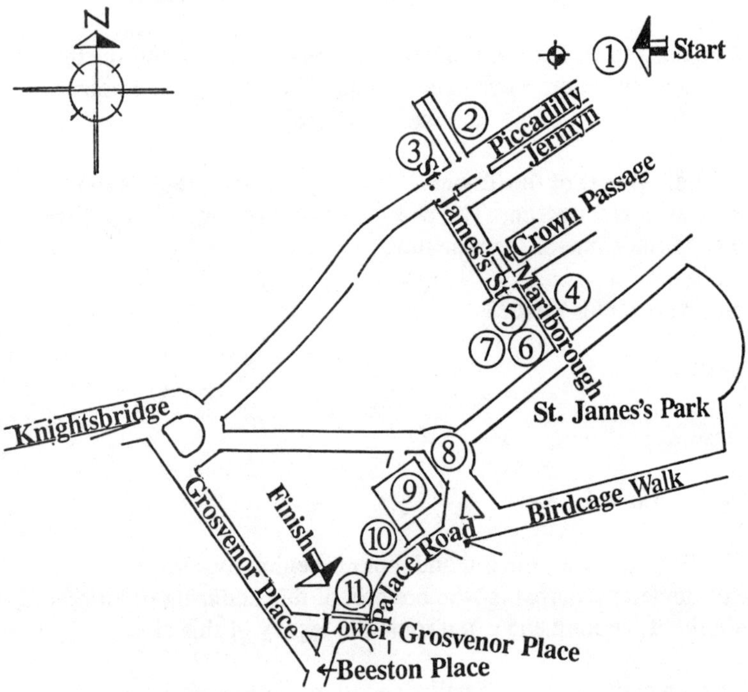

1/ Piccadilly Circus Tube
2/ Royal Academy/Burlington House
3/ Burlington Arcade
4/ Marlborough House
5/ St. James's Palace
6/ Clarence House
7/ Lancaster House
8/ Victoria Memorial
9/ Buckingham Palace
10/ Queen's Gallery
11/ Royal Mews

Royal London

Many visitors come to London like the pussycat in the nursery rhyme, "To look at the **Queen**." Chances are most of us will not even get a glimpse of the **royal family**, but you can visit the royal palaces, gardens and memorials and if timed right, you may be in town for one of the grand state events.

The **British monarchy** endows the United Kingdom with more than pomp and pageantry. It has provided stability and a sense of unity for a commonwealth which has undergone enormous changes during the centuries. It is a rare and unique phenomenon.

Just in case you are bound and determined to see the royals, check *The Times*, *The Standard* or the *Daily Telegraph* for listings of their public appearances. Other opportunities to view members of the royal family occur on state occasions

The State Opening of Parliament usually takes place late in October. The **queen** rides through the streets in one of the state carriages to preside at the opening. **Trooping the Colours** takes place in mid-June and honors the queen's official birthday. She rides horseback to the Horse Guard's Parade on Whitehall and later appears on the balcony at Buckingham Palace. On Remembrance Sunday, the Sunday closest to November 11, the **queen** remembers the heroes of the two World Wars by placing wreaths on the Cenotaph in Whitehall.

Or, if you are famous enough in your own country or have served the Commonwealth in some noteworthy way, you may be invited to one of the three garden parties held each year at **Buckingham Palace.**

About 10,000 people attend each of these galas, but it is considered a great honor to be invited.

Barring all these opportunities, you can still see *magnificent sights* and get a feel for the *extraordinary life* of the royals in and near London by visiting their *homes, gardens* and *art collections.*

Day 1

Highlights: Changing of the Guard at Buckingham Palace, Royal Academy of Art, Queen's Gallery and Kensington Palace.

Reservations: Dinner at the Ritz Hotel Restaurant, Piccadilly.Telephone 493-8181.

Morning

Since the changing of the guard is not until 11:30 a.m., start the day by visiting some of the nearby royal buildings and shops.

Take the tube or cab to Piccadilly Circus, where you will walk down Piccadilly to the **Burlington House and Arcade.** The word, Piccadilly, came from the name of a tailor who made the 'pickadillies', the famous ruff collars worn by Elizabethan dandies.

The Earl of Burlington began the Burlington House in 1664; it was converted to the Royal Academy of Arts in 1768. It contains magnificent paintings, furniture and the only Michelangelo sculpture in England, his unfinished Madonna and Child. Summer exhibitions have been held here annually for over 200 years, from May through September.

The Academy opens daily from 10 a.m. to 6 p.m., but the hours for the Summer Exhibition change, so check the daily papers. Adjacent to the Burlington House is the Burlington Arcade, a covered shopping arcade built in 1819.

After looking at these charming shops, walk down **Piccadilly** to **St. James's Street,** turn left, walk one block to **Jermyn Street**, and turn left again. You will find a number of shops which bear the seal indicating they serve the royal family, including **Floris**, the shop of perfumes established in 1730.

Walk back to **St. James's Street** and turn left; you will pass **Lobb's**, shoemakers since the 18th century and the hatters, **Lock and Company**, in business since 1700. **Berry Bros. and Rudd**, wine merchants, have been on their site since 1680.

A slight jog to your left and St. James's Street becomes Marlborough Road. On your left is **Marlborough House**, designed by Sir Christopher Wren in 1709. It now provides offices for the Commonwealth Foundation and Secretariat.

Next to it is the **Queen's Chapel** designed by architect Inigo Jones. It is not usually open to the public except by written application, but Sunday services are held here from Easter to the end of July. Attending this service is a very formal and special treat. When I went to a Sunday service one morning, I felt that I was surrounded by retainers of the royal family, very carefully and correctly dressed with their hats, gloves and well-tailored suits.

On your right, opposite Marlborough House, is **St. James's Palace**, once the home of the royal families. Remember, ambassadors are accredited to the Court of St. James! The St. James's Chapel Royal is open for services on Sundays from the first of October to Good Friday.

Next to the palace is **Clarence House**, the white stucco home of Queen Elizabeth, the Queen 'Mum'. You can walk down The Mall and around Clarence house to the courtyard of **St. James's Palace**. **Lancaster House** is across the road. It was built for the Duke of York in 1825 and has been the location of many great parties. It is not open to the public.

As you arrive at **The Mall**, turn right, but look to your left to see the full extent of this ceremonial road: the processional way for royalty on state occasions. It starts at the Admiralty Arch at Trafalgar, moves past Carlton House Terrace, Marlborough House, St. James's Palace, Clarence House and on to Buckingham Palace.

As you turn right, you will see the **Victoria Memorial** straight ahead and **Buckingham Palace**, just beyond. The Queen Victoria white marble memorial was completed in 1910. The seated monarch is surrounded by statues of Truth, Motherhood and Justice. It is also one of the best places from which to see the Changing of the Guard.

You will probably find a number of people already perched on it, trying to get a good vantage point.

The **palace** was begun by the Duke of Buckingham in 1703, taken over by George III and expanded by George IV and the great architect John Nash. Nash's work was brilliant but vastly over budget and the design work was completed by another architect.

Nash's most embarrassing mistake was his great archway, known as the Marble Arch, which now stands at the corner of Oxford Street and Edgeware Road. It had to be towed away from its original site when they realized it was too narrow for the king's coach. Queen Victoria, with her nine children, added a number of additions to the palace. She was finally satisfied with its present **600** rooms. 600 Rooms!

Here you are at 11:30 a.m., waiting for the number one tourist attraction of the city of London, the **Changing of the Guard**. I will be very candid with you: this is one of my least favorite events in London, primarily because it is almost impossible to see or hear. The crowds are enormous, the noise of the traffic is deafening and crossing the street is impossible.

Two small pieces of advice: get as close to the center of the main gate as possible and climb up on the Victoria Memorial to look over people's heads if you can.

At about 11:10 a.m., a contingent of the old guard parade in Ambassador's Court at St. James's Palace and move toward the Palace. They join the old Palace guard at the left of the center gates about 11:25 a.m.

The new guard, along with a band, march either from the Chelsea Barracks, or in bad weather, from the nearby Wellington Barracks. As they arrive at the Palace, officers of the old and new advance, touch left hands as symbols of the handing over of the keys and the guard is changed. Eight men detach themselves to relieve the sentries at St. James's Palace, Clarence House and Buckingham Palace.

At this time, music is played in the forecourt. The old guard moves out the center gates about 12:10 with the band playing, to return to the barracks; the new guard goes on duty at Buckingham Palace. A small detachment of guards with a group of drummers leaves by the right gate to relieve the guards at St. James's Palace and Clarence House.

And that is the Changing of the Guard. I wish you luck and hope you can see at least some part of what is an impressive ceremony.

Noon

Getting out of the crowd is no mean feat because you have to cross traffic no matter which way you go. Since I want you to come back here to see the Queen's Gallery and the Royal Mews after lunch, I will suggest some **nearby pubs** or restaurants.
You may choose to go back up the Mall to Marlborough Road, retracing your steps of this morning.

Walk up **Marlborough Road** and almost straight ahead, a bit to your right is **Crown Passage**, just off Pall Mall. Here you will find pleasant eating establishments.

Or you can continue up **St. James's Street** (remember it is an extension of Marlborough Road) to Jermyn Street, turn right and walk on to the **Red Lion Pub** or to **Fortnum and Mason's** for lunch.

Another more expensive place is the **Goring Hotel** on Beeston Place, just off **Lower Grosvenor Place,** behind the Royal Mews. They have both a set and a la carte menu. Lunch will run somewhere in the $20 to $25 range. Service is excellent; the room with its chandeliers, sheer Roman curtains and aqua velvet chairs is lovely. They offer a trolley with a large selection of appetizers ranging from fresh fruits to pates and mayonnaise eggs, a British favorite I don't quite understand.

Afternoon

Retrace your steps after lunch to Buckingham Palace and the **Queen's Gallery,** which is alongside the palace. Watch for the signs. It is open Tuesday through Saturday from 11 a.m. to 5 p.m. and Sunday from 2 to 5 p.m., closed Monday.

The gallery contains special exhibitions drawn from the Royal Collection, which is one of the greatest art collections in the world.

Check the newspapers for information on the current exhibition, but no matter what it is, go to see it. It will be magnificent.

If you are there on either a Wednesday or Thursday, walk down the road to the **Royal Mews.** The stables are only open those two days from 2 to 4 p.m. They contain the horses, coach rooms and the state carriages including the glass coach used by Princess Diana and Prince Charles—later by Prince Andrew and Sarah Ferguson; the Gold Coach used for coronations, and the Irish Coach in which the queen rides to the state opening of Parliament.

At this point, start walking up Grosvenor Place toward Hyde Park or hail a cab to take you to **Kensington Palace.** They can drop you on Kensington Road at the Broad Walk. Or you can walk through Hyde Park and Kensington Gardens, if you want a very long walk. Use the cab. It will be a short and inexpensive ride, saving your feet for better things.

Walk up the Broad Walk to the **Palace**. Princess Margaret, Princess Diana and Prince Charles and about 11 other members of the royal family live here. The **State Apartment** is open from 9 a.m. to 4 p.m. daily; from 1 p.m.to 4 p.m. on Sunday.

Wren was the prime architect after its purchase in 1689 by William III. Kensington Palace is much associated with Queen Victoria who was born and grew up there until the chilly night when the Archbishop of Canterbury came to tell her she was Queen of England. The State Apartments are open to the public.

Walk past the sunken gardens to the entry to the apartments. Go up the **Queen's Staircase** to her apartments. Follow along, looking at the labels if you need help, but mostly, just get the feeling of this very human royal residence.

Be sure to note the ante room next to the Duchess of Kent's dressing room, where some of Victoria's toys are on display. If this is the most moving display; the grandest is the Cupola Room where Victoria was baptized. The Council Chamber contains a most unusual ivory throne.

My favorite room is the **Presence Chamber** with its painted ceiling and superb wood carvings by Grinling Gibbons.

Return to the ground floor to see a collection of court dress. As you leave the palace, check to see if the Orangery is open. It is often closed, due to lack of staff, as they will tell you. It was built as a summer house for Queen Anne.

Evening

By now both you and the day should be fading. Try to go back to your hotel for a rest. Tonight it is dinner at the **Ritz Hotel** on Piccadilly. This may be London's most lavish dining room, with its incredible painted ceiling. A royal dinner here will cost about $100 for two

Royal Day 2

Windsor Castle

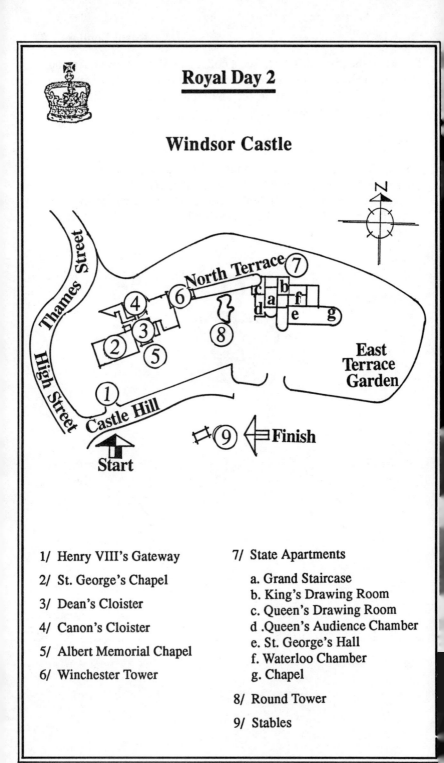

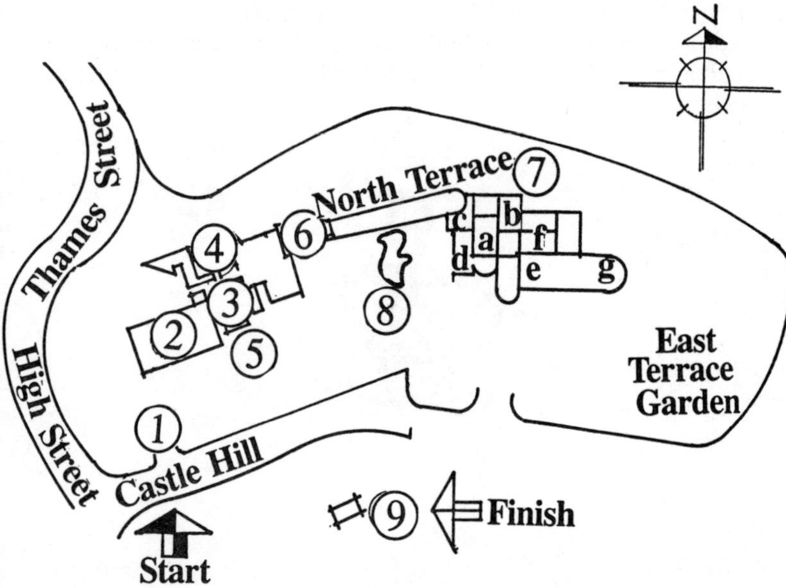

1/ Henry VIII's Gateway

2/ St. George's Chapel

3/ Dean's Cloister

4/ Canon's Cloister

5/ Albert Memorial Chapel

6/ Winchester Tower

7/ State Apartments

a. Grand Staircase
b. King's Drawing Room
c. Queen's Drawing Room
d .Queen's Audience Chamber
e. St. George's Hall
f. Waterloo Chamber
g. Chapel

8/ Round Tower

9/ Stables

Day 2

Highlights: Windsor Castle and Eton.

Reservations: The Waterside Inn at Bray on Ferry Road for lunch.Telephone (0628) 20601. Claridge's Hotel for dinner. Telephone 629-8860.

Windsor Castle. What images that evokes with its fairy tale turrets and banners blowing in the breeze. Built in wood by William the Conqueror, it was later reconstructed in stone, but still maintains its original plan.

It is not hard to remember that it was located overlooking the Thames River as a fortress to protect both the entrance to London as well as the surrounding countryside. It has been lived in constantly since medieval times and was converted into the present royal palace by George IV. Queen Victoria lived here after the death of her husband, Albert. Remember, they called her 'the widder of Windsor'? The present queen spends much time here and Prince Charles plays many of his polo matches at Windsor

Morning

You can take a train from Paddington or Waterloo stations, which leaves every half hour, or you can take a Green Line coach. The trip takes about one hour and one half. Or you can rent a car and take the M4 Motorway.

Plan to arrive when **Windsor Castle** opens at 10 a.m. It is open daily from 10 a.m. to 7:15 p.m. St. George's Chapel is open from 10:45 a.m. (2 p.m. on Sunday) to 4 p.m. during British summers.

The **state apartments** are open when the queen is not in residence (see newspapers) from 10:30 a.m. (1:30 p.m. on Sunday) to 5 p.m. The queen is in residence, usually in April, sometimes in March, May, June and December.

During the busy summer months there is usually a long line for tickets to the apartments. You can get tickets from the ticket machines at the entrance. They take five and ten pence coins. Change is available at kiosks on the North Terrace.

Enter the castle at **Henry VIII's Gateway.** Straight ahead is the magnificent **St. George's Chapel**, dedicated to the patron saint of the Order of the Garter. This is the perfect Gothic building with its great fan vaulting.

Your eyes are drawn upward by the ceiling, the helmets, crests and banners of the Knights of the Garter. In the center of the floor you will find the burial places of Henry VIII, Jane Seymour and Charles I.

Visit the **George VI Chapel**, built by the present queen as a memorial to her father. Take time to walk through the Dean's Cloister and the picturesque Canon's Cloister built in the 14th century.

The **Albert Memorial Chapel** was converted by Queen Victoria to a memorial for her husband, Albert. Winchester Tower is where Chaucer may have lived when he was Master of the Works at Windsor.

Walk on to the **State Apartments.** In a room, left of the entrance, is **Queen Mary's Dollhouse.** It was built 1 inch for each 1 foot.It includes running water, working elevators, electric lights and contains 200 tiny books in its library. The doors even have their own keys.

I will point out only a few of the hundreds of objects to especially notice. On the Grand staircase is a large suit of armor meant for Henry VIII. In the King's Drawing Room are the great Rubens paintings.

Pass through the bed chambers and dressing rooms, to the Queen's Drawing Room with the Van Dyck portraits and the Queen's

Audience Chamber and its Gobelin tapestries. Note the ceilings everywhere. I always get a stiff neck as I stare overhead.

St. George's Hall is 185 feet long and contains portraits of many English rulers. The Waterloo Chamber is decorated with portraits by the English painter Lawrence.

After leaving the state apartments, walk over to the **Round Tower** and climb the 220 steps to see the spectacular view; again remind yourself why the castle was built on this location. Do you notice how blithely I suggest climbing 220 steps? Obviously, this side excursion is for the energetic.

And do not neglect to walk round to the **Royal Mews** to see the state carriages and coaches and models of the horses with their royal trappings.

Eton, the famous public school (remember English public schools are like our private schools and their private schools are like our public ones) is only one mile from Windsor. You can walk across the bridge and up the main street or take a bus or taxi.

Visit the stately courtyards in this school founded in 1440 by Henry VI. If school is in session you will see the boys in their tailcoats and wide white collars. Visit the fine perpendicular chapel with its lovely frescoes.

Noon

There are a number of good restaurants and pubs on Eton High Street. If you choose not to go to Eton, you can get lunch at the **Old House Hotel** on Thames Street in the little town of Windsor. It was built and lived in by Christopher Wren.

At 30 Thames Street is an inexpensive Italian restaurant which is quite pleasant, **Don Peppino's.** The **Castle Hotel** on High Street, just opposite the castle, has a restaurant, bar and coffee shop.

If you have driven or want to hire a cab, **The Waterside Inn** is six miles upstream at Bray on Ferry Road. This idyllic riverside restaurant is one of the most outstanding in England. Run by Michel Roux, of the famous Roux brothers, it serves the finest food with style and flair. Closed on Mondays, this French restaurant seats about

70; lunch will be expensive, but worth it. This is an extraordinarily beautiful and elegant place, worth the extra effort and expense to plan to lunch here.

Afternoon

Depending on how long you stay at Windsor and your transportation, you should be back in London in **late afternoon**, in time for a nice **cream tea** at the **Dorchester Hotel** on Park Lane. It may not be quite the same as tea with the royals, but it is quite nice.

Evening

Dinner at **Claridge's Hotel** on Brook Street tonight, a favorite with royalty since Queen Victoria's time. During World War II, it served as a palace for three monarchs in exile. It is expensive as you might guess, but distinctly royal.

The hotel has a less expensive buffet in their **Causerie Restaurant**, which some consider one of the best buys in London.

Get a good rest, because we are going out of town again tomorrow.

Day 3

Highlights: Hampton Court and the Thames River.

Reservations: Bastian's, Hampton Court Road, for lunch. Telephone 977-0869 or 6074. Tickets for the Royal Shakespeare Company. Check newspapers or magazines for schedule. The *Practical Information* chapter provides help with ordering theatre tickets.

Today your Royal London takes you to **Hampton Court**. You can go by way of the Thames River from Westminster Pier as the monarchs used to go, or you can train from Waterloo Station or take a Green Line Coach #716 from Hyde Park Corner or bus #27 from Kensington or even rent a car.

The river trip takes almost three hours, but it is an elegant and leisurely way to travel to Hampton. You can return on any of the public transportation routes.

Royal Day 3

Hampton Court

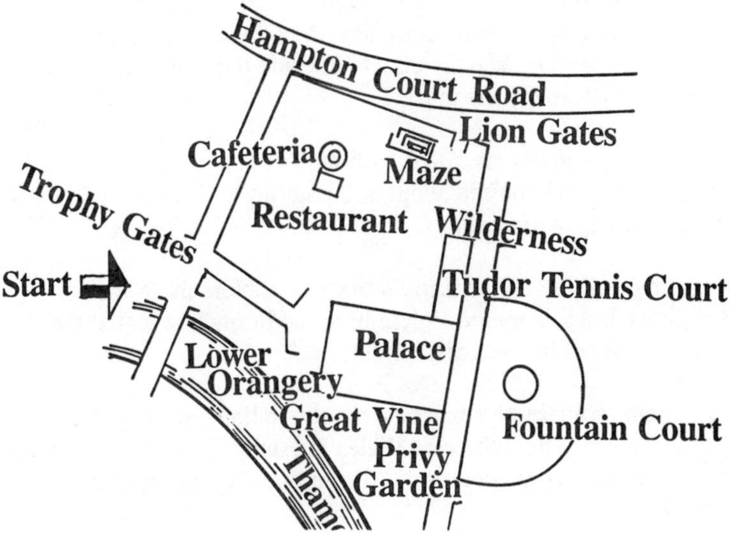

If Windsor was built as a castle and a fortress, **Hampton Court** with its gardens, galleries and ornate buildings was built as a pleasure palace. It was begun in 1514 by Cardinal Wolsey, surrendered by him to Henry VIII and added on to by William III, who hired Wren to design and build additional wings to the palace.

Open late in March to late October, daily from 9:30 a.m. to 5:30 p.m.; October through March, 9:30 a.m. (Sunday 2 p.m.) to 4 p.m. There is some variation in open times for the apartments, tennis court and banqueting house. Check when you arrive.

The State Apartments are magnificent, but if the weather is nice, it is the **gardens** you particularly want to visit. Pick up a map when you arrive, but be sure to wander through the formal and not-so-formal gardens, see the Great Vine and the tennis courts and work your way through the maze.

The **State Apartments** are filled with much of the original furniture and decorations and contain about 500 paintings. You will follow a path through the apartments.

Begin by walking up the **King's Staircase**. Note the walls and ceilings. Look in every direction: at the floors, the walls, the ceilings decorated by the artist Verrio.

All the rooms contain glorious objects; the Italian paintings are among the finest. The **Prince of Wales Presence Chamber** contains many of the best Italian paintings.Also notice the fine tapestries everywhere.

Lely's portraits of the ladies of Charles II's court, the "Windsor Beauties" hang in the **Communication Gallery**. The **ghost** of Queen Catherine Howard is said to still walk in the Haunted Gallery.

Henry VIII's Great Watching Chamber is hung with Flemish tapestries. The **Great Hall** built by Henry VIII has one of the finest hammer-beam roofs in the world and wonderful Brussels tapestries.

The **Tudor kitchens**, with their huge fireplaces and dark hallways, take you at last to the Wren Fountain Court and the Chapel.

Noon

The visit to Hampton Court is an all day excursion, but there is a **tearoom** on the grounds near the Maze, and small kiosks for food near the entrance.

If you want a lovely **luncheon**, try **Bastian's** near the palace on Hampton Court Road, East Molesey. It serves lunch and dinner on Monday through Friday and dinner only on Saturday. Expensive.

Evening

Tonight when you return to London, have a rest, eat at your hotel and go see whatever the **Royal Shakespeare Company** is doing.

They are always magnificent. No member of the royal family ever saw better theatre than you will see with this company.

For the past three days you have trod the paths of **royalty**. You have visited their palaces, seen their royal coaches, art collections, shops and parks and attended their theatres, ballet and opera.

It may not be the same as wearing the **crown**, but it should have given you a taste of the **royal life**.

Literary London Day 1

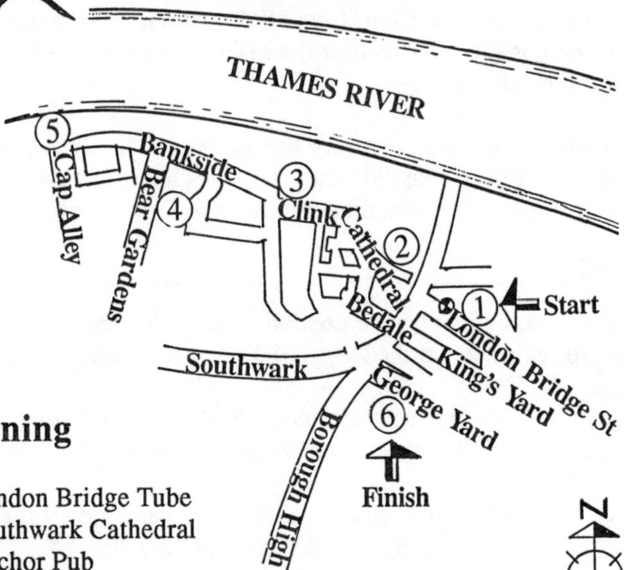

Morning

1/ London Bridge Tube
2/ Southwark Cathedral
3/ Anchor Pub
4/ Shakespeare Globe Museum
5/ Cap Alley
6/ George Inn

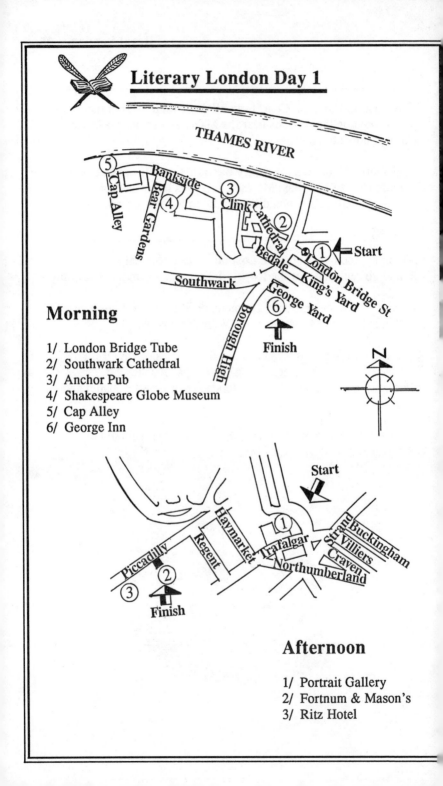

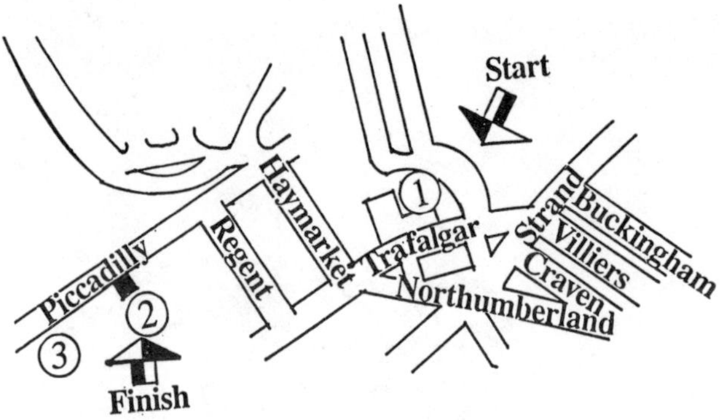

Afternoon

1/ Portrait Gallery
2/ Fortnum & Mason's
3/ Ritz Hotel

Literary London

London is the birthplace of English literature and the mother of English and American writers. Almost **every important writer** in the English language has lived, worked or studied in London some time during his or her life. Many of London's more than 600 famous "blue plaques", which identify the houses of the famous, appear on buildings which housed writers. With a little help in planning and a vivid imagination you can visit and recreate the London of Chaucer, Shakespeare and Virginia Woolf.

In the 14th century, **Geoffrey Chaucer's** pilgrims lead the way not only to the Canterbury Cathedral but to the literary tradition which followed. Their journey began at the Tabard Inn in Southwark on the south bank of the Thames.

Southwark also became home to **Shakespeare** and his great circular theatres, the "wooden O's". His earthy plays were performed for the working people standing in the pits of such theatres as the Globe, the Hope, the Rose and the Star. Across the river, John Donne was writing his love poems, first secular and later sacred, as he assumed the role of Dean of St. Paul's Cathedral.

The Great Fire of 1666 which destroyed much of central London, was reported in the great diaries of Samuel Pepys and John Evelyn, remarkable accounts not only of the fire but more importantly of the times and the people.

By the 16th century and the Age of Reason, Alexander Pope was writing satire; Dr. Samuel Johnson was sitting in the Cheshire

Cheese pub with his literary compatriots and working on his famous Dictionary.

In the 18th century, while Keats and Wordsworth were living in Hampstead and Westminster and writing about fair England and nightingales, **Charles Dickens**, the reformer and novelist, was writing about slums, prisons, thieves and London's "pea soupers."

The 20th century brought the Bloomsbury group together with Virginia Woolf and her husband Leonard; Maynard Keynes, the economist; historian Lytton Stachey; and other writers including Yeats, Forster and Eliot. All were established in squares surrounding the British Museum.

That may be the quickest summary of English literature you have ever read, but I wanted to give you just a taste of this rich stew called English literature and a desire to read more before we set out on our pilgrimage to literary London.

Before you start Day 1, I want to warn you that walking around Southwark may seem a bit solitary and tacky. Much of the area has been abandoned and in spite of some recent renovation, part of it is in disrepair. It is not heavily populated and the little side streets and cul de sacs can seem strange. But it is no more dangerous than most other parts of London. It is just a bit shopworn and typical of areas adjoining rivers.

Day 1

Highlights: Southwark, Shakespeare Globe Museum, George Inn and the National Portrait Gallery.

Reservations: Check open hours at the Shakespeare Globe Museum. Telephone 928-6342.

Tea at the Ritz Hotel. Telephone 493-8181

Dinner at Rules Restaurant. Telephone 836-5314

Theatre tickets for the Royal Shakespeare Company. Check newspapers for theatre, times and productions.

It seems appropriate to begin your literary tour of London in **Southwark** on the south side of the Thames, near London Bridge. Chaucer's pilgrims met at the Tabard Inn on Southwark's High Borough Street and Shakespeare's **Globe Theatre** vied with the brothels and bear baiting rings along the river.

Southwark was at the south end of the bridge the Romans first built across the river. It linked "The City" with this fishing village on the river's south side. Newer bridges provided the main connection from London through Southwark to the continent. The famous coaching inns along Borough High Street in Southwark supplied accommodations for Chaucer's pilgrims and other travelers.

Southwark later became an entertainment center with theaters, brothels and bear baiting rings as well as the location of the Clink and Marshalsea Prisons. Mr. Micawber, in Dicken's *David Copperfield*, spent some time in Marshalsea prison when things did not "turn up" for him. When the Thames froze, there were great frost fairs on the river. All this activity kept people amused as they waited for the morning opening of the bridge to take them into the city.

Morning

At 9:30 a.m.: Take the tube to **London Bridge** tube stop, or cab to Borough High Street and the Southwark Cathedral. If you tube, turn left as you leave the tube station and walk down London Bridge Street to Borough High Street. Cross the street to **Bedale Street.** A quick right, diagonally across a parking lot, sometimes awash in cabbage leaves from the nearby vegetable market, will bring you to the **Southwark Cathedral.**

Wander through, noting especially the altar screen. The south wall bears a memorial sculpture of Shakespeare reclining and leaning on his left elbow. Above the sculpture is a stained glass window with figures from his plays. Nearby you will find a printed hand-out identifying the figures in the window. It is not literary, but don't miss the Jacobean Tomb of Alderman Richard Humble (died 1616) and his wives along the side of the altar. Also note the very early wooden effigy of a knight, 1280-1300 and the brightly colored tomb of John Trehearne, 'gentleman porter' to James I. Be sure to visit the Harvard Chapel in honor of John Harvard, founder of our university and a member of this parish.

Exit on the South porch and walk up the steps in front of you. Winchester Walk will be directly in front of you. Turn right immediately on **Cathedral Street.** The street curves around to the left where you will find the remains of an apparently unsupported standing wall with its original rose window, minus the stained glass. It is very strange to look up and see the blue sky and clouds through it.

Take the first right off Cathedral and you will be on **Clink Street,** the site of the infamous **Clink prison** and the source of our slang expression for going to jail. Clink Street is really an alley with trucks backing around. I know it will seem wrong to you, but it's not. As you walk along Clink Street, look for the Clink Street memorial plaque and the new **Clink Exhibition,** open 7 days a week, from 10 a.m. to 10 p.m.

As you walk, turn a bit toward your right and the river and you will find **Bankside,** which not surprisingly runs along the river. During the Tudor reign, this area was outside the city's jurisdiction. Here the famous **theatres,** such as the **Rose, Globe** and Swan, thrived as well as the brothels, known as "stews" with their fancy inmates known as "Winchester geese". You will look in vain for any traces of theatres - or anything else - but here is where your imagination comes into play. Just remember, this is where London grew and is where Shakespeare and Chaucer once trod and worked.

As you walk along Bankside, you will arrive at the Anchor pub built about 1775. Its exterior remains fairly intact, although the interior has suffered some modern renovation. There is a dining deck in front of the pub. Walk across the deck and follow Bankside along the river.

Walk to the Southwark Bridge Road and turn left and continue to **Park Street.** Here you will find the site of the newly unearthed **Globe Theater** of Shakespeare's day. Turn right a short block to Bear Gardens Street, turn right again to arrive at the **Shakespeare Globe Museum** built on the site of the Elizabethan theatre, the Hope and on the location of the last bear-baiting arena which supplanted the theater. Plans are on display for the new Globe Center being developed on Bankside, which include a full-scale reconstruction of Shakespeare's theater.

The Rose Gallery looks out onto Rose Alley and the site where, in February 1989, remains of the **Rose Theater**, the first of the Shakespearean theaters, were found. Stages of the discoveries are shown along with interpretation of the excavation. Models of the old theaters are also on display in the museum. Above the Main room is a replica of a 17th-century playhouse where productions are mounted.

Walk on down Bankside to Cap Alley, where you will find a plaque on a house facing the river that says Christopher Wren lived there. This is a *private sign* and probably not true. It was most likely a brothel, along with the other houses in the area. All these buildings are old and interesting.

Retrace your steps along Bankside, past the Cathedral and back to Borough High Street. Cross Borough High Street and visit a few of the **old 'yards'** or alleys along the street. King's Yard has nice facades and lamps; White Hart Yard is where Pickwick met Sam Weller in Dicken's novel and is now a parking spot. The place you really want to see is the **George Yard Inn**, rebuilt in 1677. It houses the last galleried coaching inn in London.

Noon

Walk into **George Yard Inn's** courtyard to see the remaining two upper galleries. Dickens mentions this inn in *Little Dorrit*. They still present plays in the courtyard during the summer, while in the winter, hot food is served in front of open fires. The pub opens at 11:30 and lunch is served at noon. I recommend it for lunch. The pub lunch includes hot dishes, cold salads and pies - inexpensive and very good. You just sit at any table, joining the other eaters, which can be very pleasant.

Afternoon

Since you spent the morning on Chaucer and Shakespeare turf, I think it is now time to get an overview of the **literary figures** who graced England's history and there is no better place than at the **National Portrait Gallery**.

Take the London Bridge tube stop to Monument, where you change for either the circle or district line to **Embankment** tube stop. Walk up any of the streets north and you will arrive at Trafalgar Square. The portrait gallery is located directly behind the National Gallery. If this is too complicated, hail a cab on Borough High Street and cab to the museum.

Start on the **top floor** of the gallery. I will point out some of the special literary figures. **Room 1** has the great Chandos portrait of **Shakespeare,** the only known contemporary portrait of the playwright. The engravings for his First Folio are also displayed in this room. A miniature of Sir Walter Raleigh is in a display case with others. Remember poor Walter languishing in the tower for 13 years because of something he wrote.

Room 3 has portraits of the diarist John Evelyn, the 79-year-old Isaac Walton, Dryden, Samuel Butler, and Milton. **Room 4** has the image of Samuel Pepys, which he mentions sitting for in his 1667 diary. In **Room 9** look for Dr. Johnson and his biographer, Boswell.

Room 13 is filled with representatives of the romantic movement: Scott, Lamb, Mary Shelley, Keats, Byron in a Greek outfit, Leigh Hunt, Wordsworth and Coleridge. The early Victorian literati are in **Room 17**: Tennyson, Dickens and Thackeray along with the remarkable portrait by Branwell Bronte of his three sisters. There is a ghostly shadow at the back of this painting, which some think was an image of Bran which he painted out. I like to imagine it is him looking over the shoulders of his more talented sisters.

The full-blown Victorian writers are in **Room 21**: Christina Rosetti and Ford Madox Brown. Here you will also find the Brownings, George Eliot, and Swinburne. And at last some photographs. These are by the great photographer, Julia Margaret Cameron, and include Tennyson and Carlyle. Lewis Carroll has taken his own portrait as well as one of Rossetti.

Room 24 has the Edwardian artists: Hardy, Irving, Kipling, Shaw and Oscar Wilde's caricature. T.E. Lawrence is on the mezzanine with photographs of Sassoon, Owen and Brooke. On the main floor, sharing space with the royals, are James Joyce, W. H. Auden, Dylan Thomas and Vanessa Bell.

If you want to keep some of these images, the museum shop has black and white photographs of every item in the collection. Remarkable!

It is probably 3 or 3:30 p.m. by now. Walk down to Trafalgar and cross the Square, turn up the Strand to your left. About one block along you will come to **Craven Street** on your right. **Benjamin Franklin** lived at 36 Craven St when he was the London agent to the General Assembly of Pennsylvania from 1757-75.

The block beyond is where you will find **Rudyard Kipling's** dwelling at 43 Villiers Street. It was here that he wrote the Barrack Room Ballads and The Light That Failed.

And another block further on is Buckingham Street where you will find the home of the famous diary writer **Pepys** at number 12.

Tea time

Walk back to Trafalgar, cross the square, turn right up Haymarket til you come to Piccadilly Circus. Walk down Piccadilly to **Fortnum and Mason's** for sweets or a sandwich, or if you are feeling very elegant and have made a reservation, continue down Piccadilly to the **Ritz Hotel** for one of the fanciest teas in London.

Evening

Since this is literary London, I suggest the theatre tonight. Go back to your hotel and rest an hour or so. The tea should hold you until supper after the theatre

Since you walked in the shadows of the old Globe Theatre today, the **Royal Shakespeare Company** should do quite nicely this evening. You might want to try supper at **Rules**, 35 Maiden Lane, after the performance. Just remember they do not take orders after 10 p.m.

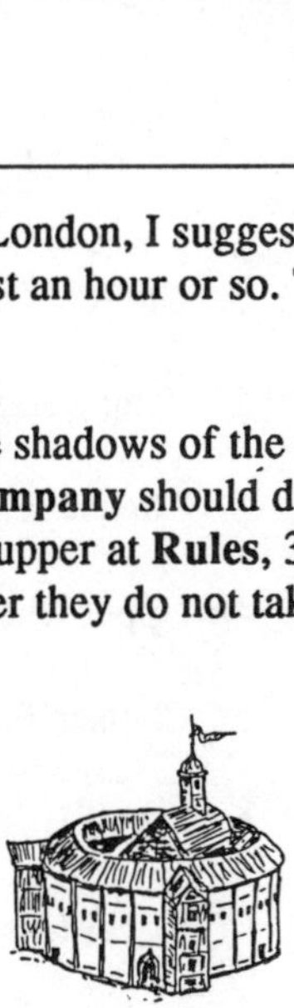

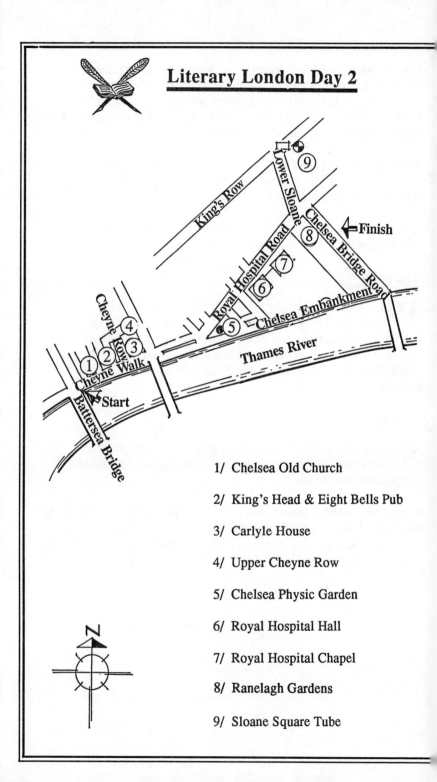

Literary London Day 2

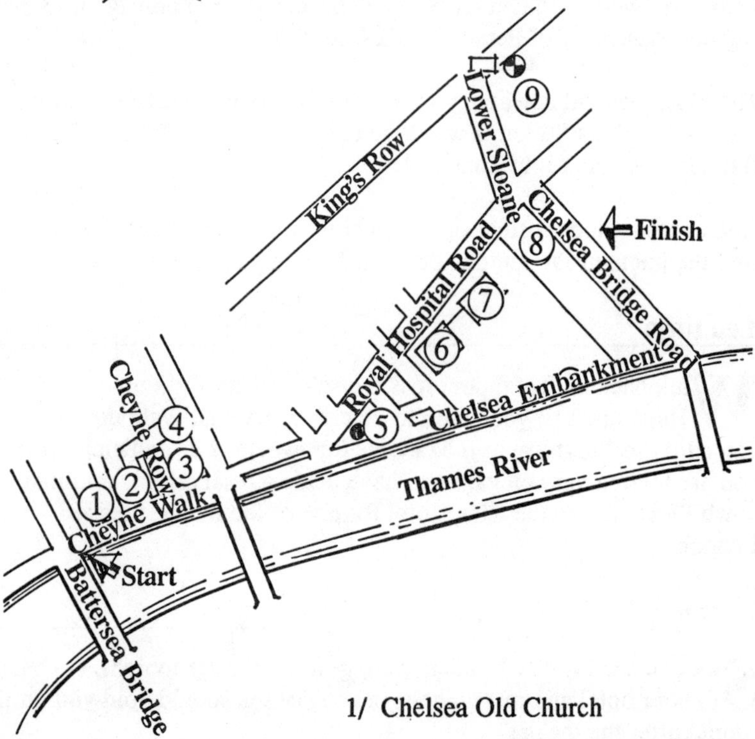

1/ Chelsea Old Church

2/ King's Head & Eight Bells Pub

3/ Carlyle House

4/ Upper Cheyne Row

5/ Chelsea Physic Garden

6/ Royal Hospital Hall

7/ Royal Hospital Chapel

8/ Ranelagh Gardens

9/ Sloane Square Tube

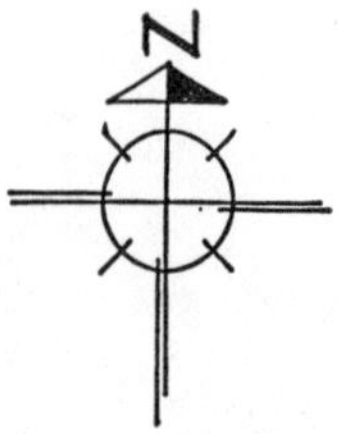

Day 2

Highlights: Westminster Abbey, Chelsea, Carlyle's House, Cheyne Walk, and the Barbican Center.

Reservations: Lunch at the King's Head & Eight Bells. Telephone 352-1820.

Theatre reservations at the Barbican Theatre. Check newspapers for productions and ticket information. Telephone 628-8795 for reservations and information. Telephone 638-8891 for credit card reservations. The Royal Shakespeare Company information telephone number is 628-3351.

Morning

Today start at **Westminster Abbey** at about 9 or 9:30 a.m. You will want to look at everything, but particularly the Poet's Corner and some of the great memorials to literary figures in the abbey. As you move down the north aisle, on your left as you enter the abbey, look for the small wall plaque in the floor in the fourth bay. It is the memorial to playwright Ben Jonson with the famous misspelling, "O rare Ben Johnson". Can you imagine making it into the abbey and then having them not spell your name right? Look also for the fine sculpture of Isaac Newton at this end of the north nave, just inside the altar rail.

Continue to make your way around the abbey. (Refer to the map and walk in *Basic Three Days in London.*) Work your way around to the South side of the abbey to the **Poets' Corner** and browse to your heart's delight. I will mention just a couple of memorials to especially look for: the great one of **Chaucer**, the not-so-great one of Shakespeare, the **burial stones of Dickens** and **Kipling** and the memorials to W.H. Auden, Lewis Carroll and Dylan Thomas. This is one of those places to just look to your heart's content.

As you leave the abbey, check out their shop. They have a very nice stock of books and cards.

Take a cab to **Chelsea.** If there is a line waiting, just go to the end and wait your turn. I "jumped" a line here one day and have never forgotten it. You are going to spend the rest of the morning in **Chelsea**, home of the great Carlyle and many other noted *literary figures.*

I suggest a cab because there is not any kind of a decent tube ride to this part of London. The closest tube stop is at South Kensington or Sloane Square, blocks from where you want to go. Have the cabbie let you off at **Battersea Bridge and Cheyne Walk**, the street along the river. Battersea is the ugly iron bridge which took the place of the wooden bridge you remember seeing in paintings by Whistler and Turner. Walk east on Cheyne Walk past the Lindsey House, the original site of Thomas More's farm.

The **Chelsea Old Church** is on a site where a church has probably been located since Christianity came to England. In 1528 Sir Thomas More rebuilt the south chapel as his private chapel. During World War II bombing, the church was extensively damaged but has been restored. Note the chained books, including a Vinegar Bible (1717).

The pulpit is a copy of the original three decker. The monument to Sir Thomas More is in the Sanctuary against the south wall. Notice the embroidered kneelers begun in 1953, each commemorating a worshipper in the church or someone connected with it. Outside the church is a handsome sculpture of Sir Thomas More, which was unveiled in 1969.

Noon

You should be at the corner of Cheyne Walk and Cheyne Row at the inn called **King's Head & Eight Bells** (50 Cheyne Walk) where you have made your reservation for lunch. This is actually two inns. You can eat and drink in a garden overlooking the Thames or in an upstairs restaurant. There is also a snack bar on the ground floor. The food is excellent and not expensive.

Afternoon

It is probably now about 1 or 1:3O p.m. Walk up Cheyne Row to **Thomas Carlyle's House**, number 24. Open April to the end of October, open Wednesday to Sunday 11 a.m. to 4:30 p.m. The house has been kept as it was in Carlyle's time. You will find portraits, furniture and letters from the "Sage of Chelsea". Visit the top floor attic study with its skylight and the kitchen in the basement where Carlyle and Tennyson used to smoke. Here Carlyle wrote his famous books: The *French Revolution, Heroes and Hero Worship, Frederick the Great* and *Past and Present.*

Walk to **Upper Cheyne Row,** turn right to number 22, Leigh Hunt's house, where he lived with his wife and 7 children and was visited by Shelley, Byron and Lamb. Walk back down Cheyne Row to Cheyne Walk and turn left. All those Cheynes are confusing, aren't they?

Walk along the river and look at the houses. Look for a plaque marking the former location of Henry VIII's manor house. Number 16, the **Queen's House**, was the home of D. G. Rossetti, the pre-Raphaelite poet and the poet Swinburn. Rosetti kept an exotic menagerie in his garden including a wombat, armadillo, kangaroo, peacocks and a Brahmin bull with eyes like his wife, Janey, so he said. Note number 6 with its Chippendale-Chinese railings and gate and the red entrance to number 4 where George Eliot (Mary Ann Evans) died in 1880 after a residence of less than three weeks.

It will be mid afternoon by now. You should be passing the **Chelsea Physic Garden.** It is open mid-April to mid-October, on Wednesday and Sunday, from 2 to 5 p.m. If you happen to be there on one of those days, stop in to see this wonderful garden founded in 1673 by the society of Apothecaries in London.

We have come to the end of our literary tour for the day, but since you are in the area, and if you have the time, walk up to the **Royal Hospital** with its Wren buildings. You will see the Chelsea Pensioners (veterans) hospital, grounds open 10 a.m. to 8 p.m. The chapel and great hall are open daily 10 a.m. to noon and 2-4 p.m. Sunday 2-4 p.m.

And if you should be so lucky as to be there in May you might see the Chelsea Flower Show, one of London's great extravaganzas. If not, walk through the adjacent Ranelagh Gardens. Take the Chelsea Bridge Road/Lower Sloane Street to **Sloane Square** and the tube stop. There are a number of lovely little shops on the square as well as the modern department store, Peter Jones.

Literary London Day 3

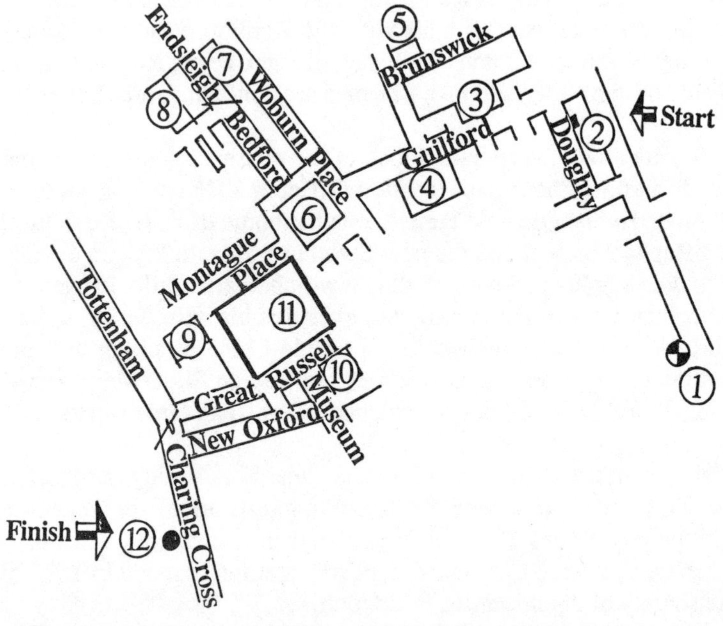

1/ Chancery Tube
2/ Dicken's House
3/ Coram's Fields
4/ Hospital for Sick Children
5/ Thomas Coram Foundation
6/ Russell Square
7/ Tavistock Square
8/ Gordon Square
9/ Bedford Square
10/ Museum Tavern
11/ British Museum
12/ Foyle's Bookstore

Evening

Back to your hotel for a rest and then the theatre again. Try the new **Barbican Center** tonight. You can take the tube to the Barbican stop where your walk to the center is very well signed and marked. In fact there is a *yellow line* painted on the walkways, which you follow right to the center. Just like the yellow brick road. The center is a modern building in the middle of this old city, but I liked its layout and the theatres have wonderful sight lines and comfortable seats. Wander around the lobbies to see the exhibitions and listen to the performance of the informal music groups. I was happily surprised by the ambience of the place and how easy it was to get around. Enjoy.

Day 3

Highlights: The Dicken's House; Tavistock, Gordon, Russell and Bedford Squares; the British Museum, Charing Cross Road and the bookstores.

Reservations: Dinner at the Ivy Restaurant, West Street. Telephone 836-4751.

Morning

Today you will visit **Bloomsbury**, a part of London which is a geographical location as well as a state of mind. I am sure everyone has a different thought when they hear the word "Bloomsbury." To some it is the home of the British Museum, to others the location of London University, and to many the bailiwick of Virginia Woolf and her friends. It is all of those things. Its geographical boundary on the east, Gray's Inn Road, even encompasses the Dickens' House, the only remaining place where he lived in London.

Today you will start with **Dickens**, wander the great squares where Virginia and her compatriots lived and visit the magnificent British Museum, with primary attention to the collections of the British Library, which is housed in the museum building.

The **Dickens House**, 48 Doughty Street, is midway between the Russell Square and Chancery Lane tube stops, and a bit of a walk from either of them. If you decide to tube, go to the Chancery Lane stop (since you will be walking in the direction of Russell Square following your visit to the Dickens House.) Or, just take a cab from your hotel. The house is open Monday through Saturday, from 10 a.m. to 4:30 p.m., and is closed two weeks in December and January.

Dickens lived here from 1837-39, after his fame had became fairly secure, and wrote *Oliver Twist, Nicholas Nickleby* and *Barnaby Rudge*. You will see the **desk** on which he was working on the unfinished manuscript for *The Mystery of Edwin Drood* the day before he died. (Broadway produced a play suggesting a variety of endings to this story.)

The house is full of letters, manuscripts, portraits, furniture and relics as well as the most complete Dickens library in the world. Near where you buy your admission ticket is a case with a little portrait of Dickens and even a lock of his hair. At one time, a reproduction of the Pickwickian *Dingley Dell* kitchen was in the basement, but it was decided this was inappropriate for the house and has been replaced by a library.

After you leave the house, walk up to Guilford Street, turn left and walk past Coram's Fields, a park for children. On your left you will see the Foundation for Children and behind it the Hospital for Sick Children.

Walk to Russell Square and turn right up Woburn Place to Tavistock Square and the adjoining Gordon Square. You are now in the **Bloomsbury** of the 20th century artists, writers and men and women of letters.

About 1905, men from Cambridge began moving into this area; it was far enough from elegant Kensington to provide a break with that past and fresh air for new ideas. **Number 46 Gordon Square** was the focus for much of this activity. The four children of Sir Leslie Stephen set up house there; Virginia Woolf was one of those young people. Later Maynard Keynes, the economist, held court here with his neighbors. Vanessa and Clive Bell lived at 50 Gordon Square, Lytton Strachey at 51 Gordon Square, Leonard and Virginia Woolf at 52 Tavistock Square.

Wander around these squares and try to imagine what it was like when the friendships which held these people together were translated into their salons, summer tennis games, attendance at new ballets by Diaghilev and the production of much of the twentieth century literature which changed our ideas.

Walk back to Russell Square and on to Montague Place and **Bedford Square**, the best preserved of all of these great squares with its three story brick houses. Bedford is along the west side of the British Museum.

Noon

Walk to Great Russell Street, turn left and just opposite the British Museum at the corner of Great Russell and Museum Streets you will find the **Museum Tavern**. It is now time for lunch and this is a fine place for a shepherd's pie or salad. Relax because you will have a long afternoon in the big building across the street.

Afternoon

By now it is about 1 or 1:30 p.m. The **British Museum** is open Monday through Saturday, from 10 a.m. to 5 p.m., and Sunday from 2:30 to 6 p.m. Walk up the impressive, wide stairs into the Great Hall. The **British Library Reading Room** is straight ahead and the galleries containing many of the treasures of that library are to your right. Visits to the Reading Room are available on the hour from 11 to 4 p.m. I suggest you take a look at the 40-foot wide dome, the 25 miles of shelving and the 1,300,000 books in the reading room which seats about 400 readers. **Karl Marx** wrote much of *Das Kapital* in this room after walking over from his dingy room in Soho.

Walk back into the Great Hall and to the Grenville Library. The first long room **Number 29** contains hundreds of manuscripts and historical documents. The cases are well marked so search for your favorites. I love the **Lewis Carroll's** handwritten pages of his "Alice."

Room 30 is filled with a collection of historical and literary manuscripts. A large case contains two of the four extant copies of the Magna Carta. Two less important but fascinating exhibits are **Essex's death warrant** signed by Elizabeth I, and **Nelson's log** of his sea battles along with his last letter to Lady Hamilton, his "dear

Emma,", written two days before he died at Trafalgar. **Scott's diaries** during his Antarctica trips are in a corner case along with other documents.

Room 31, the Crawford Room, contains temporary exhibitions which change from time to time.

Room 32, the King's Library, is the home for George III's library. Look for the case containing the **Gutenberg Bible.** At the far end of this room is the museum's enormous stamp collection. Perhaps you can find someone who will pull out the display showing the **Black Penny Stamp**, perhaps the *most valuable stamp in the world.*

It will probably be about 3:30 or 4 p.m., depending on how much time you spend browsing. Save some time to walk down Great Russell Street to **Charing Cross Road**, the street of books in London. The great Foyle's Bookstore is there. Among the special bookshops you will find along this street are: Hellenic Book Service, Colletts International Bookshop; Zwemmer Fine Art Books (maybe the best art bookstore in the world); Collets Penguin Bookshop and newsagents. **84 Charing Cross**, the bookstore made famous by writer Helen Hanff, is no more as a book store, but if you walk in you will see the memorial to it and will be treated kindly by the new proprietors who recognize the pilgrims to this site.

Evening

Dinner time. And theatre if you wish. A final suggestion. Walk down Charing Cross Road to the Cambridge Circus. To the east of the Circus, on your left as you walk south on Charing Cross, you will find little West Street and **The Ivy Restaurant**. Directly across the street is St. Martin's Theatre where Agatha Christie's *The Mousetrap* has been playing since 1952. From the sublime of Bloomsbury to the ridiculous of *The Mousetrap* might be just what you need tonight.

And **The Ivy** is sublime. It is one of my favorite dining places in London because it is so British and the management is so welcoming.

As you can guess, despite three days of retracing London's literary heritage, you have just put a sizeable dent in it. One very special place and a bit out of the way is **Keats House in Hampstead**, open Monday to Friday 2 to 6 p.m., Sunday 2 to 5 p.m/ Saturday 10 a.m. to 5 p.m.

Keats wrote the *Ode to a Nightingale* in this garden and became engaged to Fanny Brawne who lived in the other half of this semi-detached house. It was here he became ill with tuberculosis in 1820 and from here he left for Rome to spend the winter in an apartment overlooking the Spanish Steps, where he died in 1821.

You could walk up **Wimpole Street** to see the place from which **Elizabeth Barrett** left to marry **Robert Browning**, although the house is no longer there. **Baker Street** still holds the ghost of Sherlock Holmes and his friend, Watson. And **Madame Tussaud's waxworks** still feature Agatha Christie, comfortably ensconced in a chair with a pillow at her back, and Hans Christian Andersen preparing to read his rather odd tales to children.

One of the best things about London is that you never run out of new discoveries, old friends or exciting adventures. No wonder *so many writers* have lived in and loved this city.

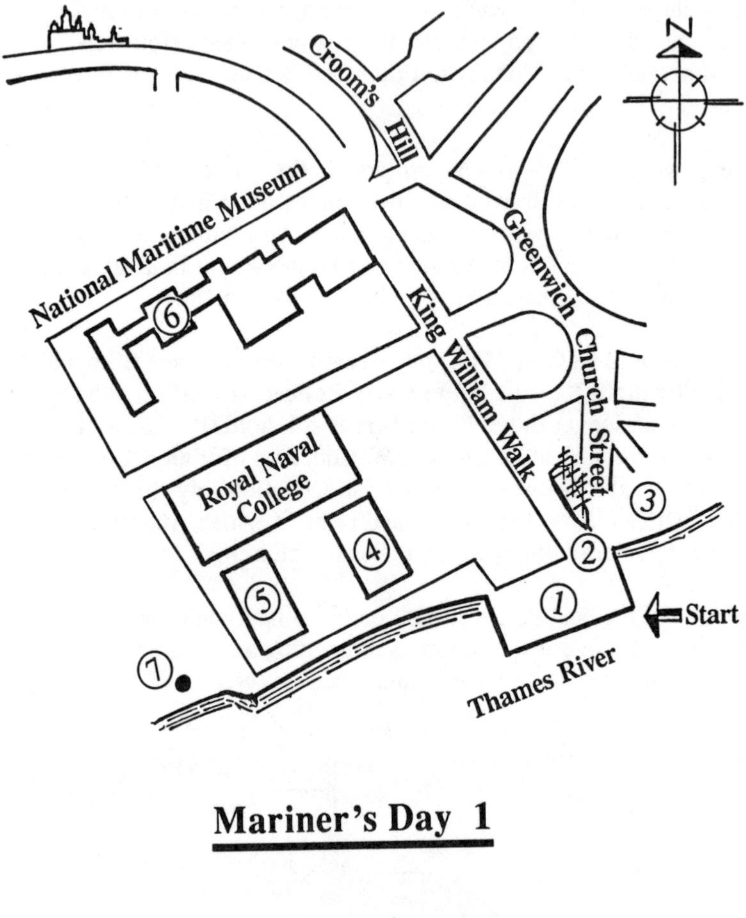

Mariner's Day 1

1/ Greenwich Pier

2/ Cutty Sark

3/ Gypsy Moth

4/ Painted Hall

5/ Chapel

6/ Queen's House

7/ Trafalgar Tavern

Mariner's London

Most people don't think of boating when they think of London, yet it is Britain's *love of the sea* that built the empire. London grew from the **Thames river**; the river was this wonderful city's first thoroughfare and its major entry to the ocean. The river was London's processional parade ground and the site for funeral processions for such illustrious folks as Elizabeth I and Winston Churchill.

As early as 60 A.D., after the Romans had defeated the Celts, London was a **busy port**. In 836 the Vikings sailed up the Thames to sack the city. In 1014, the Anglo-Saxons stormed London, tied their boats to the pilings of **London Bridge** and sailed down the river, pulling the bridge down behind them. Remember the song, *London Bridge is Falling Down?* It really did fall down. During the Middle Ages, London was the only **world port** in Britain.

In the 19th century, the **East** and **West India** trading companies began constructing docks for their sugar, grain, bananas and hard wood. Eventually there were 665 acres of dock basins and 36 miles of piers. **Thousands of ships** sailed the river and anchored at its ports. Following World War II, the bulk of the port activity moved to Tilbury and most of the docks became empty and dark.

Today development projects are underway at St. Katherine's Docks, adjacent to the Tower of London, and along the river as London **rediscovers its riverfront heritage.** What is often remarkable is the redevelopment of old warehouses and riverfront buildings into the finest studios and apartments in London---and some of its most expensive..

During this special three-day tour of London, you will see **boats galore**, from sailing barges to the most famous sailing ship of them all, the **Cutty Sark**. You'll take a quiet cruise up the historic Thames, see a three-decker pulpit, retrace some of the **glories of sailing** through the National Maritime Museum and eat aboard a restaurant ship. You will see a recreation of Lord Nelson's battle on the H.M.S. Victory, visit a 7th century royal burial ship, and boat through London's canal system.

A few notes. Doublecheck the times for boat sailings. The London Tourist Information Center has a River Boat Information Service number, 730-4812 and each pier has a phone listing. Dates and times of sailings are subject to change. Remember: the temperature on the water is usually at least ten degrees cooler than on land, so dress accordingly. A scarf or a cap can be particularly welcome on windy days. Binoculars are also very useful for spotting sights along the shore.

Day 1

Highlights: Greenwich, The National Maritime Museum, Queen's House, the Cutty Sark and Gypsy Moth, Royal Naval College, Observatory and Thames Flood Barrier.

Reservations: Tattershall Castle paddleboat for dinner. Telephone 839-6548. Or Hispaniola restaurant ship. Telephone 839-3011.

Morning

Start your tour at **Westminster Pier** about 9:30 a.m. Westminster tube stop is located near the pier on the Thames River. Today you will be spending the day at **Greenwich**, *a sailor's paradise*, with its sailing ships, naval museum and college, and old seafaring pubs. An extra trip to the Thames Flood Barrier is a part of today's visit.

Walk over to the pier. The **Houses of Parliament, Big Ben** and **Westminster Abbey** are looming over your shoulder. The river launches operate from April to October. The **boats to Greenwich** run approximately every 30 minutes, 10:30 a.m. to 4 p.m. The trip will take about 45 minutes.

As you travel east on the river you will see the Victoria Embankment on your left. At the foot bridge, notice the Hispaniola and Tattershall Castle, two restaurant boats on your left. The National theatre complex is on your right. Moored along the embankment you will see the Wellington, a World War II frigate now serving as livery hall of the Honorable Company of Master Marines and the Chrysanthemum and President, World War I sloops, now training ships of the London Division of the Royal Naval Volunteer Reserve. You will pass under the Blackfriars, Southwark and London bridges.

Soon you will see, on your right, the **H.M.S. Belfast**, which you will visit tomorrow, and on your left, the **Tower of London**, with the 19th century Tower Bridge directly in front of you. Its 1100 ton arms can be raised in an astonishing three minutes to allow tall masted ships to pass.

As you travel up the river, you will see the St. Katherine Docks. Note the Execution Dock marked with the letter E. Here is where Captain Kidd and other pirates were hung and their bodies left to permit the tide waters to 'wash over them three times'.

You can see the **Prospect of Whitby**, an old pub, and miles of wine vaults under the London Dock warehouses. The towns of Wapping and Rotherhite are on your right. Rotherhite was where the Pilgrim's **Mayflower** was built. The Mayflower's captain was buried in Rotherhite's St. Mary's church yard when he returned in 1621.

The Surrey Commercial Docks with their uncertain future are now on your right and the sweeping peninsula called the Isle of Dogs on your left. This is now home for the fish market which used to be at Billingsgate. Past the West and East India docks on your left and the Deptford.Power Station on your right.

You are now at the pier at **Greenwich**. Greenwich is the home of the Flamsteed House, former home of the Royal Observatory; the Royal Naval College; the National Maritime Museum and its connecting Queen's House, from which our White House was designed.

But the first sight you see will be the masts of the clipper ship **Cutty Sark** in dry dock at the pier. When she was launched in 1869 she was *the fastest clipper afloat*, posting 363 miles per day during her China tea trade days. Open October to Easter, Monday to Saturday, 10 a.m. to 4:30 p.m.; Easter to September, Monday to Saturday, 10 a.m. to 5:30 p.m.; Sunday, Noon to 5:30 p.m. for a small fee. Be sure to go down into her hold to see the collection of carved wooden figureheads from old ships.

Next to her is the small ketch, the **Gipsy Moth IV**, on which Sir Francis Chichester circumnavigated the world alone in 1966-67. Chichester's trip covered 29,677 miles over the space of 226 days. You can visit her during the same hours as the Cutty Sark.

The domed building next to the river is the entrance to a foot tunnel which goes underneath the Thames River. You will find 100 steps and an elevator which will take you to a foot tunnel underneath the Thames to the Isle of Dogs. It is about a 10 minute walk to the other side where you will see the magnificent view of Greenwich which Canaletto painted.

Also look for the **Greenwich Bookboat** at Cutty Sark Gardens on Church Street. This is "London's" only floating bookshop and specializes in children's books.

Noon

The historic **Trafalgar Tavern**, on the waterfront near the Royal Chapel, built in 1837, was described by Dickens in *Our Mutual* Friend, a novel about the Thames.

An old Victorian pub, the Rose and Crown, is at 1 Crooms Hill, near the observatory; the Gypsy Moth is at 60 Greenwich Church Street. There are also a number of tearooms scattered about for mid afternoon sustenance.

Afternoon

Walk up King William Walk to the **National Maritime Museum** and the Queen's House, open Tuesday through Saturday from 10 a.m. to 6 p.m. and Sunday from 2 to 5:30 p.m.

The **Queen's House** contains 16th and 17th century models of ships, maps, navigational instruments and paintings.

The Maritime Museum is the **greatest seafaring museum in the world** and is contained in two wings on either side of the Queen's House. The **East Wing** contains 19th and 20th century model ships and other materials pertaining to the Royal Navy. Don't miss the navigation room with its naval instruments or the collection of **Nelson** memorabilia.

The **Neptune Hall** in the West Wing exhibits **full size boats** such as a 1907 paddle tug, the *Reliant* ; riverboats and **Prince Frederick's 1732 barge**. This is a sailor's paradise.

When you can bear to leave this treasure house, visit **Flamsteed House**, formerly the Royal Observatory. The observatory was moved to Herstmonceux in Sussex in 1948-49 because of the growing pollution of Greenwich's atmosphere. The Flamsteed House, designed by Sir Christopher Wren, is now an annex of the maritime museum and contains a fine collection of astronomy and navigation instruments. The Caird Planetarium is nearby. They are at the top of a hill surrounded by Greenwich Park, a long, steep walk. These buildings are open Monday through Saturday from 10 a.m. to 6 p.m.; Sunday from 2:30 to 6 p.m.

The **famous zero meridian** of longitude passes through the House. However Greenwich no longer sets the world's clocks. The chronometers, long out of date, were replaced in 1985 by cesium atoms in a bureau of weights and measures in downtown Paris. For most of us, time still belongs to Greenwich.

Mariners will be fascinated with the old marine timekeepers, refracting telescope, celestial globes, quadrants, sextants and chronometers. Incidentally the second Astronomer Royal from 1720 to 1742 was a man by the name of Edmond Halley, after whom the comet is named.

Walk back down the hill and turn right to the **Royal Naval College**, open Monday to Wednesday and Friday to Sunday from 2:30 to 4:30 p.m. Christopher Wren, the architect for St. Paul's Cathedral, was also the architect for the College.

The refectory and chapel are matching buildings, placed just opposite each other. The refectory contains the amazing **Painted Hall**, a Baroque masterpiece by Sir James Thornhill. When I was there, the dining room was set for a ceremonial banquet with great silver pieces and tiny pink silk shaded lights on the long tables. This is an extraordinary room.

Walk across the open green space to the **Chapel**, which is designed in a much lighter style. Notice the altarpiece by Benjamin West and the **round pulpit** made by Lawrence to look like the *top deck of a three decker ship*.

Back to the **pier**. Boats leave from Greenwich all year from 10:30 a.m. to 6 p.m., April to September, and til 5 p.m. other months to take you on a 20 minute trip to the **Thames Flood Barrier**, upstream from Greenwich.

This is the *moveable flood barrier* built to protect London from a surge tide. When not needed, it lies horizontally deep in the river bed to allow shipping to navigate the Thames. There are viewing terraces, a buffet, a shop and an audio visual presentation.

Watch your time, since the boats back to London stop running about 5:30 or 6 p.m.

Evening

Take the return boat back to Westminster Pier. Walk along **Victoria Embankment** until you reach one of the restaurant ships you passed on your journey up the river this morning. Either the **Tattershall Castle** paddleboat or the **Hispaniola** can be very pleasant at night. Dinner will cost between $30 and $40. Or you can just have a pleasant drink on the topdeck of the Hispaniola.

Tomorrow you will be off to **Tower Pier** and a visit to the historic St. Katherine's Docks, the H.M.S. Belmont and a historic sailor's pub.

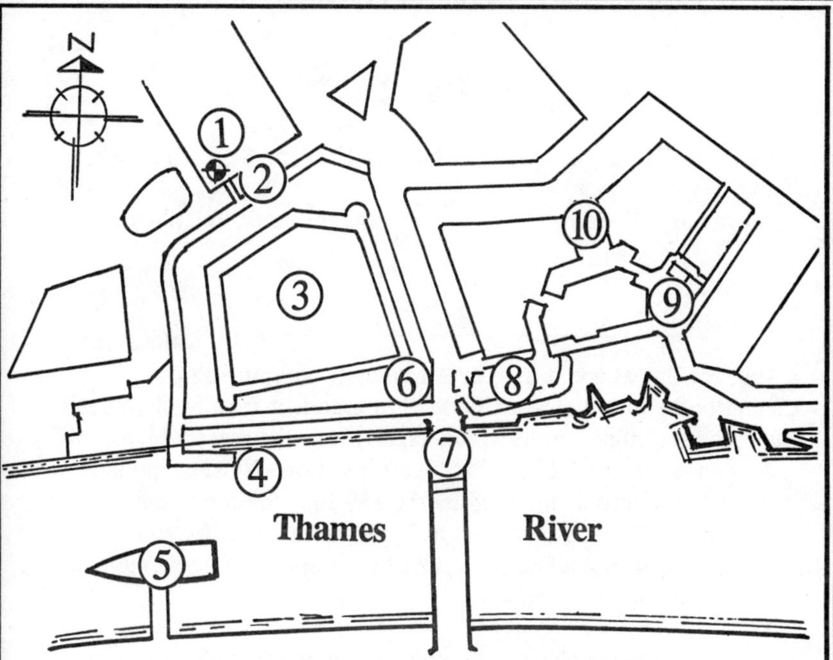

Mariner's Day 2

1/ Tower Tube

2/ Pedestrian Underpass

3/ Tower of London

4/ Tower Pier

5/ The Belfast

6/ Outdoor Cafe

7/ Tower Bridge Walkways

8/ Thistle Hotel

9/ Dicken's Inn

10/ Ivory House

Day 2

Highlights: Trafalgar Square, H.M.S. Belfast and St. Katherine's Docks
Reservations: Dickens Inn by the Tower for dinner. Telephone 488-1108.

Morning

Start the day at about 8:30 or 9 a.m. at **Trafalgar Square.** No matter the intentions of Charles I or architect John Nash to design this space for other purposes, it is clearly now the place which honors naval power and its glory. **Admiral Lord Nelson**, England's greatest naval hero, is honored by the 150-foot column in memory of his victory over the French fleet at Trafalgar in 1805. As you remember, Nelson died on the deck of his ship, the H.M.S. Victory, just as the battle had been won.

Admirals Beatty and Jellicoe were commemorated with statues in 1949 at the same time the fountains were installed. Edwin Landseer's four lions at the base of the column were cast in 1868 from cannon recovered from the ship, the Royal George, which sank in Portsmouth harbor in 1782 with hundreds of casualties. The two huge round **lamps** on the square are from Nelson's flagship, the Victory.

Proceed up **Whitehall.** The Admiralty Arch will be on your right; it honors Queen Victoria. The first large building on your right is the **Admiralty**, governing body of the Royal Navy. It is open by appointment only.

Continue up Whitehall past the Banqueting Hall, the Horse Guards, Number 10 Downing Street, the Cenotaph of 1919, memorial to Britain's war dead and on to Westminster Abbey, Parliament and Big Ben.

At this point you can **choose to boat** from **Westminster pier** to **Tower pier**, part of the journey you took yesterday, or you can take the Westminster tube stop to Tower Hill station. In either event you will arrive at the **Tower of London** from where you will visit a historic mariner's area.

If you rode the Tube, take the pedestrian subway to cross underneath the busy street separating the tube stop from the Tower. Walk toward the Tower, following the signs to **Tower Pier**.

From the pier, a **launch** will take you across the Thames to Symons Wharf where the **H.M.S. Belfast** is docked.

This World War II warship (Southhampton class cruiser) took part in the Normandy landings, the Battle of North Cape in 1943, the Arctic convoys and finally the Korean war. You can visit the Belfast from 11 a.m. to 5:30 p.m from April through September and from 11 a.m. to 4:30 p.m., October through March. The launches leave every 20 minutes.

You will be able to wander all over the ship. It has been preserved as closely as possible to its original condition. Areas open to the public are the messdecks, operations room, sick bay, boiler room, engine room, and the captain's and admiral's bridges. In addition you can see the punishment cells, and two of the four 6-inch gun turrets. A complete tour of the vessel will take about two hours. A shop provides wallcharts, postcards and other souvenirs. Be warned: some of the ship's ladders are quite steep.

Return to Tower Pier **by launch.** Walk up the stairs from the pier, turn right and walk along the river in front of the Tower to **St. Katherine Docks** where you will spend the afternoon. You will pass the Tower's **famous cannons** and see a remarkable view of the river with its continuous parade of shipping.

Noon

There is a pleasant outdoor cafe along this walkway which I recommend for lunch.

Afternoon

After lunch walk up a flight of steps to **Tower Bridge,** built in 1886-94. The 800-foot-long span includes twin drawbridges, each weighing almost 1,000 tons. They can be raised in a minute and a half to permit the passage of large vessels. Visit the twin towers and museum; enjoy the panoramic views of the river and the city from the glass enclosed walkways 140 feet above the river.

The towers are open from 10 a.m. to 6:30 p.m. Walk out a short distance on the bridge to the ticket booths and the elevator or steps which will take you to the walkways.

Level 3 features an exhibition of the structural and hydraulic engineering of the bridge with video film, drawings and photographs showing how it works. **Level 4** is the location for the two glass-enclosed walkways. Special sliding windows make it possible for photographers to obtain fine views. The **South Tower** holds an exhibition of the history of the City's bridges. The Museum contains the original boilers and engines which powered the bridge prior to electrification. There is also a shop with publications and postcards.

You will now visit **St. Katherine's Dock** area, badly damaged during World War II and abandoned until about 1968, now containing a yacht basin with about 200 yachts. Visitors can become temporary members of the yacht club on application. Wander around the marina to see the unusual assortment of **boats** tied up to the piers.

Walk back down the bridge steps, cross the street and walk past the Tower Thistle Hotel. Walk along in front of the hotel on the river side to see the plantings, sculptures and river. Pass a marina on your left, and you will come to the **Dickens Inn** directly in front of you. The collection of old ships has been moved; only the lightship Nore and the steam tug Challenge are still on view.

Continue walking along the Thames to explore the tremendous new **Dockside** development. New buildings, docks, promenades, restaurants, and dockages are being built at a rapid rate. The process is well underway, but far from complete. Do explore this newest of London's offerings.

Evening

Walk around the dock area to see the marinas with the anchored yachts; soon it will be time for dinner. Nearby **Dickens Inn** includes an ale bar with snacks, which is inexpensive, and the more costly Pickwick Room. Or, you can cab over to the famous pub, the **Prospect of Whitby**, where Whistler and Turner painted and mariners gathered.

Tomorrow you leave the river and turn inland to **London's historic canals.**

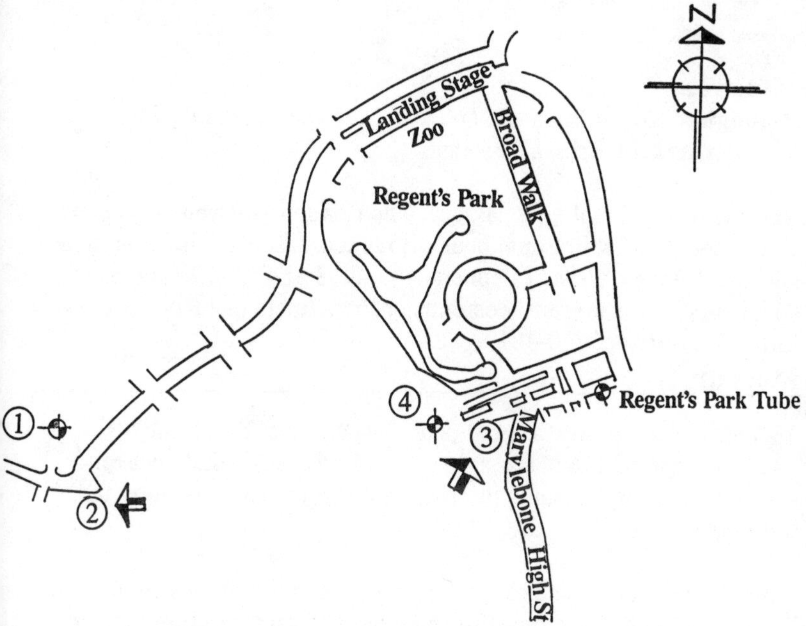

Mariner's Day 3

1/ Warwick Tube

2/ Canal Boat

3/ Madame Tussaud's

4/ Baker Street Tube

Day 3

Highlights: Regent's Canal and Park, Madame Tussaud's Wax Museum, and the British Museum.

Reservations: Canal boat passage. The London Waterbus Company. Telephone 482-2550. Canal boat with lunch. Jason's Trip. Telephone 286-3428. Jenny Wren. Telephone 483-4433 or 485-6210. Thames River supper cruise from Westminster Pier. Telephone Riverboat Information Service, 730-4812.

Morning

Today you will ride a canal boat, "experience" the Battle of Trafalgar, visit a burial ship and end your three-day visit to London's marine treasures by floating down the river to enjoy the illuminated city.

Tube to Warwick Avenue station and walk down Warwick Avenue to Blomfield Road to the **landing stage** or cab to the **canal boat pier.** You are now at *London's Little Venice* and ready to explore its eight-and-one-half mile waterway, which cuts through the city along some of its landmarks: Regent's Park, London Zoo, Primrose Hill and the great Mosque. The canal was officially opened in 1820, joining a network of historic waterways which stretched more than 4,000 miles throughout England. It is still a special way to see this city.

Three boat lines operate this part of the canal between Easter and mid-October. The **London Waterbus Company** shuttles between Little Venice and Camden Lock, with a landing at the zoo. **Jason's Trip** has a one and one half hour trip on a 1906 narrow boat, with lunch; a similar trip is offered by the **Jenny Wren.** Trips run approximately every hour from 10 a.m. to 4:30 p.m. It is necessary to book in advance.

The canal is lined with houseboats and pleasure craft, which are enthusiastically decorated by the boatmen and their families. The choice is yours, but I'd recommend the trip to the landing at the **London Zoo.** The Waterbus offers this trip for about $6 to $7, including the admission fee to the zoo. When you leave the boat, you are at the far end of the zoo. Walk through this world famous animal garden, stopping to see the pandas from China and the great aviary. Cut through Regent's Park to Queen Mary's Gardens.

Noon

Stop at either the tea house or restaurant for some sustenance.

Afternoon

Walk out the entrance and two blocks straight ahead to Marylebone Road. To your right is **Madame Tussaud's** wax museum. It is all quite remarkable, but it is for their reconstruction of **The Battle of Trafalgar** that I now recommend it to you. You enter the scene to the sound of bands playing *Heart of Oak* as they did for Nelson's fleet nearing the French and Spanish warships in October, 1805. The battle with its gunfire, smoke, dust, noise, and the dying Nelson, is quite astounding. At the last, you hear the sound of bells ringing for the dead, along with their victory toll, just as the church bells rang for the quick and the dead so long ago.

Back east on Marylebone Road to **Marylebone High Street.** At **Number 83** you will find Francis Edwards five-story shop of books on travel, maps, prints, and naval and military books. They can also find out-of-print books for you. This is a gold-mine for lovers of the nautical life.One last stop today: the **British Museum**. The tube connections are awkward, so walk back to Marylebone Road and hail a cab. You will be particularly interested in the **Sutton Hoo Treasures** in Room 41. These objects came from a **7th century royal burial ship**, excavated in Suffolk in 1939, the *richest ever found in Europe*. Included are gold and jewels, a wonderful helmet, shield and sword, drinking horns, bottles, bowls, bronze and iron utensils, metalwork and even textiles. It was an extraordinary find.

Walk out the main entrance and across Great Russell Street to the **Museum Tavern.**

Evening

Tonight take one of the **Thames River supper cruises** from Westminster pier. These often include a *basket supper* and last an hour and a half Evening cruises from Westminster Pier usually are available from 7:30 to 9:15 p.m. or 8:15 to 10 p.m. Check schedules since they are subject to change.

This is a leisurely way to end your **mariner's tour** of London and a have a last glimpse of this magnificent lighted city from its main thoroughfare.**Bon Voyage.**

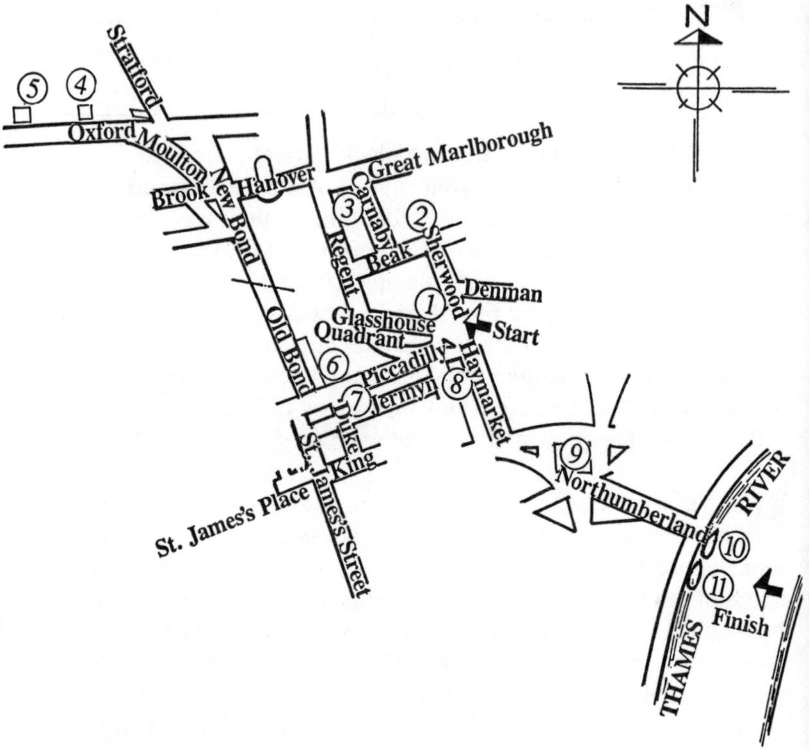

Shopping Day 1

1/ Piccadilly Circus
2/ Left Hand Shop
3/ Liberty's
4/ Selfridge's
5/ Marks & Spencer
6/ Burlington Arcade
7/ Fortnum & Mason
8/ Design Center
9/ Trafalgar Square
10/ Hispaniola
11/ Tattershall Castle

Shopper's London

London is one of the greatest shopping centers in the world. If you can't find it in London, it probably doesn't exist. London has shops so **elegant** you have probably never heard their names; it has the **largest** department store in Europe—and shops so tiny you can scarcely wedge your way through.

Remember hearing that England is a country of shopkeepers? It's true.

During this three-day tour, you will go to some of the **most famous** and some not-so-famous **shopping streets**, including Regent and Bond Street, Charing Cross and Convent Garden, Knightsbridge and Kensington. I will throw in a *fourth day* for the London markets, which are generally held on Friday, Saturday or Sunday. If you happen to be in London on one of those days, you may want to visit the markets or substitute one of them for one of the three days of shopping.

Just a few reminders and suggestions to help make your shopping more pleasant:

Hours: Most shops are open from 9 a.m. to 5:30 p.m., Monday through Saturday. A few close Saturday afternoon. On Wednesday, shops in the Knightsbridge, Sloane Square and King's Road areas stay open until 7 p.m., and on Thursday, shops in the West End are open til 7:30 p.m. Convent Garden shops are open until 8 p.m., six days a week.

If you have some very specialized shopping to do, there are several **shopping service organizations** which can provide escorts, cars and information for a fee. The charges vary according to needs and the size of the car required for the trip. Agencies include **Universal Aunts**, 250 King's Road SW3 (351-5767) and **Take a Guide**, 85 Lower Sloane Street, SW1 (221-5475). The Citizen's Advice Bureau, an independent organization, can help you with shopping problems (798-1157) and remember that The British Tourist Authority is always willing to help.

Shopping will be pleasanter and safer with travelers checks or credit cards. Although London is a *very safe city*, pickpockets work in crowded shopping streets. Remember to always get a receipt in case you want to exchange, receive credit or get a cash refund. You are entitled to ask for a cash refund in preference to a credit slip. All large shops will accept internationally recognized credit cards.

Value Added Tax (VAT): This is the scheme which enables overseas visitors to avoid paying the standard 15 percent sales tax on purchases to be taken out of the country. (See advice in chapter on Practical Information).

Just a few suggestions: Some stores are able to send goods abroad free of the VAT. Otherwise you must ask for a VAT form at the time of purchase, fill it out and present it and the goods at VAT desks at the airport when you leave the country. You must then send the form back to the store to receive reimbursement. It is a complicated, unwieldy and often financially unsound system since you may lose money on the exchange procedures. Many shops have a minimum price below which goods cannot be purchased under this system. My advice is that unless the purchase is substantial, forgo the tax relief.

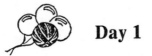

Day 1

Highlights: Regent and Bond Streets, St. James's Street, Oxford Street, Burlington Arcade and the Design Center.

Reservations: Lunch reservations at the Cafe Royal. Telephone 473-9090. Or at Estoril da Luigi e Robert. Telephone 437-8700.

Dinner reservations at the Tattershall Castle paddleboat. Telephone 839-6548. Or the Hispaniola riverboat restaurant. Telephone 839-3011.

Morning

Today you will visit the Regent and Bond Street area and spend the afternoon in the St. James's enclave.

Start the day at **Piccadilly Circus**. Walk north on **Regent Street** along the curved section known as the Quadrant. John Nash designed the original Regent Street thoroughfare, which was intended to enable the royals to drive from Carlton House to their new Regent's Park. By the time the street was finished in 1823, the royal family had moved to Buckingham Palace; the avenue was never completed according to the original plan.

Walk north up the street, crossing back and forth to see the places that most interest you. You will notice that the cross streets change names from the right to the left of Regent Street, so it is difficult to give you the names of corners. At the end of the first block at Glasshouse Street, on your right, is **Aquascutum**, the famous shop for raingear, and across the street is **Austin Reed** for the gentlemen.

Cross Glasshouse Street and you will come to **Garrard Goldsmiths,** caretakers for the Crown Jewels and shop for the most fabulous jewelry. Their window displays are smashing.

Two blocks beyond you will come to **Beak Street** on your right. Several blocks right on Beak Street is the Left Hand Shop. It is great fun in case you have a left-handed friend. As you go down Beak Street, one block off Regent and to your left you will see **Carnaby Street**. it is no longer the stylish and fun place it was during the Beatle years; it is run down, sort of sad, but at least you know where it is. It runs on for about four or five blocks.

Back on Regent Street is **Burberry's** for raingear. Expensive, but superb. On your right is Gered's for china and the great goldsmiths, Mappin & Webb. Then you come to **Hamleys** for toys and games, an amazing place. You could play there for hours. Another great toy store is Gault's, just behind Liberty's; it is smaller, but very fine.

Liberty & Company is at the corner of Regent and Great Marlborough Streets. Its Renaissance building, with a neo-Tudor addition, is one of London's most fascinating stores. This magnificent place is so filled with nooks and crannies that I almost always get temporarily lost. Their printed silks are world famous. Take some time to explore this most unusual store.

This is as far as I plan to take you on Regent Street today. If you were to proceed on Regent you would find another fine department store across from Liberty's, Dickins & Jones; Bally shoes, the Moscow Intourist Information Service, and Boosey & Hawkes musical center. Trust me.

Walk across Regent street to Hanover Street, past Hanover Square to New Bond Street and turn left. Walk south on **Old Bond Street.** Yves St. Laurent's boutique, Geiger's, Bally and Ivory for shoes and a brasserie for coffee are in the next block. Turn north on New Bond Street to Oxford Steet.

Cross **Oxford Street,** turn left. If you proceed about three blocks further west on Oxford Street you will come to two great department stores: **Selfridges**, which takes up an entire block, and **Marks and Spencer**, where all your friends have told you to go for great buys on cashmere sweaters. They do have good buys, but I always feel like I am shopping at home. If you insist, walk on down and then come back.

Retrace your steps on Oxford Street to **South Moulton Street**. It angles its pedestrian mall back to New Bond Street. The shops along here are expensive and elegant for window shopping: Brown's, with its fashionable clothes, Kristal's for wild jewelry, O'Bogaert's for gold jewelry, and shops for men's wear and children's stylish clothes.

At **Brook Street**, you re-enter **New Bond Street**. Turn right. You will come to the stationer's **Frank Smythson's** and **Chappell's** music store, in business since 1811.

Sotheby's, the *famous auction house* established in 1744, is located in a fine 19th century building. They have sales almost every weekday at 11 a.m., except in August. Viewing of the objects to be auctioned takes place from 9 a.m. to 4 p.m. Take a look. If you want to attend an auction, the usual schedule is: Books on Monday; Porcelains on Tuesday; Pictures on Wednesday; Silver and Jewelry on Thursday, and Furniture on Friday. I capitalized all those sales items because they do not auction off any lower case objects.

Ralph Lauren and the fine art gallery of **Wildenstein & Co.** are across the street. Note Tessier's 19th century front with the three round arches surrounding display windows for jewelry and silver. As you walk down the street you will pass Hermes, Ungaro's, the silversmith Georg Jensen and a little shop with elegant women's clothes, Adele Davis. Asprey & Co. with its antiques and porcelains is across the street in a fine 18th century building. Cartier, Kutchinsky and Boucheron all display magnificent jewels. Just beyond is Chanel and the famous leather shop, Gucci. Directly across the street is the oldest business on Bond Street, the hairdresser, Truefitt & Hill, set up in 1805.

New Bond Street has now become Old Bond Street, built by Sir Thomas Bond in 1686. Look for the **Royal Arcade** on your right. It is a kind of mini-Burlington Arcade and has nice shops including a fine book binding society. At the entrance is Charbonnel & Walker's, famous for chocolates, truffles and rose and violet creams. P. & D. Colnaghi and Thomas Agnew and Son, two of London's greatest art dealers, are located on either side of the street. And finally, Sac Freres, perhaps the only store in the world exclusively selling amber.

You are now on **Piccadilly** again with the **Burlington Arcade** on your left and Fortnum and Mason's across the street. The Arcade was built by the third Earl of Burlington in 1819 to stop the rabble throwing rubbish into his garden, goes the story. Some of the shops are owned by descendants of the original owners, although they no longer live in rooms above the shops. You can find lovely, though expensive things from one end to the other. Note particularly the cashmeres at both of the Peal shops, the lovely hankies in the Irish Linen shop and the miniature Hummel figures at, where else, Hummel's.

Noon

I am assuming, unless you never found your way out of Liberty's, that you could make this circle in a morning. It should be about noon and you are in front of **Fortnum & Mason's**. If you arrive at noon, take the time to watch the Fortnum and Mason clock chime the hour. Mr. F. and Mr. M. walk out of the clock, one carrying a tray, one a candelabra, all to the sound of bells playing the *Eton Boating Song*.

There is a nice restaurant in Fortnum and Mason's mezzanine which I like, and a much fancier one on an upper floor, which I don't. I have had poor food and miserable service upstairs, but downstairs is always pleasant and inexpensive.

If you want something much more elegant, walk back to Piccadilly Circus to the 120 year old **Cafe Royal**, with its superior French cooking. It will be about $30 for lunch for one. Or go across the Circus to Denman street and the Italian restaurant, Estoril da Luigi e Robert. Lunch will be about $20 to $25 per person.

Be sure to spend some time in **Fortnum and Mason's**. I love to call it a grocery store. But it is unlike any other grocery store you ever saw with its tail-coated clerks and its produce, which includes such things as quail eggs. It is easy to believe they provided groceries for the Duke of Wellington's officers during the Napoleonic Wars and that they still purvey food to the royal family.

There are several upper floors with clothing and other goods, but it is the first floor "grocery" in which you will want to spend time. They also have a corner for ordering and mailing packages of their special items to friends abroad. It is a wonderful way to provide gifts without having to carry them. The chutneys, mustards and shortbreads all make fine gifts.

Afternoon

Next to Fortnum and Mason's is Swaine, Adeney Brigg and Co., with leather goods, expensive umbrellas and incredible riding equipment. It is worth a look. **Hatchard's** bookstore is just beyond. I happen to like this book store a great deal. It has a large stock of well-chosen books and is so much more manageable than Foyle's bookstore, which you will see tomorrow. They will mail your book selections overseas, which is a great service and eliminates a lot of heavy additions to your luggage.

Walk west on Picadilly Circus to **St. James's Street**. Turn left and walk on down the street, past all the private clubs with their bay and bow windows to St. James's Place.

Back to **St. James's Street**, turn right and walk down to number 7-9 **Lobb's,** England's most famous shoemaker and number 6 next door, Lock & Co., established in 1700 and still making hats.

Walk into each shop, perhaps not so much to buy but to look. On past little Pickering Place, where the last duel in England was fought, and on to number 3 Berry Bros and Rudd, wine merchants, founded in 1680, although their present location only dates from 1730.

Back up St. James's Street to King Street, turn right to find **Christie's Fine Art** and Spink & Son, founded in 1666, specializing in coins, medals and English and Oriental art. Walk up Duke Street to **Jermyn Street** and turn right.

The Cavendish Hotel is on your right. Andrew Grima, in the hotel, sells modern jewelry.Dunhill, the tobacconists, are across the street. Walk on to Floris, perfumers to the queen; Paxton & Whitfield with their hams and cheese, and all the fine gentlemen's shops and hairdressers. Every shop is worth a look.

At **Haymarket**, turn right and walk down to the Design Center at number 28 Haymarket, a good place to end your first shopping day. This is headquarters for the government sponsored Design Council. They have a pictorial index for the best in British quality goods, prices and information as to where to buy., This is also a two-floor retail shop with textiles, cards, and household goods. Everything here is well designed and priced fairly. It is an excellent place to shop for gifts for yourself and friends

Evening

Since you have been on your feet almost all day, try to go back for a rest in your hotel, then plan a leisurely dinner. If you don't want to give up quite yet, walk down Haymarket Street, cross Trafalgar Square and angle down Northumberland Avenue to Victoria Embankment and the **Thames River.**

There are two restaurant ships tied up at **Charing Cross Pier**, right at the end of Northumberland Avenue: **The Hispaniola** and the **Tattershall Castle**. The Hispaniola floating restaurant specializes in seafood and game. Dinners will run about $30 per person. The Tattershall Castle is a paddle steamer with daily dinners for between $15 and $20. Or you can sit on the top deck of the Hispaniola and just have a drink and enjoy the scenery.

The **Players,** London's music hall theater, is nearby on Villers Street if you want to continue your evening at the theatre.

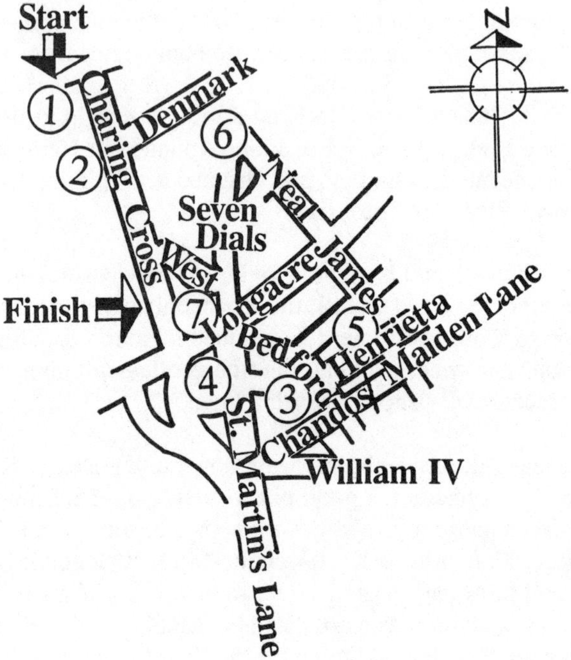

Shopping Day 2

1/ Tottenham Tube

2/ Foyle's Bookshop

3/ Goodwin's Court

4/ Cecil Court

5/ Covent Garden

6/ Neal's Yard

7/ The Ivy Restaurant

Day 2

Highlights: Charing Cross Road and its great book stores, Covent Garden, and Neal's Yard.

Reservations: Lunch at Beoty's, 79 St. Martin's Lane, Telephone 836-8768. Or lunch at Rules restaurant, Maiden Lane. Telephone 836-5314.

Dinner at The Ivy, West Street. Telephone 836-4715.

Morning

Start at the **Tottenham Court Road** tube stop this morning, which is at the north end of Charing Cross Road. Today you will visit book stores, tiny, winding old streets and alleys and the newly re-established Covent Garden.

Charing Cross is the street for scholars and musicians with its dozens of book and records stores. I will note some of the ones I particularly like.

As you walk south on Charing Cross Road, **Booksmith** will be on your left. They handle hundreds of "remaindered" books which they sell for 1/3 or more discount. As you cross Denmark Street, remember this is the home of popular music recordings.

Collett's International Bookshop features books in Russian and about Russia. Just beyond is **Foyles** bookstore on the corner of Charing Cross and little Manette Street. Remember Dicken's Dr. Manette in a *Tale of Two Cities*? Foyles is rumored to have more than **4 million** books, which I have no reason to disbelieve. I love wandering around this store and hate waiting to pay for the books I want. They have the most incredibly antiquated business system in the world. But if you love books you have to spend time here.

Several blocks on you will come to Zwemmer's, fine art books. They may have the best collection of art books of any shop in the world.

At this point you will have arrived at the **Leicester Square** Tube station. Continue to Goodwin's court on your left. You will have to look *very carefully for the entry* to this court. This is one of the special places in London with its row of late 18th century Regency buildings with their bow windows. Potted bay trees line the walk way.

Walk back to St. Martin's Lane, turn left for a half block, and on your right is **Cecil Court**, 1670. Just before you get there you will see the **Victorian Salisbury Pub**. Depending on your time, you may want to stop. This high camp pub is decorated with glass and mirrors and lots of gilt.

Cecil Court is filled with print and book shops and other nice little places. Check out **Travellers Bookshop** at 25 Cecil Court, Frognal's for rare books at Number 18, Watkins at Number 21 for mystery and occult books and Bell, Book & Radmell at 4 Cecil Court for first editions.

Noon

Time to eat. You can walk down St. Martin's Lane to Number 79 and the Greek restaurant, **Beoty's.** Very nice. About $20 per person. Or continue down St. Martin's to William IV Street, which intersects with Chandos Place. Walk straight ahead until Chandos turns into Maiden Lane and continue to the old English restaurant, **Rules**. Lovely food.

If you want a pub lunch, try the **Maple Leaf Pub** next to Rules. It is popular and crowded for a very good reason. The food is excellent, the service pleasant and the atmosphere friendly and welcoming.

Afternoon

This afternoon: the 400-year-old **Covent Garden**. Originally, this was the convent garden of Westminster Abbey. In 1662, Charles II granted charters to two theater companies which still operate here.

Theatre Royal Drury Lane opened in 1663 and the Covent Garden theatre, now the **Royal Opera House**, opened in 1732. In 1672, the Earl of Bedford received a charter to open a market for fruits, vegetables and flowers which operated until it moved to Nine Elms in 1974. The once-abandoned area has been converted into a flourishing array of shops, galleries, restaurants and theaters.

Walk up to the market from wherever you have had lunch. Although your prime interest today is in the shops, take time to walk in and around St. Paul's Church with its famous portico where the fictional Professor Higgins met his *Fair Lady*, Eliza Doolittle.

I am not even going to attempt to suggest what you should see during your perambulations around the two-level market. It is filled with book and clothing stores, restaurants and pubs and specialty shops such as Pollock's Toy Theater. This is an all-afternoon excursion.

After you finish shopping at The Market, walk north on **James Street** and **Neal Street** to find a variety of different craft shops and to **Neal's Yard**, a tiny flower-filled courtyard with health foodshops, crafts and a restaurant.

Evening

If you want dinner in this area, I can think of no finer place than **The Ivy** on West Street. Walk back to Seven Dials, the star-shaped intersection where seven streets meet. (There was once a column here containing seven sundials.) Walk down to St. Martin's Theater, turn right on West Street.

The Ivy is located just opposite the **Ambassador Theater** where Agatha Christie's *The Mousetrap* has been playing for over *30 year*s.

Or, just let your late afternoon tea take the place of dinner, and go to the theatre this evening. Check your newspapers for the current schedules and playing times.

For something different, check what is playing at the **Donmar Warehouse Theatre**, which is in this area. You may see an interesting contemporary play in London's version of an Off-Off Broadway theatre.

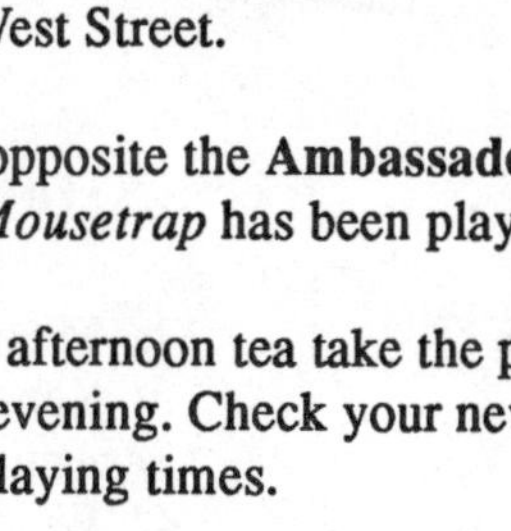

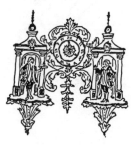

Shopping Day 3

Morning

1/ Knightsbridge Tube
2/ Harrod's

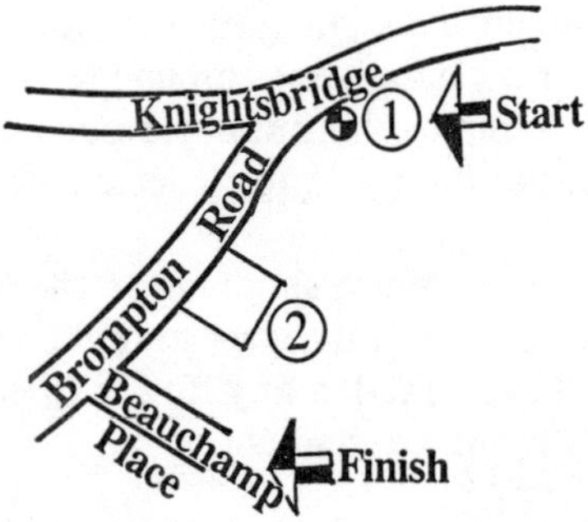

Afternoon

1/ Maggie Jones Restaurant
2/ Kensington Market
3/ Antique Hypermarket
4/ Windsor Castle Pub

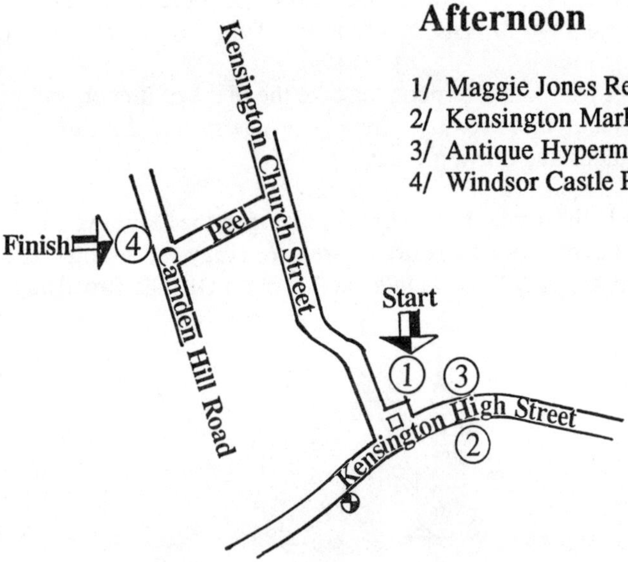

Day 3

Highlights: Knightsbridge and Harrod's Department Store, Beauchamp Place, Kensington High Street and Church Street.

Reservations: Lunch at Maggie Jones, 6 Old Court Place. Telephone 937-6462.

Dinner at Boulestin's, Henrietta and Southampton Streets. Telephone 836-3819.

The **Knightsbridge** tube stop is the starting point for today's adventure. Today you are going to shop the Knightsbridge area, where the greatest department store in Europe is located, and then go to the Kensington area.

Just opposite the tube stop at the intersection of Knightsbridge and Brompton road is the elegant department store, **Harvey Nichols**; across the street is the **Scotch House**.

The **Scotch House** has one of my favorite rooms in London. It is a beautiful dark-panelled circular room with shelves from top to bottom. Each shelf has a bolt of woolen material woven with one of the famous Scottish clan plaids. it is incredible to see them all in one place. I had no idea there were so many clans.

Walk down **Brompton** Road, not Knightsbridge. Somehow, this is one place where I always get turned around; watch the signs. Walk about *three* blocks, past Fiorucci's, Benetton (not so exotic now that they are on every block in the United States) and Charles Jourdan and the pedestrian Scholl's foodcare place. I do not know what I would do without their comforting lambswool and other products, which so lovingly care for my most precious possessions as I walk around London.

Keep going, past a number of small shops and then you are at **Harrod's**, *the Department Store*, so popular that it is often very crowded. The food halls are the **number one** attraction, with artistic displays of fruits, vegetables and fish that are *marvels of ingenuity.* The hanging carcasses of beasts and fowls, the hundreds of tempting cheeses, the confectioneries, and the dozens of pates are mind boggling. Notice the beautiful tiles set in the walls and ceilings. Copies of these tiles are on sale; they make a nice present.

You can investigate the upper floors for clothing, books and all kinds of other wonderful things.Harrod's has one of the **best tourist information desks** in town.

And if you want to get your hair done, this is the place. Fine hairdressers and tea while you wait.

In 1989 Harrod's adopted a new dress policy banning short shorts, revealing tops and cut-off jeans. Tailored shorts or Bermuda shorts are acceptable. Guards at the 11 entrances to the store are under orders to inspect shoppers and *turn away* those unsuitably dressed.

How do you follow an act like Harrod's? Walk south on Brompton Road to little **Beauchamp Place** with its Regency shops and iron balconies. It is just the right antidote for all that elegance and puffery. I love this little street with its charming shops.

Adele Davis sold me my one and only British woolen coat. The Map House is one of my favorite browsing store of its kind. Climb up to the second floor for additional exploring.

In the middle of the block is one of London's few Russian restaurants, **Borsht 'n' Tears**, for dinner only. And beyond is Luxury Needlepoint, with hundreds of needlepoint canvases.

At the end of Beauchamp Place, you will come to **Walton Street**, which is filled with fashionable shops, pubs and residences.

If you turn right for about four blocks you will come to Hasker Street and the **Saville-Edens**, a store which specializes in Lalique crystal, and the **Enterprise**, a pleasant neighborhood pub. You can walk in either direction on Walton Street to explore its elegant shops and charming buildings.

Noon

Grab a cab to Kensington high Street and Number 6 Old Court Place for lunch at **Maggie Jones.** No frills, wooden tables and sawdust on the floor, but they have very good food. Lunch will be moderate. Or, if you can't break away from Beauchamp Place, there are a number of eating places along the street.

Afternoon

Kensinton High Street has been a busy highway since Roman times, and is still popular. The **Kensington High Street** tube stop is now part of a fine shopping arcade with **Marks & Spencer** at the entrance.

Just opposite Old Court Place, where you may have just had lunch at Maggie Jones, is the **Kensington** market with 40 boutiques and 150 stalls for antiques and current fashions. The Antique Hypermarket is opposite it. They can both take hours of your time.

Rather than continue down Kensington High Street west of the tube stop, I suggest you return to **Kensington Church Street**, which winds and climbs the hill past antique shops, book stores and art shops of all kinds. Walk up **Church Street** until you get tired or until you get to **Peel Street.**

Turn left and walk to the **Campden Hill Road**. On the corner is the **Windsor Castle Pub**, built in 1835. This is the highest point of Campden Hill and at one time it was claimed you could see Windsor Castle from its windows.

Try the **Campden Bar** with its early 19th century window. When you are ready to leave, hail a cab.

Evening

Go back to your hotel and rest a bit before taking off for your dinner at **Boulestin's**, near Covent Garden, Henrietta and Southhampton Streets. Elegant and expensive. $80 to $100 for two, but worth every cent.

Extra Day

Highlights: Portobello Market, Camden Passage Market, Petticoat Lane and Bermondsey Market

This is that **fourth day** I promised you for *London's great markets* on Friday, Saturday and Sunday.

On **Friday**, the junk market south of the Thames at Bermondsey starts early, at 4 a.m. and goes on til noon. They say that if you look carefully, you may find **bargains** but you have to go **early**.

My favorite is **Portobello**, Notting Hill tube stop, on Saturday mornings. I know it is corny and crowded and there are no bargains, but I love it and the challenge of trying to find a bargain.

You can shop and eat as you go. **Sutton's Coffee Shop** sells good coconut lemon sweets and slices of pizza. The **China Kitchen** is a take-away fish bar.

Oranges and strawberries vie with derbies, leather jackets, silver and toast racks. Master butchers display whole pigs and pork bellies; the hot bread shop sells scone rings.

A good combination of markets is **Portobello** on *Saturday morning* and **Camden Passage** market in the *afternoon*, even though they are miles apart. I have to admit when I did this, I took a cab which was a bit expensive, but so convenient.

You can take the Circle Line tube from Notting Hill tube stop to Moorgate and transfer to the Northern line to Angel. It does take extra time but is not as expensive as my beloved cab.

Camden operates all week, but like many markets, Saturday is the big day. They have regular indoor shops, but on Saturday, there are dozens of outdoor stalls. Here is one of the places to look for antiques and silver. Probably no great bargains, but fun, and there are a number of good restaurants here.

On Sunday, if you love flea markets and the junk shops, try **Petticoat Lane** on Middlesex Street. Tube stops are either Aldgate or Aldgate East. (Sunday from early hours to 2 p.m; serious shoppers start at 4 a.m.)

I still remember one rainy Sunday morning when I tried to eat jellied eel which I brought at Tubby Isaac's stand. It was simply disgusting; one of the few foods I could just not handle.

Shopping in London can be as elegant or ordinary as you desire. Your choices are infinite. I have only scratched the surface.

Two final suggestions. The shops attached to museums, many of the churches and other points of interest, are almost all first rate and worth a visit.

And the last suggestion is to purchase the very inexpensive guides on famous places published by Pitkin Pictorials Ltd. and available at the places they describe and from booksellers in London. They are beautifully printed with intelligent text and exquisite color photographs and may prove the finest memory gifts you can bring home.

Good hunting.

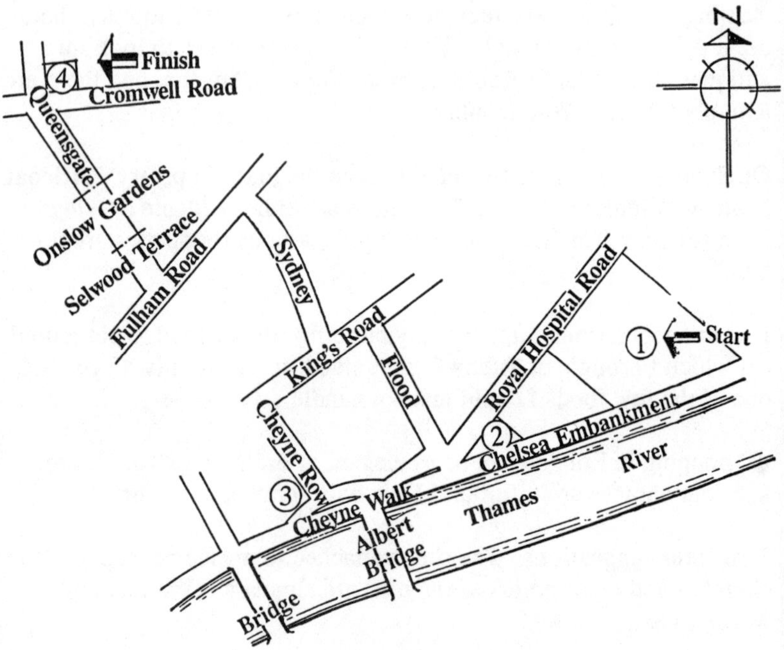

Gardening Day 1

1/ Chelsea Flower Show

2/ Chelsea Physic Garden

3/ King's Head & Eight Bells Pub

4/ Natural History Museum

Gardener's London

I**f an Englishman's home** is his castle, his **garden** is his **pride**. No matter where you go in England, you will find **gardens**. They may be rose bushes, or rhododendrons massed together on postage-sized lots adjacent to tiny cottages or magnificent gardens designed by the famous landscape architect, Lancelot Brown, better known as "Capability" Brown. Brown received his nickname because of his habit of saying that any commission had "great capabilities."

It is no wonder that gardeners throughout the world know of England's passion for plants and flowers and come to visit the dozens of **great gardens** throughout the country. But you do not have to leave London and its environs to see magnificent plantings. Three days are not long enough to do more than see some of the highlights, but it should give you a sufficient taste to lure you back for more.

One of these three days will be spent in the outskirts of London. It is easy to get to these gardens by public transportation, but you may want to rent a car for the day for more flexibility.

To see the gardens at their height of bloom and to take advantage of visiting the great **Chelsea Flower Show**, visit London in the spring, preferably in May. If this is not possible, do not fret. London blooms from May to October.

If you are interested in visiting private gardens, write for a booklet describing them and the process for visiting them: National Gardens Scheme, 57 Lower Belgrave St., London SWI.

Day 1

Highlights: Chelsea Flower Show, Chelsea Physic Garden, The Natural History Museum and Holland Park.

Write in Advance: Membership in the Royal Horticulture Society. Write Royal Horticulture Society, 80 Vincent Square, London SWIP 2PE.

Reservations: Lunch at La Tante Claire, 68 Royal Hospital Road. Telephone 352-6045.

Dinner at The Belvedere, Holland Park. Telephone 602-1238. Open air theater performance at Holland Park from June through August. Telephone 633-1707.

Morning

This day is predicated on timing your trip to coincide with the **Chelsea Flower Show**, which is held four days in May. Each year you must check to find out the exact days, usually after May 20. Have your travel agent check the dates.

The first day of the four days of the flower show is reserved for members of the **Royal Horticulture Society**. You might want to consider joining, about $20 per person. Your membership provides a free ticket for member's day at the flower show and a subscription to their monthly publication, *The Gardener*. When you realize about 70,000 people attend each of the public days, a membership might be a very good idea.

The Chelsea Flower Show, which began in 1913, is held on the grounds of **Chelsea's Royal Hospital**, where more than 400 pensioners still live. You will recognize them by their ornate red or blue 18th-century uniforms. During the show, these spacious grounds are filled with acres of floral displays from all over the world. The Royal Horticultural Society staff is present to answer questions.

To get there, either tube to the **Sloane Street** station and take a rather long walk down Lower Sloane Street, where you will turn right on Royal Hospital Road. Or, take a cab.

The grounds open at 8:00 a.m.; *go early*. You will probably spend the entire morning or longer at the show. If you choose to spend the entire day, you can skip the rest of these suggestions and plan to cab to Holland Park for dinner.

I will not attempt to walk you through the show, since each year it is different. There will be many unofficial"guides" to direct you. This is a once in a lifetime experience for the avid gardener. The show usually is open from 8 a.m. to 8 p.m., except for the final day when it closes at 5 p.m. after the sale of exhibits to the public.

Noon

If you choose to leave at noon, walk down the **Royal Hospital Road**. It is probably time to eat. I suggest either a rather expensive restaurant or a nearby pub. A Michelin two star restaurant, **La Tante Claire**, 68 Royal Hospital Road, serves lunch and dinner, Monday through Friday. Lunch will cost about $40 per person.

Or you can continue down the road, which becomes the Chelsea Embankment, till you arrive at **Cheyne Row** where you will find the pub called **King's Head & Eight Bells** on the corner. This is an appropriate place today because you can drink and snack in a garden overlooking the Thames, or eat in an upstairs restaurant. The food is excellent and not expensive.

Afternoon

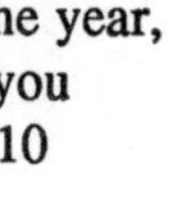

The **Chelsea Physic Garden**, on the Royal Hospital Road, was founded in 1673 for the study of horticulture. (Open during the Chelsea Flower Show from 11 a.m. to 2 p.m.; other times of the year, open Wednesday and Sunday from 2 to 5 p.m. At other times you must apply for access by writing to the Clerk to the Trustees, 10 Fleet St, London, EC 4.)

This is a **special garden**. I saw it by accident one day when the gardeners had left the door open, and I just walked in. Its research over the last several hundred years has supplied Georgia's cotton seeds via plants from the South seas; India's tea and quinine from China and South America; and Malaya's rubber plants from South America. You can walk back a few blocks from the pub to see this garden.

Walk north through Chelsea on Flood Street, cross King's Road. Turn left about two blocks and turn left on **Sydney Street.** Walk through South Kensington to see the informal gardens.

When Sydney Street reaches Fulham Road, turn left and walk to Selwood Terrace/Neville Terrace, turn right. This street becomes Queen's Gate Road. Queen's Gate ends at **Cromwell Road** where you will find the **Natural History Museum.**

Visit the **Botanical Department** on the second floor with its dioramas showing different kinds of habitats in the British Isles and other places, including an African rain forest and the Arizona desert.

Evening

This evening I suggest dinner and/or the open air theatre performance in **Holland Park.** You will already have checked on the performance and made your dinner reservations. Go back to your hotel to rest and then cab to Holland Park in time for dinner and the open air theatre production.

This **flower garden** with its exotic peacocks and geese is open from dawn to dusk. Give yourself time to wander through the gardens. There is an Orangery with exhibitions and poetry readings, often concerts on the lawn.

The **open air theater** is held in a courtyard in front of a ruined house which was bombed in 1941 and never restored. The grounds, with its more than 3,000 species of trees and plants, has been kept up.

The restaurant, **The Belvedere,** is a 17th-century mansion which overlooks the gardens which are illuminated after dark. It is a very special, pretty place.

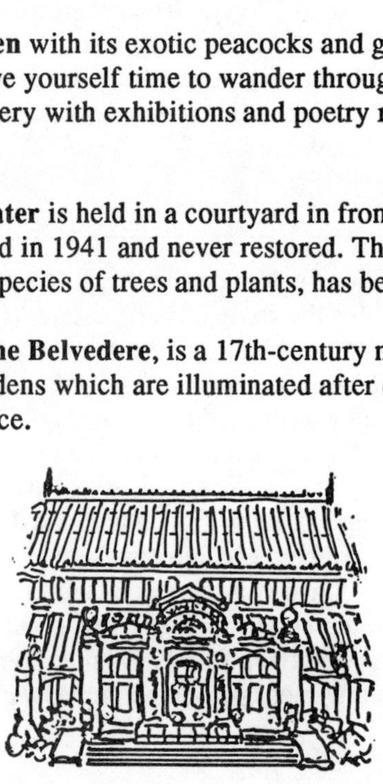

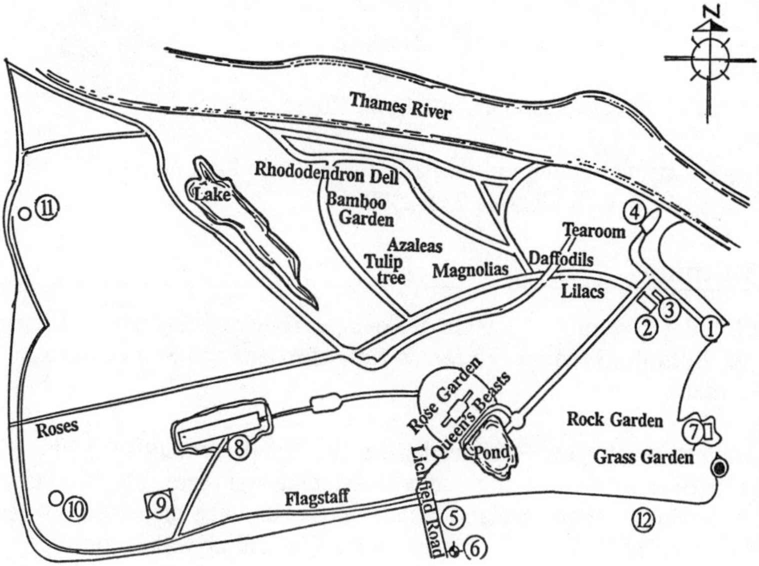

Gardening Day 2

1/ Main Entrance
2/ Orangery
3/ Filmy Fern House
4/ Kew Palace
5/ Victoria Gate
6/ Kew Station
7/ Wood Museum
8/ Temperate House
9/ Restaurant
10/ Pagoda
11/ Queen Charlotte's Cottage
12/ Maids of Honour Teashop

Day 2

Highlights: Kew Gardens, and Syon House.

Reservations: Dinner at the Park Room, Hyde Park Hotel, Knightsbridge. Telephone 235-2000.

Morning

Today is your day outside of London. You are going to the **Royal Botanic Gardens,** known as **Kew Gardens** and Syon House and Gardens.

You can reach **Kew Gardens** by the Tube (underground); the **District Line** going to Richmond will also take you there. The trip lasts about half an hour, so plan to leave in time to reach the gardens when they open at 10 a.m. The gardens are a five minute walk from the Kew Garden tube stop.

If the weather is beautiful and you want to take the time, the **river trip** to the gardens is the best way to go. Boats leave from **Westminster pier** and take about an hour and one half.

Spring is the best time to visit these 288 acres, open daily from 10 a.m. to sunset. The glasshouses open at 10 a.m., sometimes earlier; the museums at 10 a.m. There are refreshments in the summer at the Pavilion and at a kiosk near the main gate.

Your specific walk will depend on your point of arrival; there are a number of gates through which you can enter the gardens. If you take the tube and walk straight up Lichfield Road, you will arrive at the **Victoria Gate.**

If you take the boat you will probably enter at the **main gate.**

The **map** will give you an idea of where the special plantings and houses are located, but may not give you an idea of the size of the place. Even telling you that it is 288 acres may not do it. I assure you it is huge.

Let me make a few suggestions and then you pick out the places which appeal to you the most. Just remember it is a long walk from the main gate to Queen Charlotte's cottage.

Personally, I like the **outdoor gardens** better than the museums and glass houses. I love the **pond** with its Chinese guardian lions and the Queen's Beasts, the **rose garden** and the **lake** with its wonderful birds.

Kew Palace with its Dutch rooms is not very interesting to me, but I like the filmy **fern house** and all the rock and grass gardens. The Temperate House is the usual indoor botanical garden.

Very frankly, unless you are in great walking shape I would forego the far reaches of the garden with Queen Charlotte's Cottage at one end and the Pagoda at the other, neither of which can you enter.

Head for the **Orangery** first to get the **newest map**. The book's map should give you a good idea of where things are, but cannot tell you what will be in bloom or what is open on the day of your visit.

Noon

It will take the whole morning for just a cursory walk through these magnificent gardens. When you get hungry, either eat on the grounds or walk down Kew Road to the **Maids of Honour Teashop.** It usually has a single choice of soup and main dish for lunch, but also has a lovely bakery where I like to buy their maids of honour, little round flaky almond pastries.

Or, cross Kew Bridge and turn right to reach **Shand on Green** and one of its historic pubs. Either the **City Barge** or the **Bull's Eye Pub** will help alleviate your hunger.

You can spend your entire day in the gardens or you can visit Syon house and gardens. If you have a car, you can cross the Kew Bridge and go on to **Syon Park**. If you are on foot, cross the Kew Bridge to Kew Bridge Road where you can take bus 237 or 267 to Brent Lea and Syon Park and House.

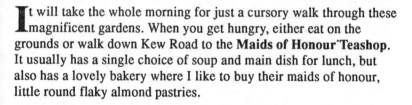

The **Syon House** grounds are open daily from 10 a.m. to 6 or sunset. The rose gardens are open from May to August and have a separate entrance south of the house. The grounds here are the oldest horticultural gardens in England, older than Kew. The were begun in the 16th century with mulberry trees imported from the continent.

Our old friend, Capability Brown, started here before moving over to Kew. The gardens are magnificent. Just wander around.

Be sure to visit the **garden center**, which is the supermarket of gardens. There is a conservatory with birds and an aquarium. The **Butterfly House** (open from 10 a.m. to 5 p.m.) across from the supermarket, is very hot, humid and sort of tacky, but is still fun. It is the only time I have been surrounded by these pretty fluttering creatures. If you have time, you might want to wander through. I do love the sign at the exit:"Check your clothes for resting butterflies."

Even though your main interest is gardens, do visit **Syon house**, at least the first **five** rooms, which were designed by Robert Adams for the Duke of Northumberland. The house is open from Good Friday to the end of September, from noon to 5 p.m. It is closed on Friday and Saturday.

The Classical entry hall leads you into a magnificent anteroom, worthy of a Caesar, with its gildings, carvings and huge columns. You then walk into the dining room, which reverts to almost total white except for some gilding around the statues in the niches. Then comes the magnificent red drawing room and the gallery from which you can view Kew Gardens. You can leave at this point; the rest is a let down after Adam's splendid rooms.

To return, retrace your steps to the underground station or drive back. The same buses, 237 or 267, will take you back to the tube stop or boat landing.

Evening

You will have done a great deal of walking today and probably will be very tired. For a lovely relaxing dinner tonight, go to the Park Room at the **Hyde Park Hotel** on Knightsbridge. They are located just south of Hyde Park and have wonderful views into the park. Dinner will be about $60 for two.

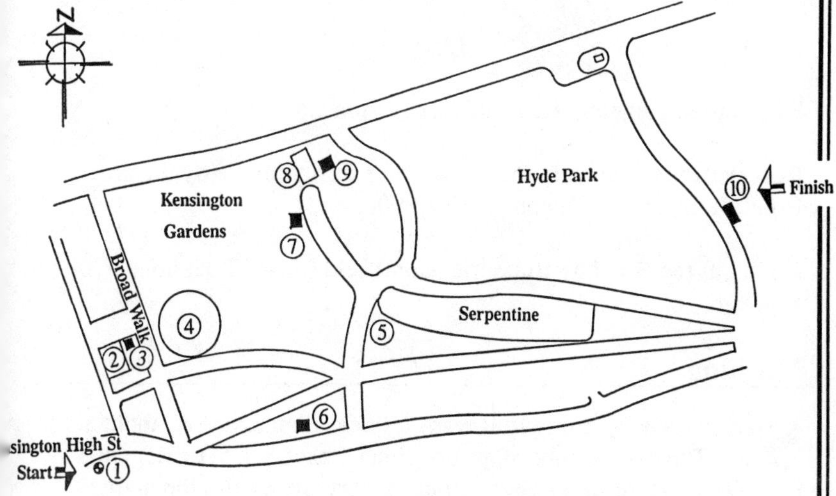

Gardening

Day 3 Afternoon

1/ Kensington High Tube
2/ Palace
3/ Sunken Garden
4/ Round Pond
5/ Restaurant
6/ Albert Memorial
7/ Peter Pan
8/ Italian Gardens
9/ Queen Anne's Alcove
10/ Dorchester Hotel

Day 3

Highlights: Regent's Park and Kensington Gardens.

Reservations: Lunch at the Royal Roof Restaurant, Royal Garden Hotel, Kensington. Telephone 937-8000.

Dinner at the Bombay Brasserie, Courtfield Close. Telephone 370-4040.

Morning

Start the day by going to **Regent's Park**. Plan to arrive about 10 a.m. The closest tube stops are either Baker Street or Regent's Park. Walk down Marylebone Road to York Street and the main entrance to the park and **Queen Mary's Gardens.**

These **rose gardens** are in their glory from May to July, and often into the fall. The beauty of the roses and the incredible scent is overwhelming. I could spend hours here. When you can wrench yourself away, you will find a Japanese garden on an island in a little lake.

The other flower beds in the park are much more formal, but have stunning displays which change, depending on the time of year. An open air theatre, where Shakespeare is performed in the summer, is located in this magical setting. The **Rose Garden Restaurant** will provide mid-morning sustenance. Just wander around to your heart's content in this special place.

Noon

Take a tube to **High Street Kensington**, an easy ride from Baker Street on the Circle Line, or take a cab to Kensington High Street and **The Royal Garden Hotel** for lunch. The hotel restaurant has a prix fixe lunch for about $25 per person, and one of the most beautiful views in town, overlooking Kensington Gardens.

If you want a less expensive lunch, try **Maggie Jones** on 6 Court Place, near the hotel. It is old and funky, but has excellent food and a lively crowd at noon.

Afternoon

Walk up Kensington High Street to Kensington Gardens. Turn left on the Broad Walk and continue to the **Kensington Palace**. The Round Pond will be on your right and the **palace**, with its Orangery and sunken gardens, on your left. Walk across the park, toward **The Serpentine**, a lake which winds between Kensington Gardens and Hyde Park. When you arrive at the water, turn left and walk along the Serpentine to the Peter Pan statue, the Italian gardens and Queen Anne's Alcove.

You can spend the afternoon exploring the 288 acres of this garden or you can wander into adjacent **Hyde Park** and explore an equally large green space.

There is a **restaurant** next to the bridge crossing the Serpentine in case you want something to eat or drink, or you can walk across Hyde Park to Park Lane and the **Dorchester Hotel** for an elegant cream tea.

Evening

Later in the evening, cab to the **Bombay Brasserie** on Courtfield Close, SW7, to spend the evening in an elegant reconstruction of the British Raj with its white wicker furniture and gorgeous plantings. It will cost about $55 for two.

Y**our three days of "gardening"** in London have come to an end, but you have barely touched the surface. Great things are still in store for you.

London is blessed with many other **wonderful parks** and **green places. Green Park** and **St. James's Park**, with its exotic flowers and birds, are in the middle of the city. Just a few minutes from the center of the city are **Greenwich Park** in the southeast and Richmond Park in the southwest. **Battersea Park**, just south of the Thames, features a boating lake, Henry Moore sculptures and a subtropical garden.

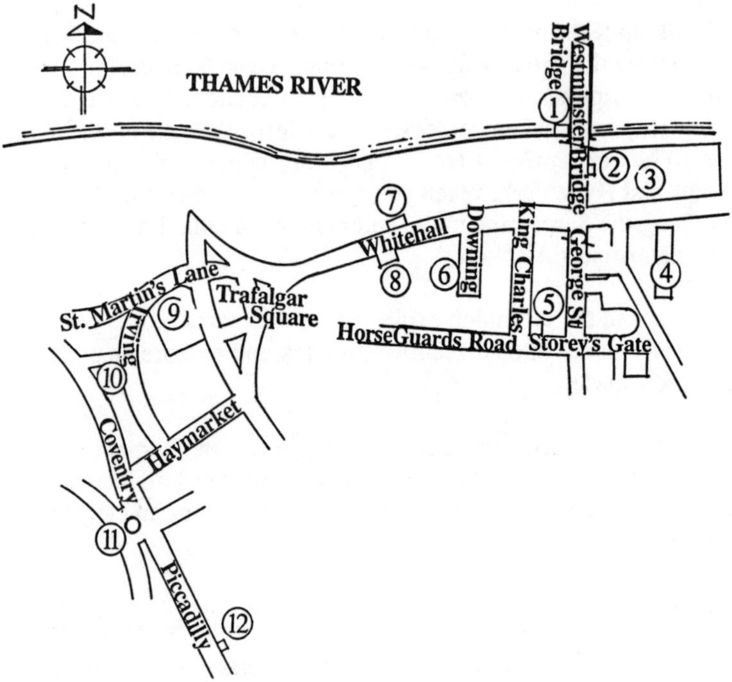

Children's Day 1.

1/ Westminster Pier
2/ Big Ben
3/ Parliament
4/ Westminster Abbey
5/ Churchill's War Rooms
6/ Number 10 Downing Street
7/ Banqueting Hall
8/ Horse Guards
9/ National & Portrait Galleries
10/ Leicester Square
11/ Piccadilly Circus
12/ Fortnum and Mason's

Children's London

London is the perfect city for children. Where else can you find castles, canals, penny arcades, the Tower of London, sailing ships, pigeons and pandas? A little careful planning can help you and your children have a wonderful time together. I can think of no other city which is such a **magic place** for children to explore.

I arbitrarily choose to define my tour for children between the ages of six and thirteen. That's because most people will not plan to sightsee with very little children; teenagers pose a whole different set of challenges.

There is one great advantage to traveling with children: Adults get a chance to do things they might be self-conscious about doing without a kid in tow. I suspect most of us are just children in big people's clothing. My daughter, Ruth, says the only difference between grown ups and children is that children are shorter and have no money. Traveling with them will give you an additional opportunity to see the wonders of London through the unclouded eyes of your young ones.

Just a few pieces of information before you start your first day's tour. For the latest information about daily events for children you can call **Kidsline** 222-8070 on weekdays from 9 a.m. to 4 p.m. or **Daily Events for Children** 246-8007. Also check the Children's pages in *City Limits* or *Time Out* magazines. The London Tourist Authority has published two booklets, *London for Children* and *Discovering London* for Children. They are available at their information centers at Harrod's, Selfridges and the Tower of London.

One special recommendation: I suggest that people traveling with children consider renting an **apartment.** It is nice to have extra room, and particularly, a kitchen. Your travel agent can help locate apartments as well as hotel rooms.

One suggestion is Dolphin Square apartments located off Grosvenor Road between Chelsea And Westminster. It is a large complex in which all apartments have a kitchen, bathroom and television. There is a heated swimming pool, tennis court, shops, a restaurant and a launderette for the use of its patrons. For information and reservations write Dolphin Square Trust Limited, Dolphin Square, London SWIV 3LX or phone 01-834-9134. A three-room, two-bedroom apartment rents for between $600-$700 per week. That will give you some idea of costs.

In case the adults want to go off on their own, your hotel will often be able to provide or locate a reputable "child minder," British for baby sitter.

Most of the restaurants mentioned in this chapter will not need reservations, but if you choose others, do book tables. Some of the suggested eating places provide "take away" food for picnic eating.

You will save the 15 per cent VAT (Value added tax) if you consume the food off the premises, a nice saving. And fish and chips make a pleasant outdoor meal.

Avoid the mobile vans on side streets; they are not always well supervised. The coffee stalls for tea, sandwiches and coffee are fine. The ice cream vans which are almost always near park entrances and other such places are fine but expensive. Try to buy your ice creams and sweets in the confectionery or tobacco shops.

Enough of the housekeeping details. Let's see **London.**

This first day you will start at the castle called the Tower of London, visit an underground bunker and explore London's version of penny arcades.

Day 1

Highlights: Tower of London, Thames River, Houses of Parliament, Big Ben, Westminster Abbey, Cabinet War Rooms, Trafalgar Square, Leicester Square and Piccadilly Circus.

Reservations: No reservations necessary if you go to the restaurants I recommend in this chapter.

Morning

Take the tube to Tower Hill or cab to the **Tower of London** in time to arrive when it opens at 9:30 a.m. This many-turreted castle with its Beefeaters in their fancy uniforms, the buildings filled with armor and weapons and the ravens hopping around the grounds, all overlooking the majestic Thames River, is a child's fairytale come true.

The **Beefeaters**, the guards for the tower, lead frequent tours of the Tower. Take the tour and enjoy both the magnificent sights and the history your guides provide en route. Incidentally, one extra sight the guides might not mention is the empty raven cages located just beyond the Bloody Tower.

The **ravens** spend their nights in the cages. As you probably know, the story goes that if the ravens ever leave the tower, England will fall. They never have and probably never will; their wings are clipped.

Noon

Take the walk in front of the tower to see the display of cannons and the outdoor cafe along the river. This is a lovely place to eat with a spectacular view.

Afternoon

Walk back to Tower pier and take one of the **river boats** to Westminster pier, about a 20-minute ride. Climb the steps from the pier and walk out on Westminster Bridge to see the famous view of the Houses of Parliament, Big Ben, Westminster Abbey and the river Thames. Walk down Bridge Street to Parliament Square, turn left to the abbey. As you cross the square notice the statue of Winston Churchill on the green and the one of Abraham Lincoln on the far side of the square.

Westminster Abbey will be in front of you. Walk through the main door and down the broad aisle to admire the lofty ceiling, great stained glass windows and dozens of chapels and statues. Just wander through without spending too much time reading labels or worrying about what is what. Just enjoy the extraordinary beauty of the place. Of special interest to children will be the **Brass Rubbing Center**, open 9 a.m. to 5:30 p.m., at the northeast corner of the Dean's Yard at the entrance to the cloisters. Replicas of medieval brass monuments are available for rubbings. This can be great fun to do and provides a wonderful present to take home.

As you leave the abbey, turn right on Storey's Gate, which becomes Horse Guards Road, to King Charles Street. Turn right and you will find the entrance to the **Cabinet War Rooms**, from which Prime Minister Winston Churchill directed Britain's activities in World War II. They are located ten feet underground in the basement of the government offices. Although a few rooms had been open to visitors on a restricted basis for the past few years, at least 17 rooms were opened to the public in 1985. The bunker is open Tuesday to Sunday, 10 a.m. to 5:50 p.m. with an admission charge, about $3 for adults and $1.50 for children. You will receive a map of the complex, but a portable audio-cassette guide is available, and I recommend using it, to hear the sounds and voices of people who made history in these rooms.

Of particular interest are the map room, the nerve center of the operation; the trans-Atlantic telephone room and the Prime Minister's bedroom. There are exhibitions and memorabilia in a number of the rooms. In Room 64 note the sign-in book with its very first entry: 29 May 1942 Dwight D. Eisenhower, Major-General, USA.

Walk up King Charles Street to Parliament Street which becomes Whitehall. Turn left and walk down past Number 10 Downing

Street, the Banqueting Hall on your right, the Horse Guards on your left. Enjoy walking into the **Horse Guards** courtyard with its clocktower. Two mounted troopers are on guard at all times.

Walk straight on down to **Trafalgar Square** with its fountains, Nelson's Column, the tourists and hundreds of pigeons. The pigeons are tame, almost too tame if you are not crazy about birds. You can get your picture taken with a pigeon on your arm or your head, if you can stand it. Your kids will love it.

Mid-afternoon snack

It is probably time to eat again. Walk up Haymarket Street to **Piccadilly Circus**, where you will find the famous statue of Eros and hundreds of young people sitting nearby. Turn left on Piccadilly and walk down to **Fortnum and Mason's** to their fountain restaurant. Here you'll find good and inexpensive sandwiches, pastries and the best sodas in London. The children will love seeing the grocery clerks in morning coats with baskets over their arms selecting groceries for distinguished looking women. Not quite like home.

Or you could walk up St. Martin's Lane on the right of Trafalgar Square to **Leicester Square**. There are statues of a number of people on the square including a handsome one of **Shakespeare**.Here you will also find the London version of **Penny Arcades**. Quite different from our American versions. Some are rather plain but others are quite palatial with chandeliers and carpeting. People under the age of 18 must be accompanied by an adult to enter these places.

Evening

On New Coventry Street, just off Leicester Square, is the huge **Swiss Centre** with its four restaurants. Check the menus and look at each one to decide where to eat; all are pleasant and reasonable in price. The Rendez Vous is for quick snacks, the Locanda for fondues, the Taverne for raclette (melted cheese, potatoes and tiny pickles, better than it sounds) and the Chesa, which is the most elegant and expensive of the four restaurants.

After the penny arcades and supper, you might just want to go back to your hotel and sack out. If you have any energy left, there are always concerts and movies.

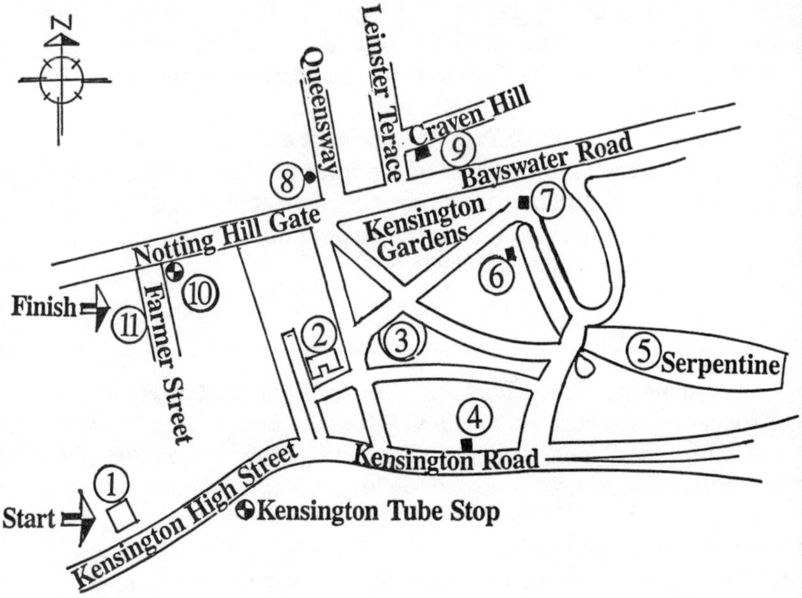

Children's Day 2

1/ Commonwealth Institute
2/ Kensington Palace
3/ Round Pond
4/ Albert Memorial
5/ The Serpentine
6/ Peter Pan statue
7/ Italian Gardens
8/ Queen's Ice Skating Club
9/ London Toy and Model Museum
10/ Notting Hill Tube
11/ Geale's Restaurant

Day 2

Highlights: Commonwealth Institute, Kensington Gardens and Palace, Serpentine Lake, Queen's Ice Skating Club, and the London Toy and Model Museum.

Reservations: No reservations necessary if you eat at the restaurants recommended in this chapter. For information on evening cruises on the Thames River, telephone 930-2062 or 4097.

Let's move over to the other side of London for a day **outdoors.** Needless to say, these days are interchangeable depending on the weather.

There is something for every child and every adult today. You can swim in the Serpentine, skate in an indoor ice rink, visit the queen's doll house, play with toys and eat fish and chips.

Morning

Start this day at the **Commonwealth Institute** on Kensington High Street. The nearest tube station is Kensington High Street. Turn left to the Institute. It opens daily at 10 a.m. (2 p.m. on Sundays); you can't miss its five-pointed green copper roof and glass walls. Built in 1962, it exhibits resources, crafts and arts through models and dioramas of the treasures of the nations in the British Commonwealth.

Walk back east along Kensington High Street to **Kensington Park.** As you pass the tube stop, notice a big McDonald's directly across the street. It is filled with chandeliers, mirrors, plantings and comfortable seating, if you want a cup of coffee or a roll at this point.

Walk up to the park and the Broad Walk which will take you to **Kensington Palace** which opens at 9 a.m. (Sunday 1 p.m.). This is now the home for Princess Margaret, Prince Charles and Diana and about ten other members of the royal family.

In 1689, architect Christopher Wren was asked to design this country house for the royal family. Of particular interest to young people is **Queen Victoria's bedroom** with her toys and **doll house.** Victoria lived here when she was princess and learned of her accession to the throne, at the death of William IV, in this room. Also notice the ivory throne and footstool in the King's Council Chamber, a gift from the Maharajah of Travancore. My favorite room is the Presence Chamber with its painted ceiling, Grinling Gibbons carvings around the fireplace and a throne.

Directly in front of the palace is the **Round Pond**, where little yachtsmen sail their **boats**. This is a very big piece of water to be called a pond. If you happen to be here on a Sunday, you will see some of the great **kite flyers** of the country. Just wander through this wonderful park.

The exotic and ornate Albert Memorial, built by Queen Victoria for her beloved spouse, is at the south edge of the park. The Serpentine, the lake which snakes through the park, separates Kensington Gardens from Hyde Park.

Noon

At the center of the park, you will come to the bridge spanning the lake. To the right of the bridge (with the palace to your back) you will see a restaurant, a bathing pavilion and bath houses where you can change clothes for a **quick swim** in the lake.

Nearby is the Serpentine gallery with changing exhibitions of contemporary art. Stop for **lunch** at this point. There is an inexpensive cafe in the restaurant building.

Afternoon

After lunch and swimming, walk north along the path on the edge of the **Serpentine** to see the **Peter Pan** statue and further on, the Italian gardens with its fountains. If you have smaller children, walk back to the west end of the park to the children's playground. Exit the park and you will be on Bayswater Road. Cross Bayswater and walk to Queensway.

If you walk north on Queensway you will come to the **Queen's Ice Skating Club** on your left, the only skating rink in central London. You can **rent skates** and have a twirl on the ice. Even if you don't want to skate, stop in and watch for a few minutes. I love this rink with its crepe paper flowers, buntings and turn-of-the-century decor. It is more like a ballroom than an ice rink.

Walk back to Bayswater Road, turn left and walk to Leinster Terrace and turn left. Turn right on Craven Hill and right again to Number 23 Craven Hill, the home of the **London Toy and Model Museum**. (Open Tuesday through Saturday 10 a.m. to 5:30 p.m.; Sunday 11 a.m.-5 p.m., Closed Monday). This old Victorian house contains **toys** and lots of working train models in its five rooms. The gardens also contain working train circuits and other wonders.

Evening

This is a good time to stop and **eat.** From the Queensway tube stop, go one station to Notting Hill tube to have supper at **Geale's Restaurant**, one of the best and oldest fish and chips places in London.

As you leave the tube station, turn left and walk a few steps to what looks like an alley, but is Farmer Street. Turn left and Geale's restaurant is a short block away. It has been a family owned business for nearly 50 years. Check the **specials of the day**; for example, mushroom soup, fish and chips and apple crumble (sort of like our apple crisp but better.) Priced at about $5. Good and inexpensive.

Tonight would be a good evening to cab to Westminster pier and take **a trip up the Thames** to see the city illuminated. Your children will love the boats, the river and the lighted city - and so will you.

Day 3

Highlights: Regent's Canal, London Zoo, Madame Tussaud's Wax Museum and the London Planetarium.

Reservations: No reservations necessary at any of the restaurants recommended in this chapter. Regent's Canal water-buses. For information telephone 286-6101.

Performance at the open air theatre in Regent's Park. For information, telephone 935-1537.

Morning

Today you will explore a curious mixture of London's pleasures - a canal boat trip, pandas from China, waxwork effigies, and a laser show.

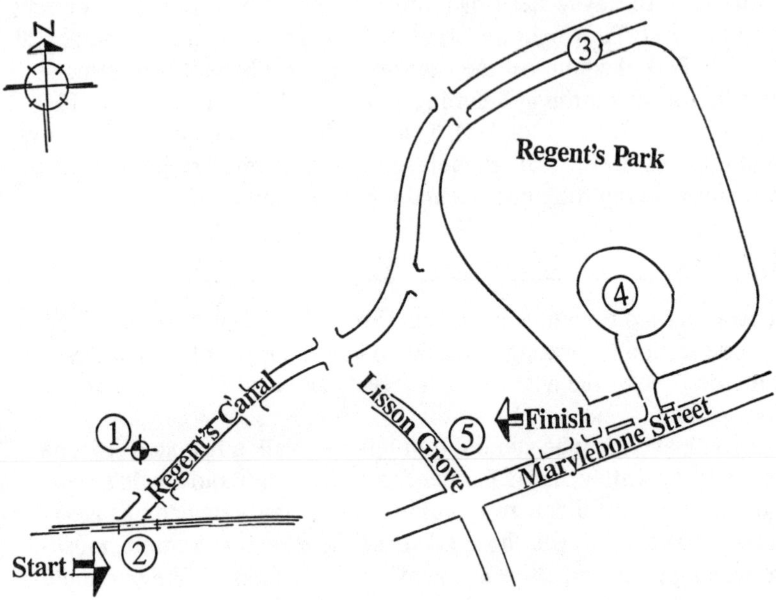

Children's Day 3

1/ Notting Hill Tube

2/ Boat Landing

3/ Zoo Boat landing

4/ Rose Garden

5/ Sea Shell Restaurant

Start the day with a **boat ride**. This would not be surprising in Venice or Amsterdam, but most people do not think of canals in London. **Regents Canal** was built in 1820 to join the Grand Union Canal with the Thames River at Limehouse, and it is *wonderful.*

Tube to Warwick Avenue tube stop or take a cab to **Little Venice**, just off Blomfield Road, where the **canal boats** leave between 10 a.m. and 4:45 p.m.

Take one of the water buses from the pier to the landing at **London Zoo** in **Regent's Park**. Get the ticket which *includes admission* to the **zoo** since that is your destination this morning.

This is a most unusual ride and the children and you will love seeing the houseboats that dock along the canal with their decorations of castles and roses.

Get off the boat at the **zoo landing**. You will be a short distance from an entrance to the zoo. Just follow the signs. The **London Zoo** is open daily 10 a.m. to 6 p.m. I will suggest a few "must see" places, but buy their helpful and handsome guide for up-to-date information about their exhibits.

This is the **world's oldest zoo**, open to the public in 1847. It was the brainchild of Sir Stamford Raffles, the famous "Raffles," founder of Singapore. The zoo has grown from the original 5 acres to 36 acres, with 6,000 animals representing more than 1,160 species.

When you arrive at the landing stage, the **Great Apes Breeding Colony** will be on your right. Just beyond is Moonlight World, where you will view animals only active at night. Cross back over the canal to visit the 80-foot-high **Snowdon Aviary,** whose more than 150 birds can be seen in their natural habitats as you walk on an elevated walk. Return over the bridge; on your right are deer, horses, giraffes, zebras, camels and llamas. Walk back toward the main gate and to your left are the giant Chinese pandas and the monkeys.

Noon

The **restaurant** is east of the pandas. Just wander through to look at whatever interests you. Be sure to see the New Lion terraces built in 1976. The children's zoo is just to the right of the gate, where you will leave the zoo to walk across Regent's Park.

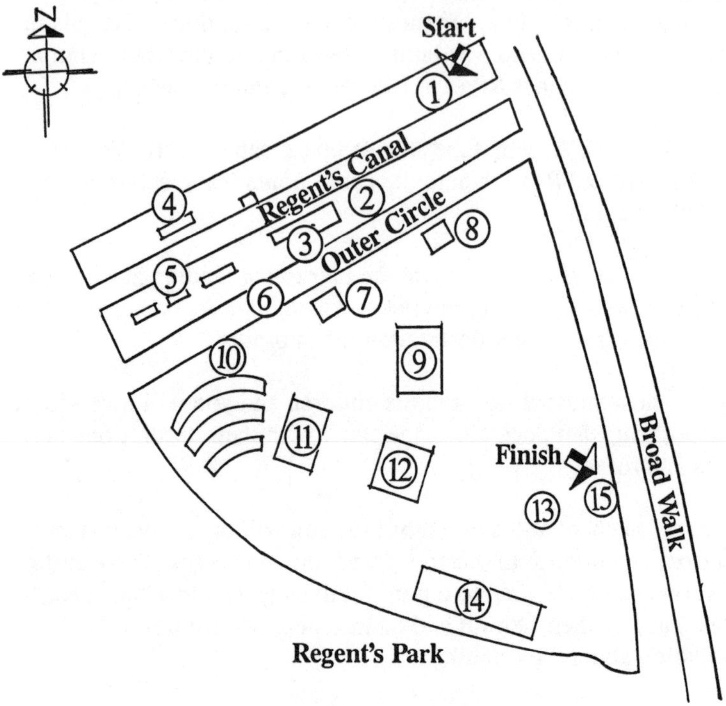

Children's Day 3

1/ Boat landing
2/ Great Apes Colony
3/ Moonlight World
4/ Aviary
5/ Horses, Giraffes, Zebras & Camels
6/ Main Gate
7/ Pandas
8/ Restaurant
9/ Playground
10/ Mappin Terraces: Bears, Sheep, Goats and Wild Pigs
11/ Reptiles
12/ Elephants and Rhinoceros
13/ New Lion Terraces
14/ Children's Zoo
15/ South Gate

Take any walk across the park; they will all lead you to Chester Road where you will turn right to arrive at **Queen Mary's Gardens**, the *famous rose gardens* and the open air theater. The walk through the roses and over the little Japanese bridges, the lake and the pools will fascinate all of you.

A **restaurant** and tea house are near the rose garden. If you did not eat in the restaurant at the zoo, this might be a good time for lunch.

Afternoon

Leave from the main entrance to Regent's Park, walk straight ahead to Marylebone Road, turn right and you will arrive at **Madame Tussaud's** famous waxwork mueum.

The **London Planetarium** is next door; one ticket will admit you to both places.

Madame Tussaud's is open daily from 10 a.m. to 6 p.m. (5:30 p.m. October through March). The Planetarium is open 11 a.m. to 4:30 p.m. daily. There are often long lines of people waiting to get in, particularly in the summer. But this is *worth a wait.* The children will *love it* and so will you.

The figures and tableaux include **entertainers and heroes**, the royals in the Grand Hall, including Prince Charles and his princess on their wedding day, American President Ronald Reagan, historical and fictional tableaux, and finally, the amazing Battle of Trafalgar.

Next door at the **Planetarium**, you will find the Astronomers Gallery on the ground floor and a one-half hour Star Show on the second floor.

Here is also what they call a **Laserium** which presents a show at 6 and 7:30 p.m. Wednesday through Sunday and 9 p.m. on Friday and Saturday. This is a fantasy in music and light using colors from laser beams; the show uses both rock and classical music.

Evening

Depending on your time (I cannot guess how much time you will spend in the zoo or other attractions) you are probably **hungry** again. Walk west on Marylebone Road to Lisson Grove, turn right to number 33 Lisson Grove to find the Sea Shell Fish Bar. This fish and chips place is very popular. You may even see some Rolls Royces waiting in front. You can either eat on the premises or take away to picnic.

After supper you may want to return to the Planetarium for the laser show or to Regent's Park for a performance in the **outdoor theatre.** Or *both.*

In three short days you and your children have tasted many of the pleasures of London, just enough to want to savor more.

Additional suggestions. The **Polka Dot Theatre** at 240 Broadway (542-4888) is one of the better known children's theatre. Call for information about times of performances.

The **Holiday Inn** at 17 Sloane Street offers a good Sunday buffet. It is a nice place to eat and relax and let the children swim in the adjoining pool. Call 235-4377 for information and reservations.

And finally, **rainy day** alternatives:

Since a good share of the foregoing three days depend on reasonably good weather, if you have a rainy morning or afternoon, go to the **British Museum.** (Tottenham Court Road tube stop).

There are **thousands of interesting things** to see. The great sculptures are on the main floor along with the Elgin Marbles. Your children will probably be entranced with the **Egyptian** galleries on the second floor with their extensive display of **mummies** and mummy cases.

Cab, tube or walk (down Great Russell to Tottenham Court Road to Scala Street) to **Pollock's Toy Museum** at 1 Scala Street. It is a small three-story corner house crammed with **toy theatres** of all kinds, dolls, teddy bears, tin soldiers, magic lanterns, toy boats and everything in between.

The ground level is a shop where you can **buy toys** and dolls. The toy theatres are up one flight and the dolls a floor beyond. There is an admission charge of about $2.50 for adults and 30 cents for children.

London is a **wonderful place** for children and for their grown up companions. These three days can be an introduction to a lifetime love affair with this ageless city.

Legal Day 1

1/ Temple Tube
2/ Charles Lamb statue
3/ Middle Temple Hall
4/ Inner Temple Hall
5/ The Temple Church
6/ Brick and Essex Courts
7/ Twining's
8/ Wig and Pen
9/ Prince Henry's Room
10/ Royal Courts of Justice
11/ Seven Stars Pub
12/ Hammick, Sweet and Maxwell Bookstore

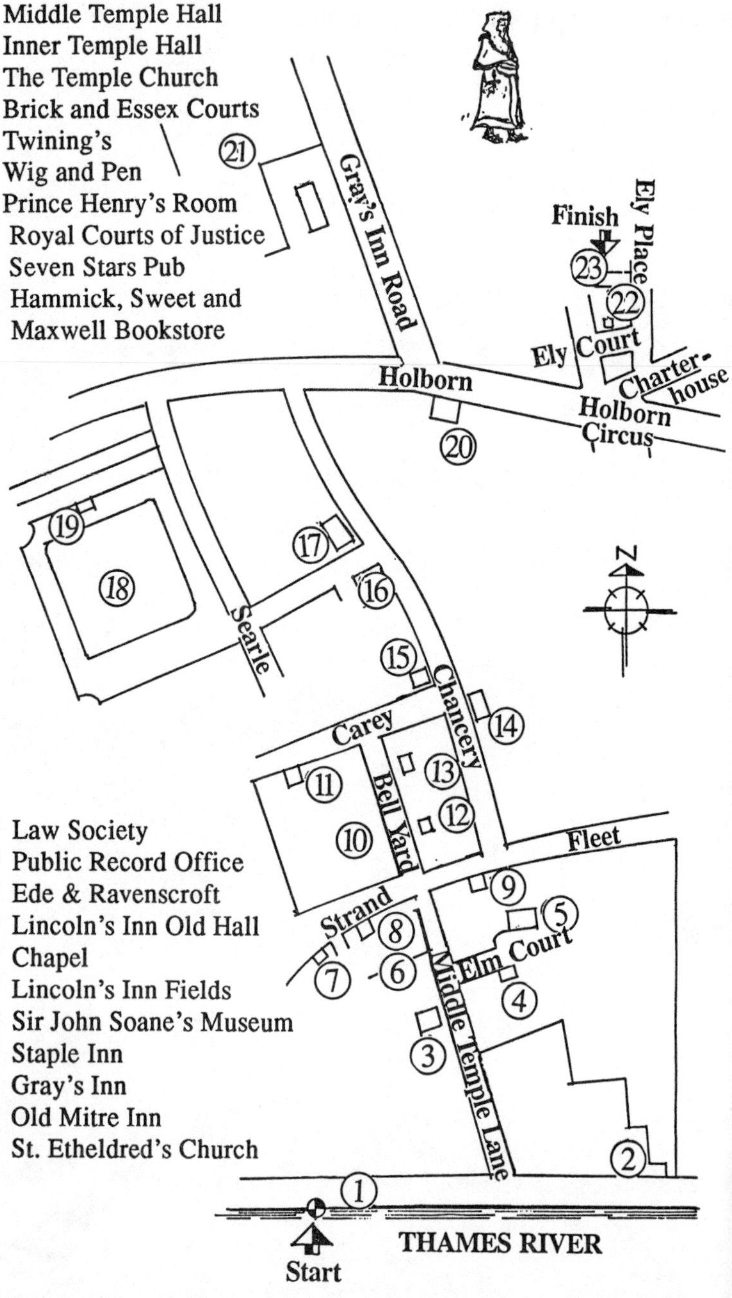

13/ Law Society
14/ Public Record Office
15/ Ede & Ravenscroft
16/ Lincoln's Inn Old Hall
17/ Chapel
18/ Lincoln's Inn Fields
19/ Sir John Soane's Museum
20/ Staple Inn
21/ Gray's Inn
22/ Old Mitre Inn
23/ St. Etheldred's Church

Legal London: Courts and Ceremonials

Legal London is of interest to many more people than just lawyers. The historical documents and buildings, the ceremonial procedures attending the administration of justice, and the unusual spaces housing and surrounding these activities *are fascinating* to any visitor to this city.

The following three days will take you to the squares of the Inns of Court; to the visitor's galleries in the **Old Bailey**; to the magnificent Houses of Parliament; and to some of the social spots filled with the men and women who make and administer the law in London.

Day 1

Highlights: Inns of Court, Royal Courts of Justice, Public Record Office, Sir John Soane's Museum and Staple Inn.

Reservations: Dinner at The Ivy, West Street. Telephone 836-4751. Theatre reservations at St. Martin Theatre. Telephone: 836-1443.

Morning

The four existing **Inns of Court**, the *Middle* and *Inner Temples, Lincoln's Inn* and *Gray's Inn* were formed in the Middle Ages and aptly called **inns** because their original purpose was to give lodging to students of the law.

They began to train barristers and solicitors to replace the clergy, which stopped practicing in the courts of justice during the 13th century. Incidentally, barristers are the lawyers who plead in the higher courts; solicitors are the lawyers who research and brief barristers on their client's cases.

Today the Inns of Courts house few law students, but they do provide offices for many lawyers. (I will use the American word for members of the legal profession). They also offer lectures, provide law libraries and examine candidates for admission to the bar. In order to become a member of the bar, a student must be admitted, by examination, to one of these Inns of Court.

Some of the ancient and quiet squares and gardens which surround these old buildings are open to the public for walking and looking. Others are open only to members of the Inn and their guests. Some of the buildings, such as the chapels, are open to the public, others only to members. Only Lincoln's Inn is closed on the weekend.

Morning

Start the day from the **Temple** tube stop about 9:30 a.m. Go east along the Embankment to a small walkway on your left, the Middle Temple Lane. Walk up the lane to **Middle Temple Hall,** dating from 1573. (Open Monday through Saturday 10:30 a.m. to noon and 3 to 4:00 p.m.) Inner Temple Hall is open these same hours. Despite announced opening times, the buildings are often closed for special occasions and always closed from noon to 3 p.m. There is no guarantee they will be open.

The **Middle Temple Hall** was heavily damaged in World War II bombing, but has been restored. Particularly note the unusual double hammerbeam roof. One of the stained glass windows features two of the Inn's "readers" (students of the law), Mr. Jekyll and Mr. Hyde. You now know where Mr. Stevenson found the names for his book. The 16th century carved screen at the east end of the hall was completely shattered by a bomb and carefully put back together like a gigantic jigsaw puzzle.

Walk Middle Temple Lane a few steps to Elm Court and **Temple Church of St. Mary**. The church, built by the Knights Templars between 1160 and 1185 as a copy of the Church of Holy Sepulcher in Jerusalem, is the most important round church in England. It serves both the Inner and Middle Temples. (Open 9:30 a.m. to 4 p.m.; closed in August and most of September.)

To enter, turn the metal ring to open the door. The first time I was there, I pulled and pushed and thought it was closed. Just turn the ring and it will open easily.

Of particular interest are the medieval effigies of knights, perhaps the oldest known English statues. Lawyers used to wait for their clients here in "the Round."

Walk around the grounds of both these **Inns of Courts** to feel the air of contemplation and learning, to watch the barristers in their wigs and robes striding through the gardens and to remember the men who lived and studied here: Charles Lamb; Oliver Goldsmith; the famous jurist Blackstone, who complained about Goldsmith's noises; and Dr. Johnson and Thackeray.

If you walk near the river, you may see the memorial fountain honoring Charles Lamb with the charming inscription, "Lawyers were children once." I urge you not to hurry. This is *a special* and *serene* place.

Walk up Middle Temple Lane to Brick Court and **Essex Court,** turn left and walk beneath overhanging sections of buildings. Another reminder to look overhead. At the far end of Essex Court you will find a glass door. Open it and walk through the glass-domed hallway.You will emerge on the Strand, number 222 Strand to be exact, just opposite the Royal Courts of Justice. It is always a shock to leave the quiet precincts of the Temple courts and spill out on noisy, busy Fleet Street.

Walk across to the impressive **Royal Courts of Justice** building (1874-82). The civil cases, which used to be heard in Westminster, are now heard in the 20 courtrooms in this building. It is open from 9 a.m. to 4 p.m. Wander through the Great Hall, with its mosaic pavement, and visit the exhibition of legal costumes in a room near the main entrance. Save your court visits for the Old Bailey Criminal Courts.

Noon

By now it should be time to think of eating. Several choices: Just across the street from the Royal Courts is the **Wig and Pen Club.** (Incidentally, it is just about here that Fleet Street becomes Strand Street. This happens all the time in London and is terribly confusing for the visitor—but be assured it is the same street, just a different name.) The Wig and Pen is a private club, primarily filled with lawyers and journalists, but foreign visitors can receive immediate free temporary membership by just asking for one. The food is good; the decor fascinating and it is an enchanting place to eat. Lots of little cubby hole rooms as well as larger areas, plus a lounge and tiny bathrooms.

Another choice for lunch. Walk up Bell Yard along the side of the Royal Courts of Justice to Carey Street, turn left to the **Seven Stars Pub**, a lawyer's hangout, with legal cartoons on the walls.

Notice two other buildings on the Strand/Fleet Street. **Twining's** tea shop, just west of the Wig and Pen, was established in 1716 and is the oldest business still on its original site in Britain. However, only the doorway survives from the original building. The store is at best 10 feet wide.

At number 17 Fleet Street, note **Prince Henry's Room**. Nobody is exactly sure about the history of this place. It was probably not connected with royalty, but its upstairs tavern room with its Jacobean panelling and its mementoes from Samuel Pepys is worth looking at, but visit it after lunch, since it does not open until 1:45 p.m.

Afternoon

Walk to Chancery Lane to the next Inn of Court, **Lincoln's Inn.** The Public Record Office is on your right as you walk up Chancery Lane (Open Monday through Friday, 10 a.m. to 5 p.m.) Admission is free.

This building houses government archives and legal documents. The most important item in the collection is the two-volume **Domesday Book**, a general survey of England ordered by William the Conqueror in 1085. Other important documents include a copy of the Magna Carta, **Shakespeare's** signed will, and **Guy Fawkes'** confession, with its very shaky signature, extorted from him after torture.

Opposite the Record Office is the building housing the **Law Society**, which controls and disciplines the solicitors' branch of the law. The law bookstore, **Hammick, Sweet & Maxwell**, is nearby at number 116 Chancery Lane, established in 1799.

Up Chancery Lane to number 94 and the shop, **Ede & Ravenscroft.** They have been purveying gowns and wigs since 1693. Even if you aren't interested in buying a wig or robe, stop in to see their display of ceremonial garments.

Continue up Chancery Lane to the Gatehouse of 1521, which will admit you to **Lincoln's Inn**. The Inn's old buildings, Old Hall and the Chapel, are just ahead. The Old Hall is open when not in use. If it is closed, inquire at the nearby porter's office. He may be willing to take you on a tour through the hall and the chapel. Just tip him. They are both fascinating buildings.

The old Hall is the finest building in the Inn with its "scissor" roof beams, stained glass and the huge Hogarth painting of *Paul Before Felix* hanging in the same place almost continuously since 1748. As you walk toward the Chapel, you will walk through an "undercroft" at ground level. The chapel stands on pillars above it. Its carved pillars and ceiling are quite extraordinary. The Chapel is usually open Monday to Friday, noon to 2:30 p.m. Note the limited open hours.

The Chapel was built from 1619 to 1623 to replace a former chapel which had become "ruinous," as they say, and was too small. The poet and churchman, **John Donne**, laid the cornerstone and preached the opening sermon. The Spanish chapel bell tolls curfew at 9 p.m. each night and also tolls the news of the death of a member of the inn. It may be from this custom that Donne found the source for his famous words: "Never send to know for whom the bell tolls; it tolls for thee."

The great stained glass window on the east contains the arms of the 228 Treasurers of the Society from 1680-1908. The arms of Treasurers from 1909 to 1962 are in the east window on the north side and those from 1963 onwards are in the west window. Lincoln's Inn Fields are just beyond the Inn of Court. This is the largest square in central London, designed by Inigo Jones, and the home for many of the famous. It was also the location for the pillory where Lord William Russell was executed.

Walk around the square and admire the lovely old homes and medical buildings. At this point I am compelled to add a side trip which has nothing to do with law or lawyers, but since it and you are both here,

I cannot let you walk past it. At No. 13 on the square you will find the most unusual museum in London, **Sir John Soane's Museum.**

Soane, architect for the Bank of England, left his home and collections to the city with the stipulation they could not be changed in any way. It is his private house, just as he lived in it. (Open 10 a.m. to 5 p.m. Tuesday through Saturday).

I do not know how to describe this eclectic collection, which ranges from the sarcophagus of Seti I to paintings by Watteau and Canaletto. The Picture Room contains two famous series of paintings by William Hogarth: *The Election* and *The Rake's Progress.*

Ask the guard to show you the folding storage arrangements for these paintings. It is not just the collections, but the house and the way things are displayed that make a visit so fascinating. The use of mirrors, recessed ceilings and walls, angled windows, half flights, arched ceilings and all manner of strange and disorienting architectural arrangements turn this house into a strange and magical experience.

It is probably now about 3 or 3:30 p.m. Walk up to Holborn Street, cross over and quickly walk through **Gray's Inn of Court**. I find this the least interesting Inn of Court, but the gardens are lovely, especially the one laid out by **Francis Bacon**, which contains his statue.

Walk on down Holborn (east) to **Staple Inn** on your right. This was part of the Chancery Inn and was both an inn and a market place for wool traders, known as 'staplers', hence the name. It is the only remaining half-timbered terrace in London. Be sure to walk into the quiet inner court.

You probably need to sit down at this point and have some sustenance. Walk west on Holborn to Holborn Circus, angle off on Charterhouse to Ely Place and look for the **Old Mitre Tavern**. You will have to search for an **ornate gaslamp** and a **very little sign,** then worm your way down the alley to one of the *smallest pubs* in London. It dates from **1546.** The pub consists of a couple of tiny rooms and an outdoor patio for summer, but I think you will find it endearing.

If you have any energy left, you can look at the 18th century houses on Ely Place and the beautiful **St. Etheldreda Church**, built about 1300, Britain's *oldest existing Catholic church.*

Evening

Go back to your hotel for a rest, if it is convenient, and then on to the theatre. *The Mousetrap* by Agatha Christie playing at the St. Martin Theatre for more than 33 years, might be an appropriate, if corny, selection for tonight. The best thing about this choice is that right across the way, on little West Street, is my favorite restaurant again, **The Ivy.** Tomorrow you will visit the courts at the Old Bailey and see some of the lawyers at work who studied in the great Inns of Court you visited this morning.

Day 2

Highlights: Old Bailey Criminal Courts, Guildhall, Bank of England, and the Tower of London.

Reservations: Dinner at the Gay Hussar, 2 Greek Street. Telephone 437-0973.

Morning

A reminder: Do not take a camera with you today - or you will not be admitted to any of the Central Criminal Court buildings. It is just too easy to hide an explosive device in a camera case. They make no exceptions.

This morning, you will start your day just east of where you drank your beer yesterday afternoon. You are headed for the Old Bailey Criminal Court at 10 a.m., but because you will be in the neighborhood, I suggest an early morning start to visit one of the city's oldest and most fascinating districts. You can stay in bed and cab to the Old Bailey at 10 a.m, but I think you will miss an exciting though bloody morning.

Take the tube to the **Barbican** tube stop or cab to Smithfield Market. Walk down either Charterhouse or West Smithfield /Long Lane Street to the market. **Smithfield Market's** 10 acres are now *the largest meat market in the world.* Smithfield, meaning smooth field, was the most important cloth fair in England during the Middle Ages. It was a horse and cattle market from 1150 to 1855; the main place of execution in the 12th century, and the site of the great St. Bartholomew's Fair from the 1100's until 1840.

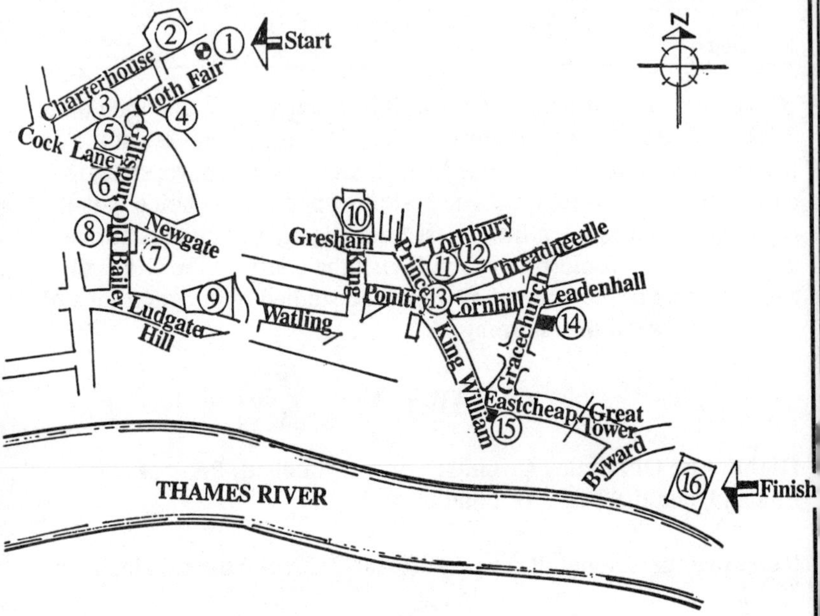

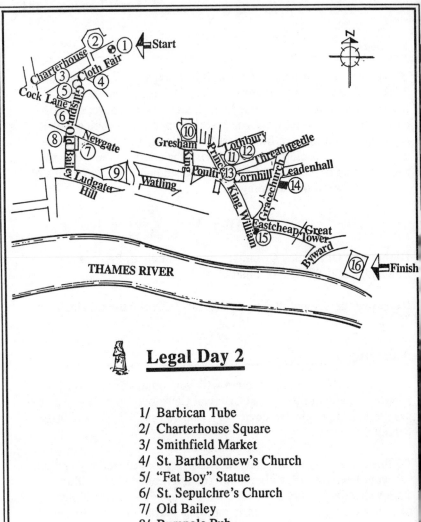

Legal Day 2

1/ Barbican Tube
2/ Charterhouse Square
3/ Smithfield Market
4/ St. Bartholomew's Church
5/ "Fat Boy" Statue
6/ St. Sepulchre's Church
7/ Old Bailey
8/ Rumpole Pub
9/ St. Paul's Cathedral
10/ Guildhall
11/ Bank of England
12/ Stock Exchange
13/ Royal Exchange
14/ Leadenhall Market
15/ Monument
16/ Tower of London

The market is its busiest between the hours of 5 and 9 a.m. Go early and wander around the market to watch the burly porters cart the enormous slabs of meat on carts around the marketplace. Believe me, if you get in their way, they will let you know. It is an incredible and amazing sight. It is not as bloody as it used to be now that most of the meat is in gauze wrapping, but you might be somewhat tempted to think about vegetarianism.

Walk to the Smithfield green and about a half a block on your left you will find the arched entrance to the little garden which will lead you to **St. Bartholomew the Great Church**, built in **1123**, the *oldest church still standing in London*. It was built by Rahere, one of Henry I's court. He began his life as something of a court jester and playboy, but following the death of Henry's beloved son and Rahere's own severe illness, he vowed to build a great church and he did.

The building is in need of renovation, but I find it perhaps the most spiritual and wonderful church in London. I love to come here for Sunday services with its small congregation and lovely choir. Note the great arches reminiscent of both Roman and Norman styles and the decorated tomb of Rahere. Walk behind the altar to the Lady Chapel to see the location of what was once a printing press where Benjamin Franklin was employed. Hogarth, the artist, was baptized at the Medieval font. Be sure to notice the needlepoint kneeling bench with its animals, fish and birds of the earth just behind the altar railing.

As you leave the church walk to your left down **Giltspur Street.** Look for little Cock Lane on your right. At the corner of these two streets, inserted in the wall above eye level, you will see the statue of what is known as the Fat Boy. The little gold boy stands shivering in the morning air. Legend, if not fact, says this marks the location where the Great Fire stopped. The lane itself was licensed for prostitution during medieval days.

Continue down Giltspur Street to Newgate. On your right is St. Sepulchre's Church and to your left and straight ahead are the **Central Criminal Courts of London (Old Bailey)**. It should be about 10 a.m. and time for the public to be admitted to the galleries. If you walk straight down what is now Old Bailey, you will come to the new court buildings. I suggest you turn left and walk east on Newgate Street.

As you walk along the side of the "old" Old Bailey, *look carefully for a door, a small marker and a bell.* It is not particularly well marked. **Ring the bell**, a guard will let you in and direct you to the steps which take you to the **visitors galleries.**

Bailiffs sit either right outside each courtroom, or immediately inside the door, and will tell you whether there is room for you in the gallery. Courts number 1 and 2 usually handle the more important trials. Incidentally, afternoon sessions begin about 2 p.m. Sit in the front row if possible.

Of all the things I love to do in London, this is my favorite. I will never forget the first time I climbed those steps, walked into the galleries, sat down and looked down into that old courtroom: I suddenly felt as though I had fallen back two hundred years in time to see the judge, in his robes beneath the great seal, the barristers in their wigs and robes, and the prisoner in the dock. As I listened to all the legal and stilted words, the formality of presentation washed over me, and I was back with Dickens and Shakespeare - all the people who have written or taught me about law, justice, the Magna Carta and democracy. I found it irresistible and almost impossible to leave.

On opening day, the judges still carry posies to court to ward off fever and herbs are strewn around the room to cover the terrible smells from the infamous Newgate prison, once located on the site of the "old " Old Bailey. Think about the figure of Justice which stands on the top of the building with its scales, but without a blindfold; and about St. Sepulchre's Church across the street, where the hand bell, which used to ring at midnight outside prisoner's cells to announce the day of their execution, is on view - but no longer in use.

Then you pay attention to the case in court today, probably a robbery or assault, much like our own, but with a legal style and presentation so different. I defy you to stay only five minutes.

Noon

As you leave the old building, turn left and walk back to Old Bailey Street and turn left again. It will probably be time for lunch. Cross the street to the**Rumpole Pub**, 27 Old Bailey. Or walk a little farther down Old Bailey Street to **City Friends**, my favorite Chinese restaurant, in this part of town.

Afternoon

This afternoon you are going to visit **The City**, the square mile which encompasses the financial district of London and includes the great Guildhall. You will also walk past the Bank of England on your way to the historic Tower of London.

Walk up Ludgate Hill, past and around **St. Paul's Cathedral**. Visit it if you are so inclined. Walk behind the cathedral to **Watling Street,** *the oldest street in London.* Turn left on Queen Street which becomes King Street and finally Guildhall Yard just in front of the **Guildhall,** seat of municipal government for London.

The Great Hall is open Monday through Saturday 10 a.m. to 5 p.m. The Hall was used for municipal meetings, the election of the Lord Mayor and sheriffs of London and state banquets. Earlier it was used for important trials. The trials are listed on a plaque on the wall. A short visit will suffice here.

Walk east on Gresham Street, turn right on Prince's Street to the **Bank of England** on Threadneedle Street. Remember *The Old Lady of Threadneedle*, the name for the Bank of England?

In 1989, the Bank of England opened its doors to the public for the first time. Visitors are now permitted to tour the building and its new museum, which features a reconstruction of the world's first stock office and an exhibition of the bank's original charter, gold bars and bank notes. A videotape program explaining the workings of the bank and its role in the financial world are shown to visitors. Admission is free.

The **Royal Exchange** across the street is usually open for temporary exhibitions. Note the glass-roofed courtyard with its unusual pavement and the historical wall-panel paintings.

The **Stock Exchange** visitors' Gallery, just beyond the bank on Threadneedle Street is open to the public from Monday through Friday 10-3:15 p.m.

Walk down Gracechurch Street past the glass enclosed Leadenhall Market to the **Monument**. This marks the approximate spot where the **Great Fire** began. The monument is 202 feet high; the spot where the fire actually started on Pudding Lane is exactly 202 feet from this spot.

Turn left on Eastcheap, which becomes Great Tower Street, and then Byward Street and you will be at the **Tower of London.** It seems appropriate to end this day of sightseeing at the Tower which held prisoners as a result of some of the most famous trials in London.

Of particular interest on this tour are the **White Tower**, where Sir Walter Raleigh spent 13 years during his second imprisonment; Byward Tower, which was the prison for Sir Thomas More and Princess Elizabeth; and Tower Green, where a scaffold was erected.

Anne Boleyn and Catherine Howard, two of Henry VIII's wives, were executed here along with Lady Jane Grey and the Earl of Essex.

Evening

Take a cab back to your hotel and rest. Tonight you might want to try a Hungarian restaurant which has always attracted lawyers, politicians and literary people, the **Gay Hussar** at 2 Greek Street in Soho. Dinner for two should be around $50-$60

If you feel like it, walk around Soho after dinner; it is lively with strip shows and sex shops.

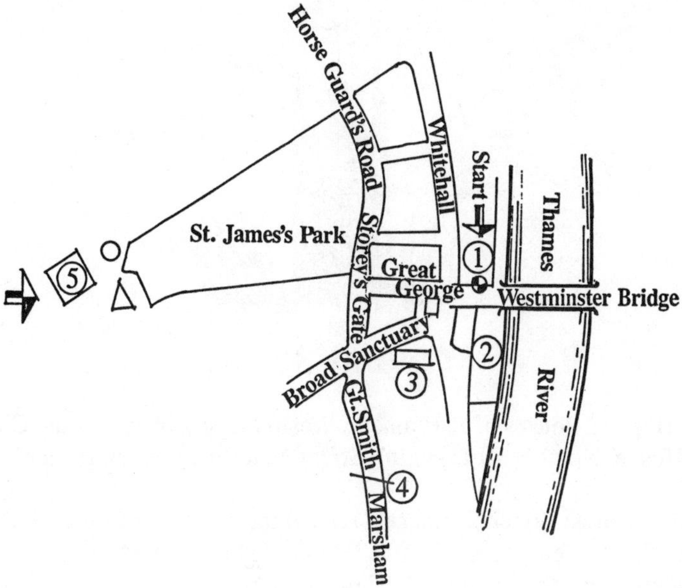

Legal Day 3

1/ Westminster Tube

2/ Parliament

3/ Westminster Abbey

4/ Locket's Restaurant

5/ Buckingham Palace

Day 3

Highlights: Houses of Parliament, Westminster Abbey and the Chapter House, Number 10 Downing Street, and Buckingham Palace.

Reservations: Lunch at Lockets restaurant, Marsham Court, Marsham Street. Telephone 834-9552. Dinner at Rules restaurant, 35 Maiden Lane. Telephone 836-5314.

Reservations for theatre tickets to see the Royal Shakespeare Company. Check newspapers or magazines for information concerning performance schedules.

Morning

This morning's tour of the **Houses of Parliament** is predicated on a simple given: that they are open. There is absolutely no way of knowing whether they will be open or closed, or what open hours may be in effect. It all depends on the political climate, when or if the parliamentary bodies are in session and a number of other variables. You must check on open times when you arrive. Read the newspapers or ask at your hotel.

Westminster tube stop is closest to the Houses of Parliament, or cab there. If you take the tube, climb the stairs and walk out on to Westminster Bridge for a look at the Houses of Parliament and Big Ben as well as the Thames.

You can take a guided tour or walk through the **Houses of Parliament** by yourself, which is more leisurely. I must admit that I like the tour because the guides are so smitten with the buildings and their history that they add a great deal to the experience.

The entrance to Westminster Hall is from St. Stephen's porch; the entrance to the Houses of Parliament from the Victoria Tower. The tour of Parliament begins as you walk up the Royal Staircase of the Norman Porch. On the right is the Queen's Robing Room. At the far end is **Queen Victoria's chair of state.**

Next is the 110-foot-long **Royal Gallery** with its lovely ceiling. The Prince's Chamber is the ante room to the House of Lords. The 80-foot-long Gothic **House of Lords**, which seats more than 1,000 peers, is too glorious to describe. You will stand in awe of this magnificently decorated chamber.

The **Queen's throne** is at the north end. In front of the throne is the Woolsack, an ordinary looking ottoman stuffed with wool from countries throughout the Commonwealth. It is a reminder that the wool trade once represented England's wealth.

At the north end, you will see the **Bar** where lawsuits on final appeal are pleaded. The House of Lords is the final Court of Appeal for all courts in Great Britain and Northern Ireland.

The Peers' Lobby, Robing Room and Library are usually not shown to visitors. The Peers' Corridor leads to the Central Lobby which is the division between the House of Lords and the House of Commons. Pass through the Commons Corridor, lobby and library. On the north is the Churchill Arch.

The **House of Commons** was destroyed during an air raid on May 10, 1941 and was rebuilt and reopened in 1950. 650 members sit on the green hide benches. The party in office sits to the right of the Speaker's chair. Two **red lines** between the benches form the boundary beyond which not one step may be taken during debate. Historically, they are *two sword lengths* apart. A formal ceremony opens each day. Visitors in the gallery can get a copy of the day's agenda from a messenger.

Return to the Central lobby. On the west is **St. Stephen's Hall** where Commons met from 1547-1834. St. Stephen's steps lead you to Westminster, one of the only parts of the medieval building still standing, built originally in 1097-9, and rebuilt after several fires.

The **hall** is the *great chamber of a royal palace*, the meeting place of the Great Council, predecessor to Parliament and the Courts of Justice. The chief court of English law sat here from the late 13th century to 1825, when the Royal Courts of Justice opened. Here Edward II was forced to abdicate in 1327; the pretender Perkin Warbeck was condemned to death in 1499; Sir Thomas More, the Earl of Essex and Guy Fawkes were tried; Oliver Cromwell was installed as protector in 1653; and coronation feasts were held. Be sure to notice the hammerbeam room with its 12 bays.

Noon

For lunch today, I suggest **Lockets** restaurant on Marsham Court, Marsham Street. Walk down The Broad Sanctuary to Great Smith Street, turn left. After crossing Great Peter Street you are on Marsham Street. Lockets is a formal English restaurant patronized by members of the Houses of Parliament. A division bell summons them for votes. It is open Monday through Friday for lunch and dinner and on Saturday for dinner.

Afternoon

Walk back to **Westminster Abbey** to the **Chapter House**, which served, in 1257, as the meeting place for Parliament's predecessor, the Great Council, and later as the House of Commons. It is just behind the Abbey

Visit the **Abbey** if you will, following the plan in the *Basic Three Days in London.*

This afternoon retrace your steps to the Houses of Parliament and walk down Whitehall past the government buildings, Number 10 Downing Street, the horse guards and the Admiralty. Turn left and walk down the mall or through St. James's Park to **Buckingham Palace**. This is a good walk to remind you that the monarchy exists, perhaps without much real power today, but a reminder of its majestic history.

Walk through Buckingham Palace Gardens and down Halkin Street to **Belgrave Square**. Here you will find a number of handsome buildings housing the Norwegian, Saudi Arabia and German embassies. Surrounding streets contain a number of other embassy and official residences.

Continue your walk through Belgravia until you arrive at Brompton Road and **Harrod's** great department store. You should be just in time for their famous 4 p.m. tea, which should hold you until supper, either before or after the theatre.

Evening

Tonight try the **Royal Shakespeare Company**. With some kind of luck they might be doing the *Merchant of Venice*, but go see whatever they are doing. They will be guilty of doing it superbly.

And sum up with dinner at **Rules**, 35 Maiden Lane, *London's oldest restaurant (1798)*. You can eat things such as jugged hare or boiled beef and finish off with English trifle. Expensive.

Legal London took you from Parliament to the Tower of London; from the lawyer's pubs to the Old Bailey. It was a long trip through history but a short three days of walking and sightseeing.

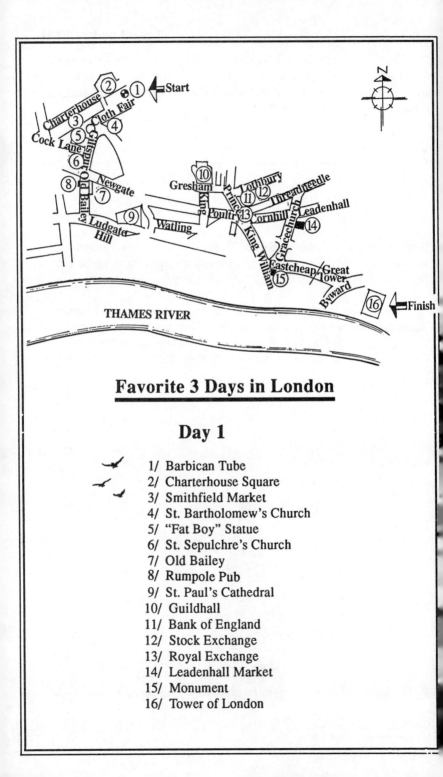

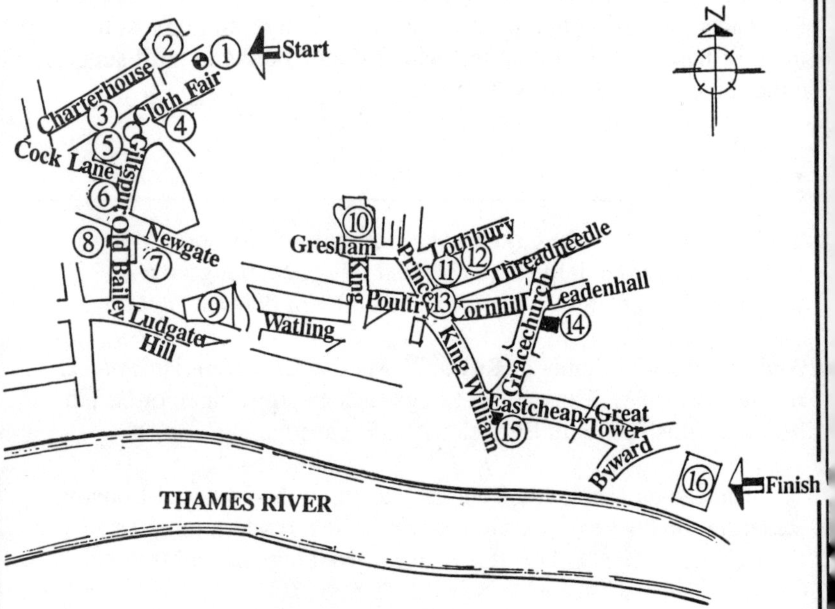

Favorite 3 Days in London

Day 1

1/ Barbican Tube
2/ Charterhouse Square
3/ Smithfield Market
4/ St. Bartholomew's Church
5/ "Fat Boy" Statue
6/ St. Sepulchre's Church
7/ Old Bailey
8/ Rumpole Pub
9/ St. Paul's Cathedral
10/ Guildhall
11/ Bank of England
12/ Stock Exchange
13/ Royal Exchange
14/ Leadenhall Market
15/ Monument
16/ Tower of London

My Favorite Three Days

If I only had three days to spend in London, I would have a very hard time picking and choosing where I would go and what I would see. I had to think about this for a long time and was actually surprised at some of the places I chose. Some were very easy and others were difficult. After all my advice to my readers, I thought this would be easy. But it wasn't.

Day 1

Highlights: Smithfield Market, Old St. Batholomew's Church, Old Bailey Criminal Court, St. Paul's Cathedral, Leadenhall Market, St. Mary-at-the-Hill Church, and the Tower of London.

Reservations: Theatre tickets for the Royal Shakespeare Company at the Barbican Theatre. Telephone: 628-8891.

Morning

I would start early at **Smithfield Market**, near 8 a.m., and wander around the huge meat market. I still am not sure why this fascinates me so much, but it does. The site is so old and the market so bustling and alive that I find it exciting.

This is the *largest meat market* in the world. I like what it is and what it was. Until 1840 the great St. Batholomew's Fair was here; England's famous cloth fair was here during the Middle Ages; and in the 12th century it was a place of execution.

century font. Then on to the old **Old Bailey Criminal Courts** for the opening at 10 a.m Nothing I ever do in London is quite so thrilling and awesome as sitting in one of the galleries in this old courthouse. Every time I suspect it will be more familiar and ordinary, but it never is. It is the best theatre in London and I never tire of looking at the robes and wigs and listening to the formal and stilted language of the barristers and judges and the street language of the defendants. It hasn't changed in hundreds of years, I am sure.

Noon

After an hour or so in "court", it might be time for lunch at my old favorite, the **Chinese Old Friends** restaurant along Old Bailey Street. They always treat me so nicely. Then up the Ludgate Hill to **St. Paul's Cathedral** for a quick walk to the American Chapel and a visit with my old friend, John Donne, in his funeral shroud.

Afternoon

Around to the back of the cathedral and a walk down Watling Street, the oldest street in London, and over to the Bank of England. Then a wander through the triangle where the **George and Vulture** pub is located and little lanes and alleys intersect. Stop and eat, if hungry.

Over to Gracechurch Street and a look in the Leadenhall Market and its meat and vegetable stands. Down Gracechurch Street to the **Monument** where the Great Fire started. And no, I will not climb it.

Eastcheap Street to Lovat Lane and a stop in St. Mary-at-Hill Church and on to the **Tower of London** for a look around. No Jewel Tower this afternoon. Just a walk around and maybe a visit to the Chapel of St. John's in the White Tower.

Take a **boat** from Tower Pier to **Westminster Pier** and out on the bridge to see the Houses of Parliament, Big Ben and the Abbey. Perhaps a quick look in the **Abbey** if I have any strength left.

Evening

Take a cab to the **Barbican Theatre** to see whatever the Royal Shakespeare Company is doing and a bite of supper after the theatre at one of the restaurants in the Barbican complex.

Day 2

Highlights: Trafalgar Square, National Portrait Gallery, Charing Cross Road, Covent Garden, Regent's Park and the National Theatre.

Reservations: Theatre reservations for a production at the National Theatre. Telephone: 928-2252 for reservations; 633-0880 for information.

Morning

Start at **Trafalgar Square** this morning. To some, Piccadilly Circus is the center of London, to others the Bank of England in the center of "The City." To me the center of London is **Trafalgar Square** with its crowds of tourists, swarms of too-friendly pigeons and Landseer's lions guarding the fountains. I love the views in every direction.

To the **National Portrait Gallery** for a quick look. I think if I had to pick just one museum that captures the essence of this country, it would be this small gallery. Actually it is not so small except in comparison to the behemoths such as the British Museum and the Victoria and Albert Museum. I always look at Richard III's sad image, Henry VIII's enormous "cartoon", and the Bronte sisters with the ghost of their brother looming over their shoulders. Everybody important in English history is here.

Then up Charing Cross Road to Cecil and St. Martin's Courts, Goodwin's Court and over to **Covent Garden**. All those tiny little alleyways with their bow-windowed shops give me the feeling of old London. Covent Garden is lively and largely renovated since the removal of the old market. But it still has lots of charm. I like to walk in the damp shady garden leading to old **St. Paul's Church** and wander around inside looking at the plaques.

Back to Charing Cross Road and up to the Cambridge Circus, looking at the book stores. This is a chance to stick my head in **84 Charing Cross**, the location of Helen Hanff's beloved book. It is no longer a bookstore, but visitors to this "shrine" are welcome. A sign tells you, yes, you are in the right place and to look around.

Favorite 3 Days in London

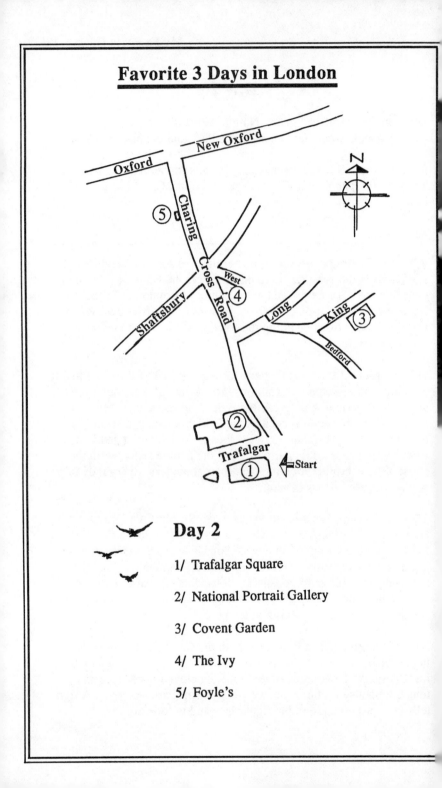

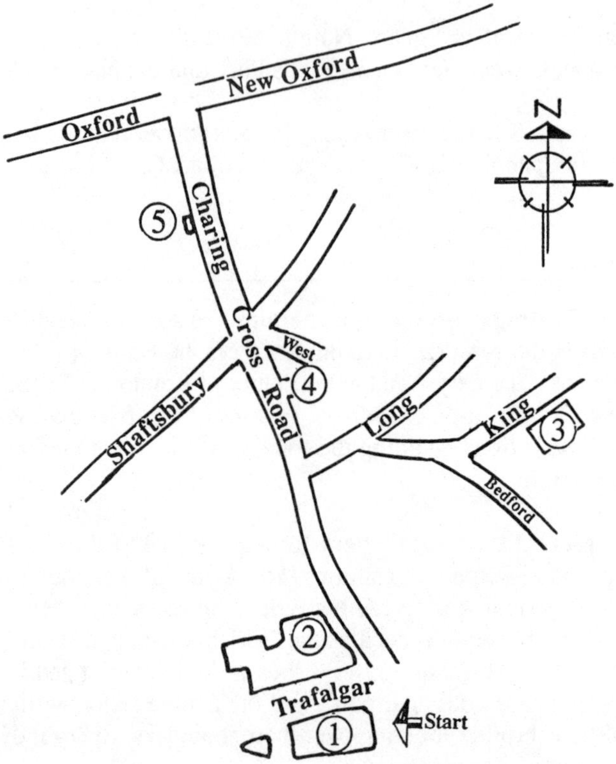

Day 2

1/ Trafalgar Square

2/ National Portrait Gallery

3/ Covent Garden

4/ The Ivy

5/ Foyle's

Noon

Turn on West Street for lunch at **The Ivy**. This is my favorite restaurant in London. I still remember the first time I arrived for lunch: no reservations, slightly damp from a long morning in the rain, dressed in slacks and my Eddie Bauer shoes - and alone.

I will never forget the way I was treated, like the Queen of England. They hung up my wet coat, offered me an apertif, commiserated about the weather and ushered me to a lovely table where I was smothered with care. I would like to think they always behave that way, but of course I cannot guarantee it. I do know that later visits for both lunch and dinner reconfirmed my earlier impressions.

This was also the site of my first encounter with "whitebait." They are often listed on London menus under Appetizers. They are a tiny fish, about the size of small goldfish, which are French fried and served in large quantities with lemon. They look exactly like deep fried gold fish and taste sort of like French fries. You just have to get over the strange sensation of eating little whole goldfish. They are very good.

Afternoon

After lunch, back to Charing Cross to **Foyle's** bookstore. I know Foyle's is enormous, crowded, complicated and purchasing a book is almost impossible, but I love it. All the things other people find difficult, I find endearing. There is no explanation for some booklover's taste. If I happen to find a knowledgeable clerk, it can be heaven. Otherwise, I just wander around and almost always find treasures.

Then a cab to **Regent's Park** and time in Queen Mary's rose garden. There is a nice restaurant and tearoom when I tire of wandering through the gardens, smelling the roses and crossing the little bridges.

Evening

A play again this evening, probably at the **National Theatre**. Afterward, a walk back across Waterloo Bridge to see the city lighted. It is an awesome and beautiful sight.

Favorite 3 Days in London

Day 3 AM

1/ Piccadilly Circus
2/ Burlington Arcade
3/ Fortnum & Mason
4/ St. James's Palace
5/ Queen's Gallery
6/ Buckingham Palace
7/ Royal Mews
8/ Ritz Hotel

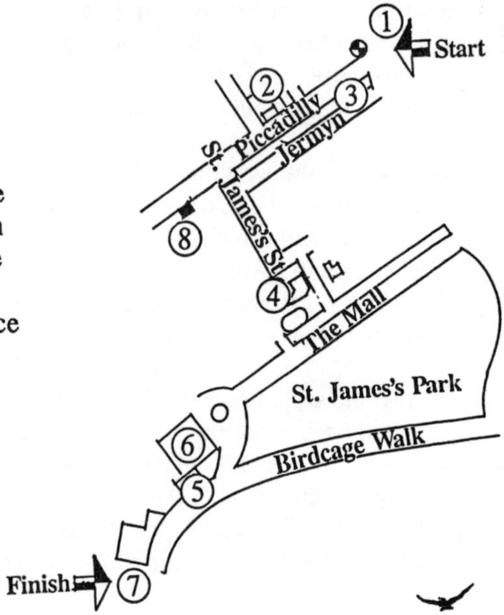

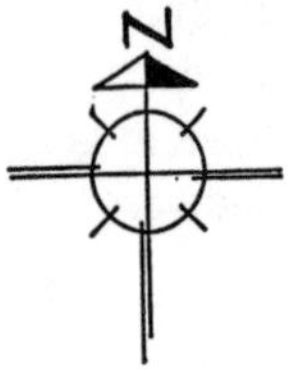

Day 3 PM

1/ Harrod's
2/ Beauchamp Place
3/ Kensington Garden
4/ Albert Memorial
5/ Peter Pan
6/ Italian Gardens

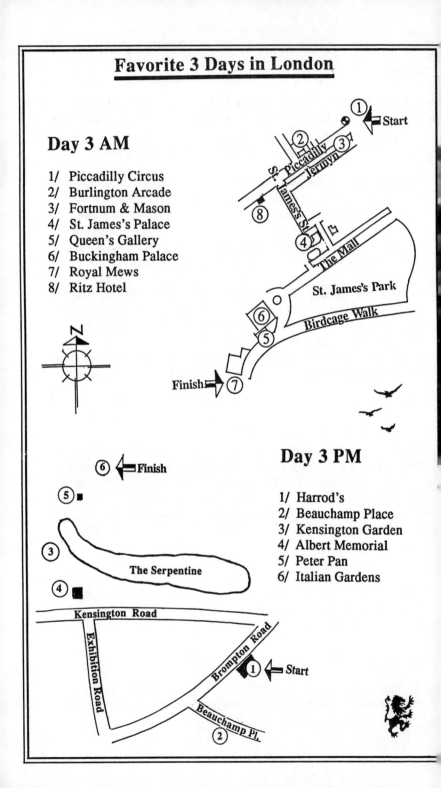

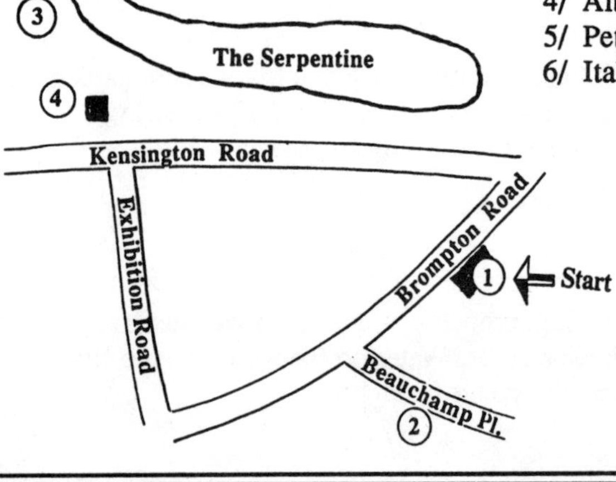

Day 3

Highlights: Piccadilly Circus, Jermyn Street, Fortnum and Mason's, the Tate Gallery, Beauchamp Place and Kensington Gardens.

Reservations: Lunch reservations at the Tate Gallery Restaurant. Telephone 834-6754.

Dinner reservations at Boulestin's. Telephone 836-7061. Or Rules restaurant. Telephone 836-5314.

Morning

Today it's **Piccadilly Circus** - and a walk down Jermyn Street with all its old shops and their unforgettable smells. Paxton and Whithead's hams and cheeses greet you halfway down the block and the perfumer Floris always smells of White Hyacinth. I don't smoke anymore, but Dunhill's tobacco shop fills the air with memories of earlier days and images of pipes and tweeds.

Fortnum and Mason's is a necessary stop. I must see the fanciest grocery in town and its "clerks" in their tail coats. Even this early in the day I wouldn't bet against my having a soda on the mezzanine. They have the best bitter chocolate soda I ever tasted.

To St. James's Street and on to **St. James's Park**. Wander around the park to see the folks stretched out in their canvas chairs and feed the exotic birds with scones from Fortnum's.

Noon

Probably time for lunch and where better than the **Tate Gallery**. With luck I will have remembered to make a reservation. After lunch a visit to look at the Turners and hunt out my friend Atkinson-Grimshaw's misty paintings of harbors.

Afternoon

Cab to Beauchamp Place and **Harrod's** for tea if the time is right. I always spend time on Beauchamp Street. It is filled with charming little shops and good restaurants.

I usually stop in the **Map House** to poke around and always visit **Luxury Needlepoint**. One time they sent me a credit after I returned home. The next time I was in the store I mentioned it, although I had forgotten to bring the credit slip with me. No problem. They sent "downstairs" for their handwritten ledger and found my "credit" meticulously entered by a lovely and loving hand.

I also bought my one and only English wool coat here on Beauchamp Place at the **Adele Davis** shop. The lavender tweed coat was in the window and I just tried it on for fun. Too much money I said, but later while I was taking a nap at the hotel, my husband went back and bought it for me. I have always loved it.

Work my way by foot or cab to **Kensington Gardens** and the Albert Memorial. I love this ornate, overblown, romantic and corny memorial of a queen's love for her husband. Any time I have left I would spend wandering in this garden, up to the Peter Pan statue and the Italian Garden and Queen Anne's alcove.

Evening

An elegant dinner tonight either at **Boulestin's or Rule's** depending on my mood. They are both favorites and right now I can't choose, but I guess I don't have to.

London will choose for me.

Special Interests in London

When I was working on this book I kept coming across little snippets of **information** which I put aside, thinking they might become special interest tours. As the manuscript developed, I realized these bits would not grow into full-fledged chapters, but might be of interest to readers with specific concerns.

Alcoholics Anonymous (AA) There are meetings located throughout central London. To locate a meeting call the London Regional telephone service number 834-8202. The General Service office is located at 11 Redcliffe Gardens (south of Old Brompton Road) Telephone 352-3001.

American London. At some point in your travels, you may want something particularly **American**. Perhaps it will be American food or an American hotel. With a little planning, you can make at least some parts of cosmopolitan London seem like New York, Chicago or Minneapolis.

American Hotels & Addresses: Many American chains have hotels in London, but be warned, most of them are very pricey. You might want to try the London Marriott on Grosvenor Square or the London Hilton on Park Lane. **Connections:** Here are a few addresses and phone numbers you may want: **American Express** at 6 Haymarket (839-6030) at 89 Mount St. (499-0288); **American Embassy** at 24 Grosvenor Square (499-9000); the American Chamber of Commerce in London at 75 Brook Street (493-0381); The American Women's Club at 1 Cadogan Gardens (730-2033/1908); and The American Club, 95 Piccadilly (499-2303/3668). **The Bank of America** is located in the Gateway house, just behind St. Paul's Cathedral. You may have noticed that **Grosvenor Square** has already been mentioned twice. This is the area known in London as **"Little America."** The **U.S. State Department** offices are also on the square. At **#20,** you will find the building where General Dwight Eisenhower's headquarters were located in 1942 and 1944; at #9, the house John Adams lived in when he was the first minister to Britain from the United States.

American Food: If you stay in an American hotel, you will probably eat American dishes, but there are a number of other **American restaurants** with recognizable names and menus throughout London. I will mention just a few of them. **Joe Allen** on 13 Exeter Street (836-0651) at the corner of Burleigh Street, is located just south of Covent Garden. It is a copy of the New York restaurant and serves from noon to midnight. You can get barbecues, eggs Benedict and pie a la mode. It is usually filled with journalists and actors who probably go more for its ambience than the food. Sort of like New York. It is extremely difficult to find. Look for a **small light** over the entrance and a very discreet brass plaque on the door jamb. I walked the street twice before I found it. The **Chicago Pizza Pie Factory** at 17 Hanover Square in Mayfair (629-2669) serves deep-dish pizzas, garlic bread, and cheesecake; it features Chicago baseball on video in the bar. (Monday through Saturday, 11:45 a.m. to 11:30 p.m.; Sunday, noon to 11:30 p.m.) The **Chicago Rib Shack** at 1 Raphael Street, across from Harrod's (581-5595), serves barbecued ribs cooked in "genuine" United States smoking ovens and onion loaves. There are dozens of other such restaurants, in addition to the **MacDonald's** and **Wendy's** all over the place. Get a copy of the *London Restaurant Guide*, published for British Tourist Authority and look at the listing for American restaurants. If you are shopping for groceries, your best bet is **Harrod's** food halls. They even sell wild rice. For all kinds of wonderful coffees, go to **H. R. Higgins Ltd.**, at 79 Duke Street; for chocolates try **Prestat**, 40 Princes Arc, Picadilly. Covent Garden has great ice cream. For American cocktails try the **American Bar** at the Savoy Hotel; Harry's Bar at the Park Lane Hotel; Trader Vic's at the Park Lane Hilton or the Palm Court at the Ritz.

Personal services: If you need a haircut or other beauty services, visit **Vidal Sassoon**, 54 Knightsbridge. **George F. Trumper's**, 9 Curzon Street, is the most famous, most expensive men's hair dressing shop - and if it is too British for you, try the barber shop in your American hotel.

Sports: If you want to keep your figure, try jogging around the wonderful parks located all over the city. Or go to the **YMCA** at 112 Great Russell Street (637-8131). You do need a membership. There are swimming pools, an ice skating rink on Queensway and tennis courts around town. Or if you just want to watch, check **Wembley Stadium** (902-1234) for the football schedule. They will even take you on a behind the scene tour daily, except Thursday, every hour on the hour from 10 a.m. to 4 p.m. Call 902-8833. The tours are only in the summer. For information on horse racing schedules call 168. This is a 24-hour information service. And if you happen to be there for the Wimbleton tennis matches, try to get a ticket and root for the American players. They also have the only **Tennis Museum** I know about, open 11 a.m. to 5 Monday through Saturday; 2 to 5 p.m. Sunday.

Entertainment: In the evening, you might try **Ronnie Scott's Jazz Club** at 47 Frith Street. This is the most famous jazz emporium in the city so reserve (439-0747) There are also "cinemas" around showing American movies. And if you look hard, you might find an American play at one of the theatres, sorry, theaters.

Churches: Finally, if you happen to be in London on a Sunday, you might want to attend a church with some American connection. In addition to the ones I have mentioned, here are a few others: **St. George's** on Hanover Square is where Theodore Roosevelt and Edith Carow were married in 1886. John Harvard, of Harvard University fame, was baptized at the **Southwark Cathedral,** and **All Hallows Barking by the Tower** is where William Penn, founder of Pennsylvania was baptized in 1644 and John Quincy Adams, 6th President of the United States was married in 1797. **Westminster Abbey** has a tablet in memory of Franklin Delano Roosevelt in St. George's Chapel and the Congressional Medal of Honor which our government bestowed on the unknown warrior in 1921. George Peabody was the only American buried here before his remains were removed to Massachusetts. **Whitfield Memorial Chapel,** now the American Church in London, is on Tottenham Court Road almost facing Torrington Place. And if you want the tiniest church in London with the longest name, try **St. Ethelburger-the Virgin-Within Bishopsgate,** on Bishopsgate north of St. Helen's Place, with its three windows showing Henry Hudson's voyage in search of the Northwest Passage. Hudson made his first communion there in 1607. This 56 foot long 30 foot high, 15th century church has the smallest parish in London. Its garden may be one of the most peaceful places in the city.

Catholic London. There are two major Roman Catholic churches and one smaller one that will be of interest to Catholic visitors to London: **Westminster Cathedral**, located on Victoria Street not far from Victoria Station, is the principal Roman Catholic church in England and is the seat of the Archbishop of Westminster. It is open daily from 7 a.m. to 8 p.m. (Check newspapers for the hours of services.) The foundation was laid in 1895. The church is designed in an early-Christian Byzantine style with alternate bands of red brick and white stone. It has the widest nave of any church in England, 60 feet across and it runs 392 feet long beneath its three domes. Sculptor Eric Gill designed the handsome Stations of the Cross on the 14 main piers of the church. Try to be there during a service to hear the magnificent music. **Brompton Oratory** on Cromwell Road, opened in 1884. It was founded by Cardinal Newman and the Oxford movement of Victorian intellectuals turned Catholic. The official name of this center is the Church of the Oratory of St. Philip Neri and The Immaculate Heart of Mary. (Again, check newspapers for the time of masses.) This Italian Baroque edifice is filled with gorgeous colored marbles of all kinds. Note particularly the Carrara marble statues of the Apostles by Mazzuoli, which came from the Siena Cathedral in Italy. Also note the altarpiece in the Lady Chapel. You may also be interested in visiting the **Church of the Assumption and St. Gregory**, better known as the 'Bavarian Chapel' on Warwick St, running parallel with Regent Street. Built in 1785, this was the only place were British citizens could legally attend Catholic Mass before emancipation in 1829.

Gay London. Homosexuality is no longer illegal in England. It does tend to be a bit more private and circumspect than in some cities in the United States. For information, check the entertainment magazine *Time Out* for a Gay London section. A Gay Switchboard offers 24 hour information and advice for men and women. Telephone 837-7324. The Gay Legal advice telephone operates nightly from 7 to 11 p.m. Telephone 821-7672. A number of pubs, discos and clubs cater to the gay community. *Time Out* magazine provides listings and open hours for these clubs. A bookstore, Gay's The Word on 66 Marchmont Street, just north of Russell Square, offers a wide selection of new, out-of-print and second hand books on gay and feminist issues. Open Monday through Saturday from 11 a.m. to 7 p.m. and on Sunday from noon to 6 p.m. The shop also hosts a variety of discussion groups and runs a coffee bar.

Jewish London. Between "The City" and London's East End, lies the old Jewish area. Here is where the Sephardi Jews resettled under Oliver Cromwell - their first home following expulsion during the Middle Ages. Jewry Street runs just south of Aldgate Street; Houndsditch just north of Aldgate. This is still the center of Jewish brokers and dealers. Just off Bevis Marks, south of Houndsditch, on little Heneage Lane is the **Spanish and Portuguese Synagogue**. Built in 1701, it is the oldest synagogue in use in England. A larger

Great Synagogue of the Ashkenazim is just beyond Bevis Marks on Duke's Place. Founded in 1690, it was bombed during World War II and has never been rebuilt. Just north and parallel to Houndsditch is Middlesex Street (Petticoat Lane), the home of a very busy and energetic market on Sunday. Back to Aldgate. If you continue north it becomes Whitechapel High Street and at number 90 you will find **Bloom's**, London's most famous kosher restaurant, handy for the Petticoat Lane market. It is open Sunday through Thursday from 11:30 a.m. to 10 p.m. and for Friday lunch. Its chicken soup, hot salt beef, pastrami, and Israeli wines are very reasonable. Don't let the busy and curt waiters and servers put you off; this is just like a deli in New York. Two other restaurants worth mentioning are **The Nosherie** on 12 Greville Street, just north of Holborn Street near Hatton Garden. (Open Monday through Friday, 8 a.m. to 5 p.m.) and **Reuben's,** 20a Baker Street. (Open Sunday through Thursday 11 a.m. to 11 p.m.; Friday 11 to 3 p.m.)

The **Jewish Museum**, north of the British Museum on Upper Woburn Street, is located in Woburn House. (Open Tuesday to Friday, Sunday 10 a.m. to 4 p.m. November to March, Friday, 10 a.m. to 12:45 p.m.) Its-one room exhibition space, opened in 1932, displays antiquities of Jewish domestic life and public worship. It contains the **Jewish Memorial Council Bookshop.** Another good bookshop is the Jewish Chronicle Bookshop at 25 Furnival Street, off Chancery Lane. The **Slade School of Fine Art**, part of the University College on Gower Street, houses the Mocatta Library and Museum of the Jewish Historical Society. It was presented to the school in 1906.

On Montague Square is located **Jews College.** From 1855 it trained rabbis and ministers and is now a world center of Jewish scholarship, recognized by London University. The **Central Synagogue** of London is near Regent's Park on Cavendish Street. Destroyed by bombing in World War II, it was rebuilt in 1958.

Stamp Collectors. There are two extraordinary stamp museums in Central London as well as a number of interesting places to buy stamps. The National Postal Museum is in the King Edward Building, next to the main post office, north of St. Paul's Cathedral. It is open weekdays from 10 a.m. to 4:30 p.m. (4 p.m. on Thursday and Friday) Closed on Saturday and Sunday. It was established in 1965 and has the most important and extensive collection of postage stamps in the world. It includes the 19th century British collection of

R. M. Philips. In addition to the huge collection, there are temporary exhibitions and a reference library. The British Museum also has a stamp collection which is on view in King's Library in the museum. It includes the Tapling Collection of Postage Stamps of the world (1840-90), the Fitzgerald Air-Mail Collection, Mosely Collection of African Stamps, the Bojanowicz Collection of Polish postal history (1939-49) and one of the most single rare and expensive stamps in the world, the Black Penny Stamp. There are a number of stamp shops. I will suggest just two. **Stanley Gibbons** at 399 Strand is reputed to be the world's largest philatelic shop. The **International Stamp Center** at 27 King Street consists of about 12 stamp stalls. Some of its merchandise is quite expensive. Cheaper stamp stalls are located on weekends in an open air market under the arches of the Charing Cross Railway bridge, just off the Strand. And finally, the post office on St. Martin's Place, just off Trafalgar Square, is open 24 hours a day, 7 days a week. Its very long counter and long lines are the place to buy first day covers and do all kinds of other post office business.

Wine lover's London. London is a wonderful place for wine lovers to both buy and drink exceptional wines. **Berry Brothers & Rudd Ltd.**, 3 St. James's Street, has been in business as wine merchants in this location since the 17th century. Even if you don't want to buy wines, do stop in this unusual shop. It has maintained its impeccable standards over the past 200 years. **Justerini & Brooks Ltd.**, 61 St. James's Street, the home of the J. & B. Rare Scotch Whisky, is also a wonderful place to go to buy wine and to get advice on laying down wine for future use. **Christopher & Co.**, 4 Ormond Yard, just south of Jermyn Street, has been selling its famous clarets and Burgundies for 300 years. There are many restaurants in London with fine wine lists, including the **Tate Gallery restaurant**, which has one of the most extensive and reasonably priced lists. The development of wine bars in London has expanded enormously over the past few years. Some of them have been in the city for centuries. El Vino Olde Wine Shades, 6 Martin Lane, off Cannon Street, dates from 1663. It is the oldest in the city and the only tavern to survive the 1666 fire. It still serves port and sherry from the wood. El Vino, 47 Fleet Street, caters to members of the journalism and legal professions, and following long precedent, requires both jackets and ties. A newer and popular cellar wine bar is the Cork and Bottle at 44 Cranbourn Street, just off St. Martin's Lane.

Young Visitors to London. These suggestions are aimed at student travelers and back packers. My suggestions assume a limited amount of money. First of all get yourself the **International Student Identity Card (I.S.I.C.)** It offers medical insurance up to $1,000; enables you to take student charter flights; gives you discounts to many museums and other benefits. You need a certificate of student status from your registrar, a passport-size photograph and proof of birth date and nationality. Cards are available in the United States through the Council on International Educational Exchange, 205 East 42d Street, New York 10017; Educational Travel Center, 438 North Frances Street, Madison, Wisconsin 53703 and Harvard Student Agencies, Harvard University, Thayer Hall B, Cambridge, Mass. 02138. In other countries, check with your nearest college or university for information about availability of the identity card. If you are backpacking I do not have to tell you to travel light. Even so, do include a small first aid kit, toilet paper and lamb's wool for your aching feet.

If you arrive without a place to stay, try the **Tourist Information Centre** at **Victoria railway station**, which runs a budget accommodation service. Another source of information is the **International Students' House**, Park Crescent, Portland Place, the house with the bust of President John Kennedy in front. Both the **YMCA** with its 764 rooms and the **YWCA** are on Great Russell Street, near the British Museum. Remember you cannot sleep in London parks or any other open urban spaces. Just a few pieces of advice about eating on the cheap. As everywhere, self-service places are the cheapest. Many provide "take away" food. There is no VAT (the 15 percent value added tax) on food which is taken away and consumed off the premises. London is filled with fish and chip places, pizza parlors, sandwich bars and hamburger joints. Other good values are at the numerous Chinese and Indian restaurants. **Bloom's** on Whitechapel offers take away Kosher food. Also don't forget the markets and groceries for the best values. Do avoid vans on side streets selling hot dogs and hamburgers; they are not policed very well and you may get more than lunch. The coffee stalls making fresh sandwiches are fine. If you want to shop, try London's West End on the King's Road and on its side streets. Carnaby is a historic relic. The weekend markets at Portobello and Petticoat Lane are fun and you can often find 'treasures'. For entertainment, check *What's On* or *Time Out* publications for the list of discos, concerts and other diversions. The **National Theatre** offers discounted student prices for its afternoon performances and many theatres offer reduced prices for seats sold just before performances.

Glossary of terms

Here are a few hints that will help you understand our London friends more easily.

Biscuit: A cookie if sweet, a cracker if unsweetened
Black or white: With or without cream in coffee
Book: Make a reservation
Chemist: Druggist
Coach: A bus
Dress circle: Mezzanine in a theatre
Ground floor: First floor
First Floor: Second floor
Interval: Intermission at the theatre or concert
Jumper: A sweater
Lift: An elevator
Lorry: A truck
Pub: A bar or tavern
Queue: Waiting line
Return ticket: Round trip ticket
Ring up: Call on the telephone
Single ticket: One way ticket
Stalls: Orchestra seats in a theatre
Upper circle: First balcony in a theatre
Vest: Undershirt
Tube: Subway or underground
Water closet: Toilet

Food

***Food and drink** have their own vocabulary in London. Here are some foods which you will find all over town.*
Bangers and mash: Sausages and mashed potato
Bubble and squeak: Cabbage and potato fried with yesterday's roast.
Crumpets: Similar to an English muffin with larger air holes
Fish and chips: Usually cod, plaice or skate served with French-fried potatoes and served with vinegar and salt
Jellied eel: You don't want to know. It looks and tastes just the way it sounds. A Cockney favorite.
Ploughman's lunch: Cheddar cheese, bread, pickled onions and bitters.
Scotch eggs: Hard-boiled eggs encased in sausage and bread crumbs and deep fried.
Shepherd's pie: Diced meat, sometimes with onion and vegetable, covered with mashed potato.
Whitebait: Tiny little whole fish, deep fried.

Drink

Bitter: Amber-colored draft beer
Cider: Strong fermented apple juice
Light ale: Fizzy beer
Shandy: Bitters with lemonade or ginger beer. Good in the summer.
Stout: Strong, dark and rich ale.

Index

Photo by Pat Horner

About the author

Ruth Humleker, who is also the author of *New York for the Independent Traveler*, has spent her life putting ideas, people and places together. During her professional career as an art administrator, publicist and consultant, she traveled extensively. She developed the unique trip-planning techniques in this book, as well as in her New York book (also by MarLor Press) for herself, her friends and later, for her own trip-planning business, "Going My Way." She has walked each tour. A graduate of Lawrence College, she is widowed and has four children and eight grandchildren.